Dudley Ashton, Ph.D., University of Iowa, is Professor and Chairman of the Department of Physical Education for Women at the University of Nebraska. She has previously taught at the University of Iowa and has also taught physical education at various elementary and secondary schools. Dr. Ashton is the co-author of a book on rhythms for children.

ADMINISTRATION OF PHYSICAL EDUCATION FOR WOMEN

DUDLEY ASHTON

UNIVERSITY OF NEBRASKA

THE RONALD PRESS COMPANY • NEW YORK

Library of Congress Catalog Card Number: 68–13469
PRINTED IN THE UNITED STATES OF AMERICA

To

E. G. B. and E. A. L.
Administrators with Faith in Youth

and

E. H.
*Inspired Teacher and Fine Example of
the Administrator at Work*

Preface

This book is designed both for courses in the administration of physical education for women and for in-service administrators. Covering elementary school, secondary school, and college levels, it sets forth aspects of present-day administration in order to prepare the prospective and the in-service administrator for today's more complex and demanding managerial roles.

The book opens with a discussion of the nature of administrative duties, together with the philosophy and principles that form the basis of administration. It then proceeds to a more detailed discussion of these duties, as well as an examination of trends in the field. Emphasis is placed on problems that are arising as the result of modern technological advances—particularly computerization.

Administration is no longer comparatively simple. It has developed overtones of management relationships and computerized structural lines. In fact, many administrators of physical education programs in the large secondary schools and colleges throughout the country now function under competitive pressures similar to those in the business world. In addition, the young teacher—in his initial teaching experience—often finds himself not only an instructor but also the administrator of his school's program.

It is precisely this kind of situation, along with a substantially increased flux in curricular patterns and the resulting experimentation in organizational structure, that is stressed in this book.

Problems are provided at the end of each chapter to encourage independent thinking and also to stimulate discussion. A comprehensive bibliography is included, along with a number of appendixes containing a considerable amount of materials designed to supplement the text discussion—especially with regard to modern standards and goals of physical education for women.

The author gratefully acknowledges the kind permission extended by various publishers to quote materials. The author also acknowledges the courtesy extended for the use of certain illustrations by the Grand Island Public Schools, Grand Island, Nebraska;

v

the Lincoln Public Schools, Lincoln, Nebraska; Education Facilities Laboratories; and The Athletic Institute.

The advice and counsel of professional colleagues have been a sustaining force in the preparation of this manuscript. Among these, the author is indebted to June Ericson, Ruth Diamond Levinson, and Elizabeth Halsey. The author also acknowledges with deep gratitude the careful work and continuing interest of Marie Hermanek Cripe, who typed the manuscript.

It is the hope of the author that this volume will be a source of both information and inspiration to young women in physical education as they enter the profession and as they contribute to its advancement.

DUDLEY ASHTON

Lincoln, Nebraska
February, 1968

Contents

ADMINISTRATION OF PHYSICAL EDUCATION FOR WOMEN

1

Shop Talk

Among the many opportunities open to personnel in the profession of teaching and to administrators in particular is that of talking to lay groups. In this situation, one attempts to explain some of the terms used in the profession and to give a thumbnail sketch of duties. This chapter, then, is a shop talk with the ramifications of the administration of physical education spelled out later in the book. The aims of an administrator and some of the problems with which he will have to contend are discussed. The reader may be familiar with certain of these problems, but there is also fresh ground broken as the problems are surveyed and the unifying lines of the general administration of physical education are presented.

What we will be concerned with is primarily education. At the start, we will leave behind us all such concepts as that of exercise for its own sake. Physical education will be taken to include a broad field of movement, both fundamental and as applied in games, sports, aquatics, dance, and gymnastics. As such, it will draw on scientific findings in biology, physiology, anatomy, zoology, microbiology, chemistry, and physics, and on psychology, sociology, and anthropology. It will recognize that all forms of physical activity contribute much toward a congenial environment for thought, and it will search the past for what it may hold and strive to satisfy the demands of the present while investigating and experimenting toward what the future may bring.

INTRODUCTION TO ADMINISTRATION

Most of us, of course, develop quickly where we find our greatest facility, and there is a tendency in social teamwork for us to contribute what we do best and leave to others what they can do with ease and competence. An administrator, although he may

3

not be called upon to exercise detailed competence in all that concerns him, will have to fully understand much that he earlier left to others and organize it all toward a common goal. Here is an acrostic that will help tie together for the moment the various aspects of administration that should make a unified whole on their own merits. Thus, Shop Talk becomes:

S — Services
H — Hopes
O — Ordeals
P — Public relations

T — Teamwork
A — Administrative details
L — Letters, literature, and loopholes
K — Know-how

Care should be taken not to see these widely divergent fields as more formidable than they are; with a little patience, everyone can realize that he has to greater or lesser extent come across them in his own experience.

S – SERVICES

For the General Student. A generous block of any administrator's time is consumed by the planning, execution, and evaluation of physical education courses, either required or elective, for the general student. Generally speaking, these courses are offered at the freshman and sophomore level. It is hoped that a carry-over of interest and participation in activities will occur in the junior and senior years, and before the student becomes too involved in the advanced academic courses.

There are numerous problems to be solved in the administration of such a program. It is necessary to consider the mechanics of scheduling and the sizes of classes. It is necessary to decide whether or not the varied experiences within the physical education curriculum shall be offered based upon a "core" course that will provide strength, endurance, and some of the skill analyses that cut across all areas, or whether the entire program shall be open to the choice of the individual student. It is necessary to ascertain the approximate level of skill and interest of these students and to plan sections or classes that will satisfy the criteria of a varied program and, at the same time, provide learning experiences that will challenge the level of maturation of a given group of students under given conditions. It would be absurd, for example, to believe that varied experiences in sports, dance, or aquatics all offered at the beginning level would completely service this program for the general student. In this phase of our services, as in other phases, the program must be carefully and tactfully administered within the context of the school or college situation in which the administrator is currently functioning.

For the Professional Student. At the college level, the preparation of students for entrance into the profession (undergraduate majors and/or minors) and for more mature contributions (graduate students) is a rewarding administrative endeavor.

In the days when undergraduate preparation consisted of some background in the basic sciences, adequate knowledge and skill in a specific system of formal gymnastics, and a minimum of practice teaching experiences, the administrator's life was complicated enough, but now the complications are compounded. We must be sure that our professional students at the undergraduate level have a wide background of general education, that the basic sciences are well covered, that the educational prerequisites for certification are part of the pattern, that the student has a grasp of both individual and community problems, that orientation for the profession and induction into initial teaching have been stressed, and finally, that the department measures up to all criteria for accreditation. These are tangibles. The administrator must also face the intangibles of personal qualifications in selection and retention of potential teachers.

The department that offers graduate study increases its administrative headaches but, at the same time, raises its professional contributions. Operative in this program are standards of admission to graduate work, details of individually tailored student programs, adequate staffing, and opportunities for experimental problem-solving.

For Recreational Interests. Schools and campuses today are reacting to the impact of increased enrollments. In elementary and secondary schools, this may mean physical education classes that are too large to secure many of the benefits in physical skills and social relationships, or it may mean double sessions. In college, this may mean oversized classes, but even more serious, living conditions that necessarily have eliminated some of the space usually reserved for recreation rooms. In response to these pressures, recreational services in the form of Girls Athletic Association, Women's Athletic Association or Women's Recreation Association, intramural sports, dance and synchronized swimming clubs, and the open gymnasium are a must. Physical education departments recognize their role in providing recreational opportunities for the total college community; so, included in these recreational responsibilities are provisions for faculty participation in activities.

For the Community. Frequently, the elementary or secondary physical education teacher is asked to help with various phases of community recreation. These may range from serving on a community recreation council to teaching a night class for exercise and/or fun, or even to organizing and administering a full summer recreation program. These same community services are operative for the college teacher. In addition, the college department, especially in state-supported institutions, is expected to contribute assistance by answering letters of inquiry that range from a source for volleyball rules to complicated community surveys of administrative responsibilities. Colleges are expected to arrange clinics, workshops, and conferences to assist with in-service education of teachers in the local and state communities. Among these services may be off-campus classes. Last are the consultant services available for school surveys or for curricular studies.

H – HOPES

The hopes of any department may well be wishful thinking founded upon vague dreams, or they may be tangible intangibles that have been fostered by plenty of spadework. Too often, curricular changes that involve complete faculty action are classified by a particular staff, consciously or unconsciously, in the realm of wishful thinking. One may identify this reaction by the rationalizations offered in favor of the status quo. Interest in newer designs for curricular emphasis is stated but is immediately qualified by reference to lack of facilities, lack of key administrative interest, or even by indifference on the part of the physical education staff. The destruction of hope under such circumstances is an indictment against professional advancement. Later in this volume, ways and means of lifting this problem from the category of wishful thinking to the category of feasible reality will be discussed.

One of the tangible intangibles that exists, in the beginning, on hope is that of either staff or individual research projects. These are usually "beams in the eye" when they first occur. If the administrator of the college department or of the secondary school listens, but at the same time casts doubts and obstacles in the way, these ideas suffer an early death. It is seldom possible to implement research ideas on the spur of the moment. Equipment, space, personnel, and student cooperation are involved. Sympathetic attention, however, can be extended to research proposals. The administrator then has an obligation to investigate avenues for support for such staff projects. These may be local in nature, such as provision for the purchase of special equipment in a fiscal budget. The support may consist of reference to avenues for state or general grants. An important phase of an administrator's duty is that of maintenance of staff support and interest until the research project has been completed and reported.

In this day of constantly increasing enrollments, the hope for additional staff must become a concrete achievement. Contrary to the simple fact that we have more students, therefore, we need more teachers; additional staff is a complicated administrative problem. Available space or more teaching stations is one facet of the problem, and proof of the need for additional help rests upon accurate records that state the number of students served over a period of time plus faculty load across the same interval. It is obvious that financial provisions are necessary before additional staff may be employed. Finally, there is the problem of recruiting competent personnel either before the bulge occurs or frequently as late as the opening of the academic year. We shall suggest ways and means to handle these problems later, having in mind the goal of realization rather than hope.

A corollary to the hope of additional staff is that of either expanded or new facilities. Although many of the newer secondary schools and numerous colleges have erected adequate buildings and increased the acreage for sports use, we still find gymnasiums located as the central core of buildings and buildings located as the central core of grounds! Women, who are not worried about provision for spectators for sports events, have inherited facilities from the men that cut the size and use of teaching stations because such provisions are part of the permanent setup. Even the fortunate in our midst who have modern dressing rooms and showers, multiphase teaching stations, and regulation-size fields and courts are feeling the constant pressure of greater numbers. In some phases of the present economy, tax levies are sufficient and bond issues have covered the needs for excellent physical education facilities. Under these circumstances, expanded and new facilities become a reality; but, in all too many cases, these basic requirements must be classified as hopes. Certainly the author does not intend to indicate that too many programs are limited by facilities but does intend to point up the administrative problems that exist under such circumstances.

O – ORDEALS

All administrators walk tautly stretched tightropes in dealing with innumerable personnel problems. Since availability is one mark of efficient administration, the "open-door" policy has become a tradition. So, to the administrator's door comes daily a procession of personalities seeking help; presenting alternatives for decision; seeking support for both new and old projects; and searching for funds to underwrite research, curricular changes, and/or extracurricular activities; or students needing academic or personal advice. No one of these problems may be lightly considered or casually tossed aside. The administrator must study each situation, frequently making a decision based upon the circumstances as well as the presentation. What to say, when to say it, and how to say it are factors in this "advise and consent" framework that may decisively alter staff morale. The administrator must balance carefully and step lightly but firmly as he moves along the wires of personnel problem-solving.

The reference above to the discouraging situation of poor or inadequate facilities leads naturally to the matter of providing excellent programs in spite of inadequate facilities. Usually, this experience starts as an ordeal and ends as a challenge.

One of the most important laboratories used in the physical education program is the athletic field. Over the years, areas varying in size as related to the needs of children, youth, and adults have been set aside for outdoor participation in sports activities. Many suburban communities are now planning school facilities early in their development and making provision for such needs. Colleges have practiced a policy of provision for playing areas for use by classes, intramural teams, and recreational pursuits. However, a new ordeal has arisen for the administrator of physical education—the preservation of these playing areas in the face of rising enrollments and the need for space to be used for classroom buildings. In addition, the automobile in steadily increasing numbers is in competition with all campus activities for parking space.

There is one ordeal that no administrator desires to face. That ordeal is the defense of the department or some phase of the work of the department. Often, this ordeal becomes necessary because of lack of communication with other subject-matter areas within a school or a college. It may be misunderstandings with regard to scheduling of extracurricular events such as athletics, it may be the dissatisfaction of parents with basic curricular offerings as reported by students, or it may be academically minded proposals to curtail requirements or even entire programs. One could hastily conclude that such ordeals involving the protection of departmental programs and policies can be completely avoided by the use of correct means of public relations. Unfortunately, this has not always proved to be the case. Academic bias and personal experience prejudices stay underground and suddenly emerge when least expected. So, departmental protection must necessarily become an administrative task.

When one first enters the administration of physical education, the many interviews with higher administrative authorities are mental and nervous hurdles to be crossed. There are increasingly finer and better prepared personnel in higher administration and in physical education with the result that such interviews are fast becoming a source of professional pride in conference situations wherein the "give and take" of objective discussion predominates. There are no free agents in administration. Each of us is subject to some authority above us. Much friction can be avoided and better programs produced when we face this fact, and correlative to this is the fact that budget conferences, staffing conferences, schedule clearances, personnel adjustment conferences as well as a myriad of other facets of this phase of administration should be regarded as professional opportunities by the administrator.

P — PUBLIC RELATIONS

The relations of a department of physical education to its various publics is a matter of grave concern for any administrator. Too frequently, public relations has been administered as crash programs in moments of either crisis or need. Even more disastrous is the business of considering that the pattern of public relations is a matter of placating all questioners. Such public relations tactics belong in the category of too little too late. The problem of the administrator is one of foresight—implementing a program of physical education that speaks for itself and a program that convinces the student that physical education lives up to its value claims. Foresight marks the use of fine media. Careful analysis of the best activities for TV presentations, thoughtful editing of materials for school and community publications, and judicious use of demonstrations as an educational outlet make for better presentations. Sensing the pulse of the interest of the community in casual contacts with the ability to present the principles of physical education in short addresses will help to enlighten such key groups as the PTA, women's clubs, and luncheon service clubs. Other media exist and are sources for excellent contacts with the various publics.

Probably, one of the greatest access routes for presenting the values of the physical education department to the publics lies in the interrelationships that necessarily exist between the departments and colleges in the area of higher education. Many times these are pleasant lanes that have not been followed. Instead, they have been beaten into slippery rocky paths that do not lead from "farm to market." Violations of procedures, policies, or principles set up by higher administrative authorities will lead to friction that no amount of explanation entirely clears. Disregard of health status, health standards, and health regulations often builds disrespect for personnel and eventually for entire departments. Reputation is a nebulous state. Public relations is fostered by the reputation of accuracy in recording data and/or records, promptness in expediting schedules and other necessary mechanical needs, integrity in counseling students, and supporting the value systems of the educational institution and the community. Evidences of irresponsibility in such instances create an atmosphere of distrust of departmental procedures and incentives. "Mending the fences" in situations of this kind is usually patchwork. One finds oneself in the position of wishfully thinking that one had used "public relations"—not "postscripts."

T – TEAMWORK

The concept of teamwork is basic to the sports culture found in this country. It is certainly a major factor in the development of the games and sports programs in physical education. As our cultural emphases have changed and will continue to change, so will the administrative needs in our sponsorship of sports change. Out of cultural impacts have arisen many problems that relate to the administration of the broad canvas of sports and physical education. We have in the past endured sports managed by students and in due time realized the importance of institutional management of such activities. We know the influence of changes in dress on women's sports. Changes in cultural setting on men's sports are quickly evident as witness the growth of interinstitutional contact when the automobile was finally established as a pillar of our society. We know that economic conditions such as the prosperity of the 1920's and the technological prosperity of today affect physical activity outlets. We know that economic depression has a reverse impact. We know that agencies with vested interests can and do influence the administration of the sports world.

Regardless of all these factors, we also know that basic to any game or any sport is the necessity for teamwork. Unless the team operates as a unit—thinking, planning, and playing together—the game becomes chaos. We have identified this pattern in the world of sports and in the world of business and named it cooperation. This sense of oneness, this sense of subjugating selfish interests for the good of all, this sense of "give and take" in the roles of both leader and follower are traits that permeate our culture. At one and the same time, we have the spirit of competitive endeavor. At first glance, cooperation and competition would appear to be in opposition to each other. But, as we put our shoulders to the wheel to compete in the academic world, all phases of cooperation come into play. The staff must work as a team in the development of fine curricular offerings if the department is to win its place in academic prestige in the school or college, or in state or national reputation. The staff must work as a team if the department is to contribute any research in the field. The staff must compete by supporting its members if the department is to be represented on committees and by key appointments within the institution, the community, the state, and the nation. The staff must exhibit the cohesion of team effort in its daily contacts with students, with other faculty, and with top administrative units.

Finally, teamwork on a staff means a willingness on the part of staff members to help each other. It means unselfishness in sharing one's experiences and prior knowledge with a newcomer. It means willingness to give of one's time to work diligently on staff committees and staff projects. It means that one looks on the positive side of the opportunities inherent in a democratic exchange of ideas. It means that in teamwork, one of the keys to fine staff morale is present in facing both the major and the minor crises that confront every department with an objective professional focus on the problem and with faith that by working together the staff (team) will be able to find satisfactory solutions to most difficulties. It means also that the "lifts" that come with accomplishment are accepted as staff accolades.

A – ADMINISTRATIVE DETAILS

There are moments when an administrator wishes that it were possible to wave a magic wand and thus take care of the myriad details inherent in the day's duties. The mechanics of administering any program are concerned with being sure that all the cogs of the wheels mesh correctly so that the wheels will turn smoothly, accurately, and silently. Because these details are cogs in the wheels, they cross-reference with every phase of administrative endeavor. We shall select a few of these details for mention at this point and leave amplification of this subject to a later chapter.

One administrative chore that has many ramifications is the planning of schedules. One has to be very sure that the schedule planned for students can be adequately staffed. One has to be sure that in planning student schedules, one has not discarded the guidelines for staff loads. In relation to class size, one must check existing facilities and possible use of additional spaces and/or feasible additional hours (noon or night) in plotting student, staff, and facility schedules. Schedules must be established for cleaning, repair, and maintenance of the building that will not interfere with maximum teaching time.

Policies must be established for the use of all facilities. These range from community demands for swimming and exercise programs and provision for staff supervision of inherently dangerous activity areas to prohibition of smoking in locker and dressing areas, gymnasiums, and potentially hazardous buildings.

The many report forms that cross an administrator's desk demand that time be planned to prepare these. After a year's experience in an administrative setup, one can establish a calendar that anticipates the deadlines for such details as departmental reports, schedules of classes, schedules of staff meetings, accident reports, reports on staff load, and grade or progress reports on students.

Budgets, inventories, purchasing, and ordering of equipment and supplies are additional cogs in the wheels that require time and careful attention. For example, it is necessary to plan allocations within a departmental budget that will take care of needs for sports, dance, and aquatic equipment under conditions of increased enrollment. Accurate and well-timed inventory practices are basic in this case. How and where orders are placed and how purchases are made determine, in large part, the timing of these procedures.

These plus other administrative details must be enmeshed into the needs of the curricular programs of the department, the contacts made with the public, and the plans and hopes of the department for the future; and, above all, the staff must cooperate as a team if the cogs of the wheels are to run true.

L — LETTERS, LITERATURE, AND LOOPHOLES

Letters that cross an administrator's desk run the gamut from important to ridiculous. Among the important types that must be carefully phrased are requests for additional personnel, recommendations of qualifications of either staff or students in teacher education, letters relating to policy implementation, and letters relating to budget needs. If a department is to advance, letters must be formulated to recruit both staff and students. One must reply to many requests for services from the field (community or state) in which one is located. It is necessary to write letters of congratulation and letters of condolence. Although letters seem to many persons to be a minor matter, practice is necessary to phrase succinctly, to state propositions and/or decisions clearly, and to convince the reader that the matter at hand is both relevant and important.

Memoranda of various types must be prepared. Sometimes these relate to protection of facilities such as use of building requests for odd hours, or notification of campus police that groups will be in activity at specified locations. One very important duty is that of notes of appreciation when departmental needs have been recognized.

It is an axiom that every professionally minded individual must keep in touch with new developments by constantly reading the literature in his field. The many changes in physical education in this century have multiplied this professional obligation, particularly in relation to research findings. An administrator is charged with stimulating interest in the literature by use of the latest articles and books for staff study. Staff need to be encouraged to develop personal professional libraries. Moreover, if the newer materials are to be available to all personnel, the coordinator of physical education in the public schools and the administrator in the college must see that acquisitions for professional libraries keep stride with the developments in the field. Staff members who have both the interest and the ability should be encouraged to write professional materials. Finally, the administrator must facilitate research on the part of those staff members who have the capacity to pursue such studies.

For want of a better term, we have labeled the myriad odds and ends of an administrator's life the "loopholes." One spends a great percentage of one's time attending both professional and commu-

nity meetings. The nuances of college and/or community reaction
and interaction, as well as the biases, both pro and con, are loopholes worthy of an administrator's attention. One may be catching up the loops by inspecting the building, representing the
department on a committee, or serving at a tea. The opposite
phase of the loophole concept, however, is that of the administrator's need to guard the academic interests of the department,
to keep an ear on the ground for unusual developments that may
affect the department, and to be willing to fight for the best interests of all departmental affairs.

K – KNOW-HOW

In administration, there are no pat answers. The problems in
local situations demand local considerations and local answers.
From preschool to doctoral and postdoctoral study, to programs
for the aged, administrators in physical education need knowledge
of growth, development and maturation factors—both physical and
mental. They need knowledge and ability in motor skill patterns
over a wide range of interests and activities. They need insight
into the characteristic behavior to be expected from students and
from staff. They must have the "know-how" and the willingness
to work with a myriad of details and yet to see the "larger wholes"
in a given problem or a given situation.

Know-how in the administrator's book has two sides. First,
there must be staff members with the best possible qualifications
for the job at hand. In some instances, this means that the staff
member must have a high level of motor skill in sports, dance,
aquatics, and gymnastics, as well as teaching ability. In some instances, it means that beyond teaching ability in motor skills, the
staff member must know how to present the scientific, historical,
and theoretical bases of this profession. In other instances, it
means the staff member must have the patience and know-how
to direct graduate students.

Second, there must be know-how on the part of the administrator. The administrator must be well qualified academically
if respect for the department is to be maintained. An administrator's qualifications must include experience in every phase of
the program in order that he may both foresee problems and understand difficulties as they arise. Academic preparation and experience will assist the administrator in many cases, but know-how
extends to the area of human relationships. The administrator

needs tact, insight, and sympathetic understanding to handle the problems of students and of personnel.

Know-how is the integrating factor in administration. With know-how, one may solve equipment needs, curricular problems, crowded class situations, personnel difficulties, and the numerous other demands on the administrator's time. How, when, and why one uses know-how is the theme of this book and the foundation upon which this "shop talk" has rested.

WHAT IS ADMINISTRATION?

Within the last two or three decades, a mass of material has been compiled on the subject of administration. As the organizational structures of public and private school systems and of colleges have become more complex, more and more attention has been focused upon the problem of how to manage the concrete phases of operation and how to structure the abstract problems in personnel relationships. We have run the gamut of administrative name-calling from casual indifference based upon an erroneous concept that all the involved factors in the problem may be resolved by the use of common sense to the concept of administration as an art. In physical education, we are cognizant of these varying opinions, and in preparation for our administrative functions, we have studied these points of view. As a result, we reject complete dependence upon common sense since such a solution would disregard scholarly endeavors in many phases of administrative functioning, while we retain common sense as an integral part of some administrative functions. For example, it is only common sense to investigate long-range availability of water before building a swimming pool, but the reverse has been known to happen. If, on the other hand, administration is to be considered an art in the connotation of "art for art's sake," we are forced to reject this as an impractical situation. However, if administration is an art in the sense of an administrator becoming a "maestro" in striking a fine balance between the concrete and abstract demands in any given situation, then we must subscribe to this point of view. Along a continuum between these extremes lie the functions of the administrative process.

It would be simple to administer if we were concerned only with things. Things must be handled by people, and people must be managed by people. Administration, then, concerns itself with facilities and equipment, the legal implications of a specific situation, publicity gadgets for communication with its various publics, and concrete curricular content, but a large portion of an administrator's time is concerned with the interactions and interrelationships of people. These interactions of the personalities involved in a specific administrative problem carry implications for the things made available or used in physical education.

Who administers a program of physical education? If you are the only physical education teacher in an elementary or secondary school or in a college, you assume a dual role—teacher and administrator. If you are a member of a staff in a large department, you will find yourself assigned certain administrative duties. If you have engaged in the necessary preparation, planned your teaching experience on a broad base, and, finally, conditioned your thinking to the administrative function, you may find yourself in the role of the top administrator. This role has many scenes in which it may be played: supervising teacher for the physical education program in several elementary schools, consultant or supervisor in a public or private school system, chairman of a secondary or college department, and director or dean of a school of physical education, to name the obvious ones. The duties and responsibilities in the above position may differ in degree, but there are basic responsibilities common to all.

ADMINISTRATION—ITS BASIC RESPONSIBILITIES

Any enterprise to be successful rests upon sound preparation, carefully designed allocation of duties, timely and responsive completion of the project, and, finally, judgment or evaluation of the results. At this point, the enterprise, probably embracing new facts, repeats the cycle.

Tradition is a part of sound preparation in that the best learnings from the past are combined with the best thinking of the present. To embark upon an enterprise means that one must know where one is going. Every phase of administration must, therefore, have its aim, its objective, or its goal clearly set forth. We need to define and state our purposes. Are we concerned with the development and the potentials of every student with whom we come in contact? Shall we confine our program to physical fitness in a limited way, or shall we be concerned with fitness for enriched living experiences? Are we building gymnasiums and establishing play areas for 1970 or for the year 2000? Are we pointing our public relations media toward a segment of the population, or are we interested in the reactions of many groups in our communities? Are we selecting staff who may be able to make individualized contributions, or are we employing "Yes" men? We repeat, we must know where we are going. Call this phase of administration, aim, objective, or goal, as you please. Call this phase a one-year, three-year, five-year, or ten-year plan and you have encompassed immediate, intermediate, and remote purposes. The fact remains that you must aim your weapon—your total program—and that this weapon should be carefully chosen.

Planning is the wheel of administration. The hub (stated purposes) is connected by the spokes (details of the pattern of operation) to the rim that passes along the path of the educative process, either cutting a deeper rut or blazing a new trail. The spokes of this wheel may be large in scope at one time and smaller at other times. In the larger scene, we find the administrative planning necessary for curricular revisions, for enlarging the scope and functions of a department, for creating the need for and support of new facilities, for structuring staff thinking relative to the needs of professional students twenty or fifty years hence. Among the smaller spokes, we find a number of the organizational factors in administration of a staff, of a class, or of an office. These finer bits of organization are extremely important. They are the fine wires that absorb the stress and strain of many an administrative problem. In the words of William Morris: "There is no beauty without order." The structure of the organization, whether set by higher administrative officers or by staff within the subject area, greases this wheel. Without grease, the wheel either will not run or will move in a sticky, jerky fashion. Daily, weekly, seasonal, yearly, and decade planning and organization are basic administrative responsibilities.

Implementing, or putting into operation, the purposes and plans for any physical education department demands executive ability. The administrator is involved in coordinating the work of his department with that of other departments. In this introductory material, we mention only two parts of this coordination: scheduling of classes with due respect to total scheduling or college layouts and curricular demands, and coordinating participation by individuals in relation to the recommendations of the personal physician and/or the health services of the institution. The implementation of even a partial change in curriculum is a task of formidable proportions in terms of equipment, use of facilities, and reactions of all personnel touched by such an operation. Communication is needed in both these problems. Often, it is that of supplying information on a current or proposed project, but one of the great needs in a physical education department is communication that will educate, that will stress its values for colleagues, parents, higher administrative officers, and students. The keystone to implementation is the right person for the right job, including the administrator's qualifications both professional and personal. Ramifications of these executive responsibilities will be discussed at length in this book.

The last major responsibility that we shall discuss here is that of judging the results of the program and one's actions in relation to these results. Several divisions of this responsibility are indicative of the scope of this operation. One of these is supervision. A dilemma faced in putting administrative responsibilities and relationships in black and white is where to ignore overlaps and how to classify these duties. Supervising practices certainly are present as one plans the total physical education curriculum; it is an inherent portion of the coordinating functions as follow-up occurs; and it is definitely called into play in judging the results of a physical education program. A widely accepted short definition of supervision is that it is any activity concerned with improvement of instruction. Thus, supervision and administration are twins. It is in the supervisory role that an administrator views the efficacy of the teaching within a staff and the values apparent, hidden, or even non-existent within the curricular offerings. It is in a supervisory role that the administrator notes the reactions of personnel to the total school or college situation, the individual contributions of staff members to school and community life, and the interplay of personalities in staff relationships. There are many ways both formal and informal of evaluating and finally judging the results of the physical education program. Evaluation plus the resulting changes is a constant in the administrative equation.

A second phase of judging results is concerned with research before judgments can be made. Most administrative research is practical in nature. The facts may be gathered from all classes regarding attitudes and/or reactions to a program. Samples of opinions, effective standards, or organizational methods may be sought in situations similar to one's own problem. The administrator often cannot find the time needed for intensive research, but he can surely stress this need and support members of the staff who are qualified to do so.

The administrative process is involved. Not the least difficult is this matter of judging results. The presence of constructive leadership is revealed if the administrator maintains a functioning program that strives to support administrative lines, to reach high standards, to establish fine personnel relationships, and at the time to move ahead creatively in thinking and planning for the future. Thus, the wheel turns with provisions for progress as the guiding central traffic line on the road to better physical education.

PRINCIPLES OF ADMINISTRATION

In physical education, we usually reserve the intensive study of principles for the senior major and/or the graduate student. Because principles involve abstract thinking based on both inductive and deductive reasoning and because physical education is so highly objective in its practices, many persons have come to regard principles as difficult concepts. In reality, we cannot operate unless we know what we believe and why we believe it. Only by establishing basic truths may we set our goals, our standards, and our priorities in administration. In bringing these truths into practical use, we find ourselves reaching for policies and procedures to make the task feasible.

Policies have been variously defined as guidelines for action, structure for action, and statements of intended action. Any one of these phrases will suffice as long as we realize that any policy to be effective must have support from both staff members and administrators and must consider the best interest of students. Support implies action. Action implies authority. As we develop the administrative network, we will discuss policies that should be discussed and agreed upon by staff members and policies that, because of authoritative limitations, are the prerogative of administrators. Procedures, by definition, are the ways, the means we use to carry out our programs. An interesting simile for these concepts is that of a tree. Our basic beliefs (roots) form the body of our principles (trunk); our policies (intentions) branch out in many directions, while the procedures bring us to full maturity (leafing).

It would be impossible to include all the principles operative in administration. A few sample principles will be stated followed by a policy and one or more procedures for each.

Facilities and Equipment

Principle I   Designs for new facilities in physical education should be based upon a projected program that encompasses the needs of all students.

Policy   The program shall be pointed to classes for instruction, intramural and extramural participation, as well as recreational opportunities for students and/or the members of the community.

Procedure   The staff shall be divided into committees, based upon interest and expertness, to prepare details of the program with needed facilities in specific areas.

Principle II   Equipment and supplies in sufficient amount are imperative to the best development of a well-rounded physical education program.

Policy   The administration of physical education must be cognizant of departmental needs in equipment and supplies in the preparation of department budgets.

Procedure   Staff in charge of program areas should be asked to state equipment and supply needs in terms of quantity, quality, and costs.

Interrelationships

Principle I   Any department of physical education receives its authority and structures its action within the framework of the school system or institution.

Policy   The administrator of physical education should orient staff with regard to the lines of authority and the organization in use in a given educational setting.

Procedure   Staff must be counseled and advised when any proposed project exceeds the authority of the department.

Principle II   Participants in physical education should be protected by a full-scale physical examination before entering any activity.

Policy   It shall be the policy of the physical education department to respect the recommendations of the physician or health service with regard to classification of students for activities.

Procedure   By mutual conference, a form for activity classifications (classes, intramurals, and extramurals) shall be formulated and used.

Principle III   Environmental health, as evidenced by the facilities in physical education, is a responsibility of the administrator in physical education.

Policy   Gymnasiums, pools, shower and locker rooms, office, and consultation areas shall be kept scrupulously clean.

Procedure   Cleaning schedules shall be prepared for custodial staff, and supervision shall be established to insure

environmental conditions conducive to acceptable
health practices.

Legal Responsibilities

Principle I The administrator of physical education should become familiar with the laws of the city, the county, and
the state governments that affect his function.

Policy The operation of the swimming pool shall comply with
the sanitation codes in a given situation.

Procedure Water samples shall be tested daily for compliance
with sanitation standards.

Principle II The administrator of physical education shall be aware
of the local and state laws concerned with personal
legal liability as contrasted with vicarious liability.

Policy By consultation with the legal librarian, these laws
shall be obtained, and the legal implications of supervision shall be carefully explained to all staff.

Procedure Lines of supervisory authority and standards of supervisory practice for use of physical education facilities
and equipment shall be established for school and departmental personnel.

Public Relations

Principle I The public, paying the bills for education in the form
of taxes, has a right to information about the physical
education programs in the schools.

Policy Publicity in the form of newspaper releases and/or
pictures should be cleared with the chairman of the
department to be sure of clearance with higher administrative authorities and to avoid embarrassing circumstances.

Procedure Dates for releases are established when news of importance is available. Releases are prepared by the
department, taking care to include pertinent facts and
to check accuracy of the details of the story.

Personnel

Principle I Standards of preparation and experience will be agreed
upon for staff members in a given situation.

Policy Only candidates who meet these standards will be
considered in filling a staff vacancy.

Procedure Available resources will be canvassed to secure applicants to fill such a vacancy.

Program

Principle I   The curriculum should be planned to serve the best interests of students in a given locale, stressing progression in materials and continuity in learning experiences, with due consideration of the facilities available and the competencies of the staff.

Policy   Students will be scheduled for progressive units in any given activity, and repetition of a unit will be discouraged.

Procedure   Instructional units of sufficient length to offer opportunity for the development of skill for participation in the activity will be scheduled.

PHILOSOPHY OF ADMINISTRATION

There is little to be found in the literature regarding the philosophy of administration of physical education. Presumably, the assumption is made that administration deals with such concrete details that abstract thought is out of the picture. Presumably, also, administrators and their staffs have been exposed to current theories with regard to the application of realism, pragmatism, idealism, and/or existentialism in the conduct of physical education. As one studies these schools of thought, one identifies oneself with either a specific philosophy or blends one's beliefs into an eclectic point of view. The ramifications of these ideas have no place in this book, but the manner in which one's beliefs are carried out becomes the administrative philosophy of the school system or the college department. It is a moot question whether to base one's philosophy upon the principles that one accepts or to determine one's philosophy and then derive one's principles from the accepted philosophy.

The administrative philosophy in physical education necessarily is influenced by the philosophy of the school system or college in which the department is located. If all matters of principle and policy are determined by top echelon, then the department is limited in its use of democratic participation by staff members. In many colleges and universities, we find a faculty senate in which decisions are reached relative to college calendars; liaison channels for horizontal as well as vertical staff-to-staff contacts are established; and policies on library services, scholarships, and student loan practices are formulated. In public school systems, one must face the fact that, by virtue of the varied duties and size of the faculties involved, it is often not feasible to involve more than one specific faculty in decision-making of a democratic nature. Therefore, the philosophy of a particular school system as far as policies and practices go is set by a superintendent and his staff of assistants, consultants, and school principals. This does not mean that opinions of all persons involved are not sought, nor does it mean that an individual faculty would be prohibited from using democratic techniques in the administration of the functions assigned definitely to that specific school, but a central authority frequently makes final decisions.

If the use of democratic techniques is part of the administrative philosophy of a specific situation, several pertinent points of view follow. The first of these is belief in the potentials of all individuals who are on the scene—the students, the staff in parallel positions or in lower or upper echelons, and other administrative personnel or units. In this instance, we hint at one of the value structures that forms the spine of school morale. Only if we believe in individuals will individuals believe in us. Perhaps, this is the thread from which loyalty is woven.

If we believe in the potentials of individuals, we are willing to provide opportunities, administratively speaking, for the best programming for all students, and for participation by staff in growth and development activities and in departmental functioning. In both cases, opportunity spells privilege and privilege spells responsibility. Thus, students who have the privilege of fine programming must be stimulated to accept the resulting responsibilities. By the same token, staff members who participate in certain departmental decisions must be willing to accept resulting responsibilities. The democratic process is a two-way street.

Without leadership, democracy becomes a lost cause. The role of the leader in democratic administration of physical education then becomes a focal point in determining success or failure. If democratic leadership is defined as complete permissiveness, the frictions that may ensue between staff and students, students and other students, and between staff members will rub away the administrative structure. If permissiveness is constructively used in freeing staff to experiment with new ideas in curricular approach, in introduction of interesting materials, in use of newer teaching media, or to consult with other staff and/or authorities on professional problems, then permissiveness becomes a cohesive force.

The example of the leader has critical significance. If the leader of the group is willing to work, then the group will follow suit. If the leader sets an atmosphere in which contributions may be made, then the group is willing to state their own experiences and to formulate judgments based on group thinking. If the leader disregards details, fails to make reports, and in general is careless about group planning, then one may expect the group to follow suit.

Thus, the role of the leader in the groups helps to cast a mold for the philosophy embraced and the values that ensue and, in so doing, points out the goals or objectives that are the milestones along the way.

SUMMARY

In the acrostic "Shop Talk," the duties of an administrator have been indicated. Reviewing these responsibilities briefly, the reader comes to realize that a department exists for the services that it may perform for people. In the performance of these services, the adequacy of facilities and equipment influences programming, but staff competency and staff morale overshadow this influence. Organization and coordination of the myriad details of department functioning are indicated in this acrostic. The teamwork and know-how needed for a successful program together with dedicated leadership point the way toward *esprit de corps.*

There follows a discussion of the administrative process, emphasizing both the concrete and the abstract phases of the work. We become aware of the responsibilities of the administrator with regard to setting up goals, planning short- and long-range programs and projects, organizing for the task of implementing changes or coordinating the many factors in any situation toward completion of the work, and finally evaluating what has happened.

The literature in physical education contains numerous books and articles concerned with the general principles and philosophy of this field. The author cannot hope to add to these fine statements. The use of principles of administration as a basis for policies and procedures has been discussed and several examples included. Finally, the role of the philosophy of the staff and/or department as it relates to administration has been indicated.

Here are the nuclei of the administration of physical education. The growth and development of each nucleus is the concern of the following pages of this book.

PROBLEMS

1. Using the acrostic "Shop Talk," list two administrative duties in each category for an elementary school consultant, a secondary school teacher, and a chairman of a department in a small college.

2. Define administration in your own words. How does organization differ from administration?

3. As a teacher in a large city school system, state in order of priority the five most helpful administrative duties your coordinator of physical education could perform.

4. Select an area of administration, such as program planning (others), and construct two or more principles for this area. Work out carefully a policy and a procedure to implement each basic belief or truth.

5. In your own words, construct your philosophy of administration in physical education.

2

Administration
of the Program

In this chapter, an effort will be made to describe the problems of and to suggest possible solutions for the administration of the program of physical education in public school systems and colleges. No attempt will be made to present definitive philosophies and their resulting programs in physical education. Necessarily, indications of the trends and changes in thinking regarding programs in physical education will be involved, but the logic and analysis of such ideas will be reserved for the texts in philosophy and curriculums in physical education.

By definition, the curriculum in physical education will be concerned with all the physical activity programs controlled by any specific educational institution. These programs will include class instruction, intramural sports, extramurals or interscholastic athletics, as well as informal recreation such as activity clubs (dance, sports, aquatics), noon-hour and before-school recreation, faculty and family recreation, and special events conducted by the educational institution. In short, those experiences of an activity nature that are sponsored by a school or college all come under the term "physical education." This does not mean that we intend to exclude the mental learning and stimulus of the socialization opportunities or the emotional-moral-spiritual values that may accrue from participation in physical education activities but simply to pinpoint the administrative responsibilities in this program.

Since activity is a biological necessity all through life, the administration of the physical education program will be concerned with the elementary school, the secondary school, college (for the general student and for the professional student), and graduate programs. The complexities that result when the various phases of the physical education curriculum are meshed into the organizational patterns in our educational continuum give rise to the problems one meets in administering these programs.

Administratively, harmony must exist between the general philosophy and the overall objectives of the educational institution and the physical education program if learning is to take place. Some of the personnel problems that arise result from differing philosophies and striving for goals that are in conflict. An administrator at any level or for any phase of the program must be aware of the philosophy of the institution and must support this philosophy in his selection of activities in order to attain mutually satisfying goals. The general policies and procedures of the institution should be well understood so that the administrator in physical education may again support these policies and procedures. This is a situation in which the pillars support the roof while the roof maintains the stress that holds the pillars in place. Therefore, the policies and procedures developed in the physical education program should be supported by the general administration of the school or college.

THE ELEMENTARY SCHOOL PROGRAM

Currently, there are two administrative patterns for the teaching of physical education in the elementary school; namely, (1) all activities are conducted by the classroom teacher, and (2) a specialist in physical education is employed for grades three or four through grade six. There are excellent reasons, both philosophical and practical, for each of these patterns. The wealth of information available about the child, the possibility for integration of the learnings in physical education with other subject-matter areas, and the improvement in skills and posture possible in daily schoolroom tasks enable the classroom teacher to handle the physical education program as a phase of the general education of the elementary schoolchild. Particularly in the lower grades, the warmth that exists between teacher and child sets a climate in which all types of learning are facilitated. Increasingly, we are finding teachers in the elementary school who have a background of the broad curriculum but who have, in addition, specific preparation in a subject area and who may either teach this subject or act as consultants within the school. The second pattern uses a specialist employed to teach physical education from grades three or four through grade six. The specialist in physical education may offer to the elementary schoolchild a widely varied program based upon knowledge of growth and development, ability to teach and improve motor skills accurately, and intense interest in all phases of physical activity. Usually, such specialists are assigned two or more elementary schools. When the time can be arranged, these specialists will act as consultants for the lower-grade programs. In either pattern, a top administrator known as a supervisor, city-wide consultant, or coordinator sets the pace and the scope of the physical education program for the elementary schools.

Brief comment on the physical education program of the elementary school is necessary before consideration can be given to the administrative problems. For many years, within the structure of the "informal" program, a rather formalized presentation of activities has been the practice. Thus, games, dance materials (basic rhythms, folk and square dances), stunts, free exercises, basic postural concepts, and lead-up materials for sports, planned with definite progression from grade to grade, became the established procedure. Courses of study or curricular guides were written by experienced teachers or by supervisors. As we have changed our concept to the highly expert appraisal needed of classes and children to foster individual growth and development patterns and to challenge the intelligence of the children of this century who have been stimulated by advances in communication and technology and by the opportunities of the atomic age and the new horizons in the space age, we are planning our programs more flexibly. So, we plan for graduated levels of growth and development for early childhood (six to eight years), middle childhood (nine to eleven years), and early adolescence (twelve to fourteen years).[1] Thus, it would be feasible to use the more advanced materials of early childhood with children whose backgrounds demand this and to use easier materials at the same level for classes with limited ability or limited understanding of play situations. In other words, we no longer depend upon an exact grade placement for physical education materials in the elementary school. We are also interested in what the children say about our materials and how the children use these materials in free-play situations at school, at home, or in the neighborhood play areas.[2] Although the

[1] *Spotlight the Children in Physical Education* (City of Detroit: Board of Education, 1951).

[2] *What We Like To Do. A Report by Fourth, Fifth and Sixth Grade Boys and Girls,* Physical Education Standards Project Bulletin 5, New York State Education Department, Division of Health and Physical Education, Bureau of Physical Education (New York: University of the State of New York, 1954).

skills of movement have been taught for many years, they have been treated as entities in themselves (the serve for volleyball, the punt for football, the skip or the step-and-hop for folk dance). We restricted the fun of exploration of movement to the unsupervised hours of playwork that the child pursued on his own initiative. Far be it for the author to deny the value of these hours; we need more hours of release from pressure. Children always have and always will explore movement. But today we realize that we have failed to apply to the daily teaching of physical education all we have known for years of the laws of anatomy, kinesiology, and physiology. Add to this the information that we have from psychology and sociology of the child's need for self-determination, for recognition, for stimulating experiences, and for group interaction and we have unlimited opportunity for movement education. In movement education, the child is encouraged to explore *space*, to grasp the significance of *time* (length of movement, timing, and relationships within a group), and to discover how much or how little *force* he needs to perform a movement or a series of movements. Movement is set forth as a problem for him to solve. In so doing, he develops personal skill and endurance, as well as extending his knowledge and his appreciation of his own movement and that of others.[3, 4] Every child counts in this approach. Our games, stunts, dance materials, and body-building activities are not didactically presented; each is a problem that requires creative thinking from the child. Each of these possibilities in a program results in certain identical administrative problems and certain other differing problems.

All these programs demand consideration of the adequacy of the teacher, the space(s) available for activity, the play equipment necessitated by the activity, the time allocated to the lesson or free play, and the scheduling feasible within a specific school. Please note that all these programs are instructional, not merely allocation of a few minutes for "recess," or noon-hour play, or unsupervised play. At this point, the similarities in administrative demands cease.

The traditional grade-by-grade program is the easiest to administer. One checks credentials to be sure that the teacher, either classroom or specialist, has taken at least one course in plays and games, rhythms for children, or, even better, a survey of physical education in the elementary school. One hopes that such a teacher

3 Elizabeth Halsey and Lorena Porter, *Physical Education for Children, A Developmental Program* (New York: Holt, Rinehart & Winston, Inc., 1961), chap. 9.

4 Gladys Andrews, Jeannette Saurborn, and Elsa Schneider, *Physical Education for Today's Boys and Girls* (Boston: Allyn & Bacon, Inc., 1960), chaps. 4, 13, and 14.

is either well prepared with a card-index file of activities and several good books on physical education or knows where to find them. A checklist of equipment needs for the elementary school physical education program is consulted, and a supply (available on a rotated basis) for class use is provided. The playground is carefully scheduled class by class; indoor space, often quite limited in nature, is made available when feasible (see Chapter 7). Scheduled time, also often limited in nature, is provided for these activities. This scheduled time is liable to hazards; it may be placed on the total program at an hour that is poor (such as the start of the day or immediately following lunch), it may be low in relative placement to the more academic areas, or it may rotate with art or music. The teacher is charged with the responsibility of definite instruction in the skills and activities planned for each specific grade level.

It would be quite possible to plan and administer a program giving consideration to levels of growth and development within a grade-by-grade class scheduling. The teacher, in this instance, would need to be astute and to have a flair for organization. Groupings within a graded class would identify those children with advanced skills and interests, the average group, and the group whose maturity is at a lower level. Using similar materials, the teacher would need to plan different approaches and organize different activities for these varied groups. This approach is constantly used in reading, mathematics, and social studies; but the teacher of physical education has seldom realized the possibilities in so organizing his activities.

Either the traditional-materials approach or the movement-exploration approach lends itself to a final administrative setup. Careful selection should enable the administrator to find teachers who have been introduced to movement exploration, to observation and careful analyzation of the reactions of children, and to cognizance of the potentialities within a play situation for social interaction and resulting personality development. The total school program then becomes the administrative unit with flexible use of scheduled time. Thus, a social studies unit of language arts materials that lend themselves to integration of subject matter might well carry the scheduling of the physical education materials as a part of a larger block of time. In another unit, where integration would not prove feasible, the physical education materials would return to basic scheduling, and the teaching emphasis would stress skills. Flexible scheduling would necessitate both flexible use of facilities and availability of play areas when needed. Particularly in the movement approach, the child's exploration of space demands that space be there to be used. The use of small or hand apparatus is encouraged in a movement approach as well as balls, large apparatus, and sundry other kinds of equipment. Because movement exploration delves into individual reactions, play supplies must be on hand in sufficient quantity to enhance this program. In the long run, no more time is devoted to physical education in this administrative setup than in the traditionally set periods; the time is simply distributed differently. No additional play areas are needed, but they must be kept available for the use of the physical education program. No more teachers are needed, but they must be teachers with a high degree of insight, the courage to explore subject matter, and the know-how to guide learning experiences.

The reader, by this time, is probably wondering where the current emphasis on physical fitness may find a place in this program. In and of itself, physical fitness cannot be designated a subject-matter area since it is a state or condition of well-being that results from the physical education program. Administratively, in the elementary school, the phases of the program that are concerned with posture and free exercise may well place emphasis upon the concept of physical fitness. Schedulewise, the detailed work in this area will be scattered, depending upon type of activity and weather factors throughout the school year.

The figures in Table 2–1 represent composite percentages of time allotment calculated by the author from varying estimates in leading studies. These percentages are suggested as a suitable guide. See Table 2–2 for a listing of suggested seasonal activities.

Within the past decade, there have been increasing pressures toward intramurals and even interscholastic participation for upper elementary schoolchildren. This is a highly controversial area with implications for teacher and parental ambition and pride, shadowy gray areas of the emotional effect of such participation, and unsolved problems of individual physiological age as the basis for such participation. It would appear that children may not, in the past, have been challenged enough by the rather vague play and games programs conducted in certain elementary schools. On the other hand, we know that elementary schoolchildren are malleable, and any activity from complicated square dances to competitive sports can be thrust upon them if the adults will keep on pressuring long enough. Because of the unknown and possibly negative factors involved, it would seem wise to achieve educational ends rather than personal satisfaction. Therefore, it is strongly recom-

Table 2–1

Time Allotment—Recommended Percentages

	Primary Grades (6–8 years)	(Intermediate Grades) (9–11 years)
Movement exploration	20%	15%
Self-testing	15	20
Games	30	40
Dance	30	15
Fitness and posture	5	10

Table 2–2

Suggested Seasonal Activities

Fall (September–November)	Winter (November–January)	Winter (January–March)	Spring (March–May)
Outdoors	*Indoors*	*Indoors*	*Outdoors*
PRIMARY GRADES			
Self-testing (apparatus play)	Movement exploration	Movement exploration	Self-testing (rope jumping)
Ball handling (fall activities)	Indoor games	Indoor games	Ball handling (spring activities)
Active games (low organization)	Self-testing (stunts and tumbling)	Self-testing (stunts and tumbling)	Active games (low organization)
	Dance	Dance	
	Fitness and posture	Fitness and posture	
INTERMEDIATE GRADES			
Relays	Movement exploration	Movement exploration	Track and field
Lead-ups to fall sports	Dance	Dance	Lead-ups to softball
Active large group games	Lead-ups to winter sports (volleyball)	Lead-ups to winter sports (basketball)	Softball
Team games	Active large group games	Active large group games	
	Stunts and tumbling	Stunts and tumbling	
	Indoor apparatus (ropes, etc.)	Indoor apparatus (ropes, etc.)	
Fitness and posture	Fitness and posture	Fitness and posture	Fitness and posture

mended that informal grade-by-grade (Fifth I vs. Fifth II) games of an intramural type be the pattern with an occasional invitational game with a neighboring fifth grade. To avoid a buildup of neighborhood pressures, it is further recommended that the invitations be rotated from school to school. Track and field events are fascinating, and fourth-, fifth-, and sixth-graders enjoy an afternoon meet with other classes in the same school. This would seem to be an acceptable practice.

A word must be said about the special events that occur within the elementary school program such as school assemblies, PTA demonstrations, and fun nights. Elaborate costuming, exhaustive rehearsals, and star performers defeat the educational purposes of such events. Administratively, these special programs should be planned as culminating events for the regular instructional program.

Noon hour in the elementary school has also often been a source of irritation to the classroom teacher who has been forced to eat her lunch under trying circumstances. Increasingly, we are finding one of two administrative patterns in operation. Teacher aides are now being employed to supervise the noon hour. The second pattern is the development and use of leadership by children from the highest grade in the school. These children are given the opportunity to assist one teacher or an aide by supervising small groups of younger children at play. Correctly set up and guided, this is an excellent experience for these older children.

A summary of the administrative practices in the elementary schools includes:

1. A progressive program based upon the growth and development characteristics of children at varying ages. Included in this concept is the maturation scale (mental, social, and emotional).

2. Since the elementary school experience lays the foundation for future experience in physical education, administrative decisions must be concerned with the competency of the physical education teacher.

3. Scheduling physical education in the elementary school must be an instructional period with due regard for a short period of informal play (tension release) on the alternate half of the school day. Therefore, a fifth grade with a thirty- to forty-minute instruction period in the morning would be scheduled for a fifteen-minute relief period in the afternoon. Staggered scheduling (i.e., all grade-one and grade-two classes use the playground at one period, grades three and four another period, etc.). In this way, smaller play areas are used to advantage and safety hazards are reduced.

4. Due consideration must be given to the scheduling of physical education for indoor areas, especially during the winter months. A

ratio for proportionate use of multiple-scheduled areas should be established (multipurpose room shared by audio-visual, music, and physical education; combined auditorium-gymnasium; or combined lunch areas and gymnasium).

5. The principal or physical education consultant should confer with the classroom teacher or physical education specialist in the interest of a balanced program of activities.

6. Provision should be made in the general scheduled budget for yearly purchase of small items of equipment such as balls, recordings, and ropes. From time to time, changes or additions in larger playground equipment should be considered. If facilities and teacher competency are adequate, provision for larger items of indoor equipment, such as mats, should also be considered.

7. Provision should be made for communication among the school nurse, parents, and the teacher regarding the health status of each child. This is particularly important when outbreaks of the so-called children's diseases occur in a neighborhood.

8. Evaluation of the program should occur constantly. Children should be taught that they have "learned" in a physical education program and this learning should be reported by the teacher.

9. Supervision of before-school, after-school, and noon-hour activities should be carefully scheduled with due regard to teacher load and teacher comfort during the school day.

THE SECONDARY SCHOOL PROGRAM

In spite of considerably more "know-how" and "know-why" than fellow alumni of former years, the beginning teacher of physical education at the secondary school level faces a vastly complex educational structure as he launches a professional career. This being true, the complex of problems, in spite of additional preparation and teaching experience, that faces a neophyte administrator is not only challenging but often staggering. There are problems of personnel, facilities and equipment, type and scope of curriculum, and finance, to name only a few. In due time, these varied problems fall into their respective niches, progress is made, and the neophyte teacher and/or administrator finds that the secondary school is a rewarding place in which to work.

For purposes of this discussion, the junior and the senior high school will be a continuum. Such a continuum would recognize that distinctive differences exist in growth and developmental factors and in the philosophy supporting the junior high school program in contrast to the senior high school program. These differences will receive proper reference. But the continuum has many identical administrative problems, such as the need for specialized facilities and equipment, the need for competent personnel, the need for adequate time allotments and practical scheduling, and the need to establish evaluation techniques. It seems redundant to spell out these identical administrative needs.

In this day of accreditation at the secondary school level, one or more teachers are assigned the responsibility for physical education and related activities. It is increasingly true that physical education, especially in large secondary schools, is taught by competent, well-prepared personnel. As consolidation of school districts occurs, it is the optimistic opinion of the author that the physical education curriculum of the future will be manned by well-prepared specialists. Administratively, then, the solution for the problem of personnel for secondary school physical education becomes that of careful selection—teachers whose professional competence and personality traits indicate adaptability to a specific local situation (see Chapter 6).

The preadolescent, adolescent, and young adult students who make up our secondary school population are at a crucial point in their growth and developmental patterns. They need and demand sympathetic guidance to face many conflicts in ambitions, hopes and desires, success and failure, and emotional groping toward maturity. Not only is the adolescent worried about himself, but he is also frequently in conflict with the mores of the adult population or the mores of his peers. To the boy or girl caught in the vortex of several conflicting needs or interests, a casual incident may be built up into a crisis. Each of these boys or girls is developing physically at his own rate, meeting or rejecting intellectual challenges on the basis of his own fluctuating estimates of his present and future needs, and structuring his own values of a social and moral nature as he tackles his daily problems. The complexity of all these drives toward maturity results in one of two solutions—either he sorts out the issues and faces them, or he becomes emotionally harassed. Years later, adults look back and wonder how they managed to survive this ordeal of growing up. Credit should be recorded to each generation for the thoughtful care that brings each of us to adulthood.

Administratively, what do the above generalizations about secondary school students mean? The objectives of the secondary school must recognize these characteristics. Differences in growth rate and development must be acknowledged by differences in objectives for junior and senior high school students in both age and sex adaptations. The uneven growth patterns must be covered by attention to individual objectives as well as group relationships. The need to accept responsibility must be met by intellectual and social challenges within the framework of a physical education program that aims to reach every student. Such a program must find a focus of interest for each student; therefore, it must encompass a wide range of activities and a wide range of skill levels. The objectives must take into account the demand for strength status on the part of the boy and for grace in daily living skills on the part of the girl. These objectives must be concerned with the awakening interest in the opposite sex, and programs must be provided that give some opportunity for coeducational experiences. Finally, these objectives must provide ways and means for learning leadership and followership roles, for emotional outlets that can be constructively channeled, and for the establishment of certain values, such as fair play, sportsmanship, honesty in action, sticking to the end of the activity (tournaments), ability to think under stress, and positive calm reaction at a moment of decision. A big job—but one that is worth the effort.

Cowell and Schwehn express a generally accepted idea that the curriculum uses experiences as building blocks in a desired position or sequence.[5] It follows, then, that a primary responsibility of administration is to arrange the program in such a manner that the objectives may be feasible. This arrangement is commonly called a design or a pattern for the program. In listing experiences to help in shaping this pattern, one must include classwork, extra-class experiences such as intramurals, varsity sports, cheerleading, and pep clubs. One must be concerned with selecting activities that provide ways and means for effective teaching with resultant learning. Both the teacher and the administrator face problems of planning progressions, avoiding repetitive participation, and tailoring the curriculum to fit the needs and interests of secondary school youth within a framework of available facilities and equipment, adequate and competent personnel, and the competing needs and interests of other subject-matter areas. This program needs to be carefully weighted and its components balanced in several directions. Overemphasis upon body building, varsity competition, or physical skills may result in negative reactions from the academicians. Little or no attention to individual needs may result in student and justifiable parental criticisms and also in inquiries from the guidance staff. Little or no attention to development

[5] Charles C. Cowell and Hilda M. Schwehn, *Modern Principles and Methods in Secondary School Physical Education* (2d ed.; Boston: Allyn & Bacon, Inc., 1964), p. 87.

of leadership skills, sportsman-like conduct, and the moral learnings that may be concomitants of a sound program refute the objectives related to attitudes. Participation without attention to the historical, regulatory, aesthetic, and appreciation learnings in an activity ignores the knowledges that are possible. Selection of the specifics for the program from the range of sports, aquatics, dance, body-building, self-testing, camping, outdoor, and recreational activities of a social nature then must run the gamut from the low to the highly skilled and from the restricted to the highly active individual. The program is also dependent upon seasonal interests, weather conditions, geographic handicaps or advantages, and the mores, customs, and traditions of the community. Time allotments and schedule slots also exert controls over this program. (See Table 2–3.)

The junior high school years form the bridge between the elementary school and the senior high school. It is during these years that the student is expected to sound out and find a sense of direction for senior high school experiences and even for higher education. The curriculum, in general, offers opportunity for exploration, experimentation, and experiences leading to the wider choices available in later educational settings. The same is true in physical education. The administrator must plan variety in this program, utilize the energy and enthusiasm of this age, and lay the groundwork for the more advanced programs that follow. Team sports on a seasonal basis receive heavy emphasis. Provision must be made to introduce some of the individual sports. Coeducational activities (dance, recreational games) are valuable at intervals but not as a constant diet. Body building, fitness activity, self-testing, and stunts, tumbling, and gymnastics satisfy many needs of these students. The program should be broad, but because of social immaturity, the student should be carefully guided in an exploratory program. Irregular growth patterns reduce the advisability for making heavy demands on endurance activities.

For many students, the senior high physical education program is not only the place for the development of recreational skills but it is, unfortunately for many, a terminal experience. The program should be administered to touch lightly upon the team sports, unless new experiences can be introduced, but there should be a heavy emphasis placed on individual and dual sports that have a carry-over value. If at all possible, an aquatic program should be offered that includes instruction in water safety. Increasingly, there is interest in free exercise, creative gymnastics, and apparatus. Dance in both social and creative forms should be available.

Table 2–3

Types of Activities and Their Respective Time Percentages *
in the Secondary School

Types of Activities	Boys †		Girls †	
	J.H.S.	S.H.S.	J.H.S.	S.H.S.
Organization	5%	5%	5%	5%
Team sports	40–30	25–20	35–30	20–15
Individual and couple	10–15	15–25	10–15	20–30
Dance (modern, folk, square, social)	10	10–5	20–25	25–30
Gymnastics	15	15	10	10
Track and field	5	5–10	5	5–0
Combatives	0–5	5–10	0	0
Aquatics	10	10	10	10
Body mechanics and conditioning	5–10	5–10	5–10	5
	100%	100%	100%	100%

* Percentage figures are given here to designate trends and should therefore not be considered unchangeable.

† The types of activities and percentage time allotments have been given separately for boys and for girls; certain activities such as dance, individual and couple activities may be taught and played in coeducational groups.

SOURCE: Arthur G. Miller and M. Dorothy Massey, *Methods in Physical Education for the Secondary School* (Englewood Cliffs, N.J.: Prentice-Hall, Inc., 1963), p. 127. Reprinted by permission.

Administration of the secondary school program carries the following considerations:

1. The program (grades seven to twelve) must be planned for progression in skill, the junior high years being used for basic skill development with opportunity for advanced skills during the senior high school experience.

2. The program (grades seven to twelve) must consider the problem of repetition of the seasonal sports. Involved in this situation is scheduling by grade levels so that some homogeneity is assured. Alternate-year scheduling as well as providing for sports that have similar characteristics but use different skills and equipment are two ways to work with this problem.

3. The program must be carefully scheduled. Decisions must be made within the framework of the local situation. In states where daily physical education participation is a requirement, it must be so scheduled. However, if there is leeway and if the entire school is organized for module scheduling or a modification of this plan, it would be wise to investigate and to try this plan of operation in the secondary school physical education program.[6]

[6] John E. Nixon and Ann E. Jewett, *Physical Education Curriculum* (New York: The Ronald Press Co., 1964), chap. 10. This is probably the clearest and most concise explanation of flexible scheduling.

4. The aquatic program demands attention to safeguards in health practices, pool regulations for swimmers, and sanitation of the pool, suits, and towels.
5. The dance program has administrative needs such as provision of accompaniment, correct and safe floors to use, and special costuming needs.
6. The body-building, gymnastics, and apparatus programs necessitate administrative emphasis on protection devices and safety precautions plus careful selection of trained personnel.
7. The administrator must be aware of the need to balance the program with due attention to sports and athletics, to aesthetics (dance and swimming), and to cardiovascular needs (fitness).
8. Constant evaluation of the program must be planned and carried out (see Chapter 10).
9. Guidance within the physical education program should be provided based upon cumulative records that provide health information and leadership experiences as well as skill and activity competence.
10. The need for coeducational experiences must be evaluated within a specific situation and activities scheduled as indicated.
11. Teacher loads in physical education must be structured along similar lines with other subjects in the school. The physical education staff should expect to carry its fair share of extras but not the total load.
12. Physical education as a required subject in the secondary school is open to questions of legal liability. All personnel must be aware of this factor and should be encouraged to carry liability insurance. It is imperative that physical education personnel be alert to the need for constant vigilance, safety precautions, and inspection practices that may help in avoiding accidents.
13. The programs of physical education demand clear communication from teacher to student, teacher to teacher, and teacher to administrator if they are to be effective.

Administrative problems found in the secondary program using flexible scheduling include the following:

1. Curricular units would be structured to permit a flexible number of weeks per unit based upon student needs and interests.
2. Classroom space, equipped with projectors, public address systems, and other audio-visual devices, must be available for large lecture groups.
3. Additional smaller space must be available for discussion groups of ten to twenty students.
4. The school library must include books and periodicals that will enable both the teacher and the student to study a topic in depth.

5. The gymnasiums, outdoor play areas, and auxiliary play areas must be adaptable for use by both large and small groups.
6. Teaching personnel must understand the problems of structuring the program to individual needs and must have the know-how and patience to conduct physical education activities in this manner.

NEWER PATTERNS

One should not leave the subject of program planning in physical education without pointing to certain trends and frames of reference relative to the curriculum in the schools of both today and tomorrow.

Several years ago, educational TV began to occupy a place of prominence in the thinking of administrators as they faced the challenges of increased numbers plus increased emphasis on programs for the highly gifted. Physical education has only scratched the surface in the use of this medium for programming. There have been a few in-service classes to upgrade the teaching of physical education at the elementary school level [7, 8] and several fine public school system presentations directed toward health education and fitness,[9] and institutions of higher learning have used closed circuit TV to cover large numbers in basic classes,[10, 11] and there have been programs presented at local levels to inform the public of the work of the school and college departments. We have left untapped the use of closed circuit TV in the education of students in the background, the reasons for activity, and the aesthetic appreciations possible. We have also failed to explore the teaching of specific skills—for example, golf—by means of live TV presentations by an expert at the time a specific skill is needed. The author feels that additional programs such as consumer education programs in this day of heavy buying of sports equipment, boating, water safety, and traffic skills could be augmented by use of this medium. Administratively, the problems are old as well as new, and usual as well as different. Securing the finances to back such a venture is an old problem; the distribution of well-prepared kinescopes is a

[7] Virginia Robinson, "An Experiment in Instructional TV," *Journal of Health, Physical Education, and Recreation*, XXXIII (May–June, 1962), 31.
[8] Martha A. Goble, "Fit as a Fiddle—Via TV Teaching," *ibid.*, 27.
[9] A Team Effort in Atlanta, Georgia, "Fitness and Fun on Educational Television," *ibid.*, XXXIV (February, 1963), 24–26.
[10] Jean McIntyre and Dorothy Kurth, "In Focus for College Classes," *ibid.*, XXXIII (May–June, 1962), 29.
[11] Marjorie Souder, "Exploring with Television To Find New Concepts," *ibid.*, XXXII (April, 1961), 28.

new problem. Sequence structure of motor skills is one of our usual problems, but how to plan these sequences so that they will portray the skill accurately is a different type of problem in this field. We have only scratched the surface of the possible uses of this educational medium.

Programmed instruction is another teaching aid that physical education has not used to any great extent. It has been stated that the machine in use is only as valuable as the program that has been written for it. With the interest in individualized instruction and the possible new approaches to physical education in team teaching and flexible scheduling, we may see a number of programs written that delve into the principles of movement, analysis of sports skills, strategies in sports, historical backgrounds, and the aesthetic appreciations to be found in physical education.

Team teaching and flexible scheduling seem to be developments that tie into one another. When two or more persons combine their abilities in the teaching of a unit, a course, or a complete subject, we have a team. With the addition of more teachers, each with specific talents, we are able to cover more material with more individual attention to each student. When the team is a large unit, it is feasible to use teaching aides or student assistants for certain practice areas. Certainly, secretarial help for a large team, or even for two teams, would free teachers to perform the teaching acts more thoroughly. Team teaching functions well when large groups may meet for presentation of basic materials. In physical education, this could well be the historical background of a sport plus the general scope of play; the climatic, historical-political, and social culture of a country whose folk materials are under scrutiny; or the principles of movement for a basic course (core) in fundamentals of physical education. After such a presentation, the large group would break into smaller groups for presentation of skills and game participation. These smaller groups could break into fours, couples, or individuals for practice as needed or body building as demanded by the activity. When plans of this type are put into effect, the schedule must be flexible. More time may be demanded for physical education at one time than at another time. Module scheduling (based on a time unit from fifteen to thirty minutes) has been tried and found to be successful. Therefore, the large group might meet only once a week for one module, the smaller groups two times a week for four modules, and the individual practice modules may depend on the skill of the player (or dancer or swimmer). Administratively, this approach means that the entire program shall be so structured and that the facilities must lend themselves by number and type to these uses. It demands teachers who are sympathetic to the idea and whose teaching skill is such that the students will profit by individualized instruction. This is a new idea in physical education. It is still too early for complete evaluation of its feasibility over the long run or for its inherent faults or advantages to have emerged. Physical educators and administrators, however, should be cognizant of these trends and be willing to test out these newer approaches. We have been searching for a long time for a way for the neophyte citizen to handle the responsibility for his own future activity. As Chisholm succinctly observes: "The most neglected part of an adequate health and physical education program in the schools is the part which seeks to develop in each individual that degree of maturity whereby he will be able to direct his own activities in a high degree of effectiveness in the field of health and well-being throughout life." [12] It would seem advisable to investigate these newer trends for newer approaches to this ideal.

PROGRAMS FOR THE EXCEPTIONAL

Little mention was made of this phase of physical education in discussing physical education for the elementary school. It was pointed out that class games or neighborhood school games might be scheduled. This would be one means of caring for the individual differences of the highly skilled child. Leadership for groups of younger children also gives the skilled child a sense of his worth to the total group. The child restricted by physical difficulties is seldom privileged to have activity classes provided for his peer group; and, unless supervision is available and specially prepared instructors are placed in charge, he is often better scheduled in a regular elementary school program. We are seeing today increasing attention to the needs of the mentally retarded child. Special schools or special classes now give attention to these children. Realizing that play therapy is an integral part in the development of these children, physical education must provide personnel for such classes. The needs of the elementary school do not differ to any great degree from those of other educational levels in providing for the two extremes of skill ability or capacity and will be discussed as part of the total picture.

At the secondary- and college-age levels, it is generally assumed that extracurricular activities (interscholastic and varsity athletics;

[12] Leslie L. Chisholm, *The Work of the Modern High School* (New York: The Macmillan Co., 1953), p. 228.

special clubs, as dance, swimming, outdoor education) together with intermediate and advanced sections in sports, gymnastics, dance, and swimming will care for the needs of the students with advanced-skill interests. It is possible that the use of flexible scheduling and team teaching may improve physical education for the highly skilled student since this approach is based on individual student needs.

The adapted program at the high school and college levels has been developed to provide opportunity for students with limitations to participate in activity. The safety, restrictions, capacities, and interests of these students must be carefully evaluated, and the program must be conducted by teachers who are subject to medical supervision. The following administrative measures are necessary:

1. There should be: individual attention for each case, including medical referral of type of activity tolerated by the student.
2. Close cooperation between medical services and the department is needed.
3. Provision must be made for personnel specifically prepared in this area.
4. Provision must be made for facilities and equipment adequate for the general types of handicaps or limitations usually identified.
5. Careful records must be kept indicating the activity or exercise program planned for each student.
6. Selection of staff for this program should be meticulous. Adequate scientific foundations, background in general physical education, as well as specialized training in the conduct of physical education under physical and/or mental limitations are basic considerations. The individual chosen to teach this area of physical education should possess excellent mental hygiene in order to "live with" the conditions he meets and in order to pass on to the student an optimistic, yet realistic, outlook.
7. Provision must be made in the general program of physical education to provide space in classes where activity is on a moderate level (for example, golf or archery) for individuals leaving the adapted program.
8. The goal in these classes should be the return of the student to the regular program. It has been suggested that, particularly in the secondary school where peer opinion is treasured, these students should be scheduled to regular activities certain days of the week and to the adapted program the remainder of the week.

Guiding principles for these programs have been carefully spelled out by the American Association for Health, Physical Education, and Recreation (AAHPER) Committee on Adapted Physical Education, endorsed by AAHPER Board of Directors, Joint Committee on Health Problems in Education of the American Medical Association (AMA), and the National Education Association (NEA) (see Appendix No. 1).

Another phase of exceptional physical education that is beginning to receive attention is physical education for adults. Many women, in particular those who have interrupted their college years to marry and rear children, are now returning to complete college degrees and, subsequently, to enter the working world. In this day of concern for activity at all ages, physical education must be prepared to induct these adults into the program based upon the capacity as well as the recreational interests of the individual student. Administratively, this situation calls for scheduling enough low-activity classes to accommodate these persons, opening the adaptive program for their use if necessary, and, above all, stimulating an interest in the staff in the needs of this group of mature students.

INFORMAL CURRICULAR EXPERIENCES

INTRAMURALS

Intramurals at either high school or college level have similar administrative demands. These activities, which follow in general the schedule of the instructional program, may be organized as an entity or they may be sponsored by an athletic association (Girl's Athletic Association, Women's Athletic Association or Women's Recreation Association, Boy's Athletic Association, Men's Athletic Association). Intramurals are designed as an enrichment phase of the program and as a means of providing recreational or additional activity for the instructional program. These games, within the walls, provide competition for all students. Organized and sponsored by student activity groups, intramurals provide opportunities for leadership and for acceptance of responsibilities. The student has a chance in the intramural program to make friends, engage in the fellowship of common endeavor, and begin to establish participation patterns in selected activities in which he is interested.

Intramurals are financed through regular school channels. The person in charge of this program is usually a regular staff member (man for the boys, woman for the girls). This person must like people, have the ability to organize the activities and to stimulate and guide student leaders, but above all else, this person must display his enthusiasm for the program. In many colleges, an intramural director is employed, and in some instances, buildings constructed specifically for this student recreational program have been erected. Smaller schools and colleges must ask the regular instructor to assist with this program. In larger colleges, better staff support of intramurals and better schedule loading is established by rotating some of this responsibility among staff members.

Student leadership is often organized into a council of sports heads plus officers of the sponsoring agency and faculty advisors. Such a council sets up the schedule of activities for the year, formulates policies and procedures for securing participants, approves budgets and other related financial matters, adjusts grievances, and sets up ways and means of providing officials for games.

Some system of establishing teams must be provided. In secondary schools, class identification, homerooms, or floor teams are practical. In colleges, housing units, floors, or residential zones may be the answer. A perennial problem is the inclusion of independent or town students in the team classification scheme. Frequently, a representative assembly from each unit identified is used as a means of communicating with teams and of securing cooperative assistance for officiating the games.

There are a few eligibility problems that need to be faced. Varsity players (college or secondary) and majors in physical education must be limited in the number allowed to play in a game, or intramurals will become the victim of either personal aggressiveness or domination by the more highly skilled players. Players may not transfer loyalties during a specific intramural season. The medical recommendations for regular participation hold true in intramurals. A student who is considered a poor risk in the regular program should not be found on the intramural courts. Only students belonging to a specific population should be allowed to participate in the program for that school (legal liability). Because the philosophy of the intramural program is based on opportunity for all, participation should not be limited by skill or scholastic eligibility requirements.

Awards of little or no intrinsic value (for example, cups or plaques) are usually offered in the intramural program. Generally, these awards point toward participation in a number of activities by individuals or by homogeneous groups. An administrative problem at this point is the devising of a simple but accurate record system.

A serious administrative problem in intramurals is that of scheduling. In large consolidated, township, or urban secondary schools, the expanded school day may provide time either immediately be-

fore or immediately after classes for this activity. Module scheduling, as it increases, may also allow short periods for intramural
play as a phase of the total time allotment for physical education.
In many cases, facilities must be shared by boys and girls and by
intramurals and varsity sports. Some equitable arrangement needs
to be considered. Perhaps short intramural periods followed by
longer varsity practice periods, ratio scheduling between boys and
girls based upon the possible percentage of participation, and use
of floors, courts, and tracks on an off-season schedule for intramurals may suggest ways of solving this problem in a specific
locale.

Officiating intramurals also poses problems. The game must be
well called and official rules should be used, but if modifications
are necessary, these should be understood by the players. Intramurals exist for participation, however. If the players are skilled,
they appreciate closely called games. The official needs to be
aware of the skill level of the teams playing and to adjust his
officiating skills accordingly (often an explanation of the call is all
that is needed). At the secondary level, volunteer officials who are
interested in future officiating experiences are frequently used. The
students and the intramural program will benefit by several clinics
on officiating the various sports. At the college level, if majors in
physical education are on campus, this is an excellent laboratory
experience for them. In addition, there are students at the college
level who either enjoy being officials or who want to learn the art.

Because of the more informal situation operative in the intramurals program, an adequate protection program is a must. Previously, we mentioned the need to carefully check the medical record
of participants. This can be expedited by the health services of the
institution in the form of an intramural participation card issued
only for restricted cases. Items are *not* checked in which the participant may engage (Fig. 2–1).

The protection program involves careful supervision of equipment, facilities, and apparatus in use. Prompt first-aid measures
with referral to medical authorities are needed in case of accident.
The same accident report form may be used as that for the regular
program.

Communication with the student body is a serious problem for
the intramural program. It is necessary to set up channels by which
students will become aware of the entire program. Devices that
have been used successfully are small handbooks, calendars of
events arranged to catch the attention, bulletins giving tournament
information, and articles in the school or college paper. While

University of_____   University Health Services

PERMIT FOR
INTRAMURAL AND RECREATIONAL PARTICIPATION
FOR WOMEN

This is to certify that:

Name _____
          Last   First   Middle

may participate in the activities NOT CHECKED below. This evaluation is based on the medical information available to the medical staff on this date.

Vigorous	Moderate	Mild
____ Volleyball	____ Soccer Baseball	____ Bowling
____ Basketball	____ Badminton	____ Table Tennis
____ Tennis Singles	____ Softball	____ Riflery
____ Swimming Meets	____ Tennis Doubles	____ Archery
____ Orchesis	____ Golf	
____ Aquaquettes		

Date _____   _____ M.D.

(Send Permit to Department of Physical Education for Women.)

Fig. 2–1. Sample permit for participation in activities.

tournaments are in process, machinery is in motion to notify teams of playing dates and to assign officials to games. The results of tournaments are of great interest to the student body. Articles, scores, and special-event items in the school paper are appreciated by the student body.

In closing this discussion of intramurals, we would like to mention the clubs that frequently form part of the organization. These clubs emphasize specific sports, or dance, or synchronized swimming. In the sports, they organize for practice and play either invitational or limited-schedule games. In dance and synchronized swimming, the emphasis is upon creativity, with recitals and water ballets climaxing the work of the season or the year. These programs bring into action responsibilities for deadline dates and tickets, use of facilities, and many items of staging specific to the particular presentation.

In the intramural program, there is a steadily increasing trend toward more coeducational activities. In certain sports, such as volleyball, slight modifications of rules enable the girls to participate more fully. Archery, badminton, bowling, tennis, golf, and similar recreationally orientated sports lend themselves to coeducational use.

A final trend that we find is the provision of intramural facilities (buildings, courts, pools, fields) as a campus center for students. Such a setup lends itself to the "open gymnasium" for informal play and informal participation.

EXTRAMURAL SPORTS

At the moment, the majority of administrative concerns exist in connection with the interscholastic or varsity programs for men and boys. These contests, started by student initiative and, in the beginning, rejected by faculty and administrators, soon developed some questionable practices. The college program at the turn of the century began to realize some of the problems, and by 1905 the Intercollegiate Athletic Association of the United States (later known as the National Collegiate Athletic Association) was in operation. The National Association for Intercollegiate Athletics and other conference groups also help to set standards in collegiate varsity programs. By the time of World War I, the athletic program had seeped down into the secondary school, and there were numerous community agencies, each with worthy aims but frequently with no professional educational guidance, trying to sponsor programs for children and youth. Gradually, educational institutions and professional organizations began to realize the implications of an athletic program and began to assume leadership roles. The National Federation of State High School Associations was organized, and many controls of secondary school athletics followed. Beginning with the Women's Division of the National Amateur Athletic Federation and evolving under several titles, today the Division for Girls and Women's Sports (DGWS) of the AAHPER gives leadership to all forms of athletics for girls and women (see Appendix No. 2).

Numerous complete books have been written on the conduct of athletic programs. Space demands that the present volume suggest only certain administrative problems with due respect for the philosophical reasons underlying these programs. In other chapters, associated problems are presented.

1. Anatomical, structural, and strength differences between the sexes should be recognized and programs planned accordingly.

2. The standards established by the regulatory agencies should be carefully and conscientiously followed.

3. The type of financial support offered the athletic program helps to amplify or reduce certain problems. If athletics is a part of physical education, then it deserves relative support. Gate receipts, used for total support, by virtue of dependence on winning teams increase the chances for overemphasis upon the total program, participation of key players under unadvisable physical conditions, and local pressures for community prestige. The author has taught, at the graduate level, a number of very fine coaches who believe that one solution lies in the use of gate receipts to support the program under limited conditions. It has been suggested that all receipts be turned over to school financing offices with any profits going into this common fund but with provision for limited support of the program (a stated amount) in case of deficits.

4. All phases of medical and physical protection (pre-examination, conditioning, availability of first aid and medical assistance at games, postgame care, and postseason care) need to be established.

5. Legal liability constitutes a major problem in athletics. Players should be covered by accident insurance policies; coaches and school officials should be covered by liability insurance. Travel in bonded public carriers is highly recommended.

6. Travel standards and limitations in distance are being increasingly controlled in the interest of the academic program and the fatigue element for the player. Standards of conduct by all personnel on a trip may become the source of some fine personal values.

7. Schedules for games should be provided that enable a fine season to take place but are not extended to the point where the academic standing of the players is jeopardized.

8. In the highly organized varsity program, it is necessary that a number of contracts be legally executed (games, officials, transportation, concessions). Such contracts should be carefully drawn, their terms adhered to, and their termination established.

9. One of the keys to fine athletic competition is competent, unbiased officiating. Officials should be drawn from pools where ability has been proved. Reliable officiating can foster better and more open play.

10. Both safe and sanitary practices are responsibilities in this program. Equipment should be well selected for protection purposes; it must be constantly inspected, and sound health procedures demand that it be clean at all times.

11. Crowd hysteria is an administrative problem for the coach. Judicious preparation of cheerleaders and pep clubs may assist with this problem. The attitudes and reactions displayed by the coach to decisions during the plays are keys to this situation.

There has been controversy regarding the advisability of excessive or highly demanding schedules of interscholastic athletics for junior high school boys. The question arises out of the irregular physical growth and developmental patterns prevalent in this age group. It is hoped that, in the near future, a reliable, simple, and inexpensive index of physical maturity may be identified. Development of pubic hair has been successfully used as one of the indices. Classification formulas are also used to match players more evenly. Our culture demands that we do more and more things earlier and earlier. Therefore, a lot of cultural pressure exists for interscholastics at the junior high school level for both boys and girls. Some administrators have solved this problem by emphasizing intramurals (team sports) at the seventh- and eighth-grade levels with the winning (or champion) team playing an invitational game with another school. Short schedules played late Friday afternoon with very limited travel involved are planned for the ninth-grade students.

As previously mentioned, senior high school and college interscholastic sports for boys and men are now regulated by agencies based upon voluntary school memberships. It is to the credit of the fine men we have coaching in this country that many of the questionable practices of the past have been eliminated and conferences concerned with the future of athletics are based upon the ideals of our society.[13]

With the steadily increasing emphasis upon excellence in all areas and the need of the currently few highly skilled girls in mind, DGWS has gradually encouraged a more highly based competitive program for girls. Moreover, DGWS is interested in fostering such programs for girls and women rather than avoiding this issue with the result that non-educational agencies might assume control. There are a number of factors of administrative interest to be considered in sports programs for girls. There is little or no tradition in the women's program for the hiring of special coaches for specific sports. Women physical educators must then take care of the majority of the girls in the school and add these advanced-skill programs to their schedules. The tradition of "every girl in a sport and a sport for every girl" is still the philosophy of the women of this country. To sacrifice this principle would be to sacrifice participation for the majority of the girls. In addition, DGWS has exerted leadership over the years to avoid exploitation of women

[13] American Association for Health, Physical Education, and Recreation, *Values in Sports* (Washington, D.C.: AAHPER, 1963). A report of a Joint National Conference of the Division for Girls and Women's Sports and the Division of Men's Athletics.

in sports (publicity, curtain-raisers), to avoid overemphasis on winning, to keep public pressures at a minimum, and, in general, to avoid some of the problems that men have faced. Frances Todd states the thinking with regard to sports for women concisely:

> Although the rules and skills of most sports are similar, there are two real differences in the manner in which the same sports are played by men or by women. First, women rarely achieve as high a degree of speed, endurance, and skill as do men. Second, most women are much less eager to participate in sports on as high a level of intense competition as are men.

. . . .

> Girls today achieve both physiological maturation and social sophistication at an earlier age than did girls of previous generations. Even so, and even considering that girls mature earlier than do boys, the adolescent girl cannot compete physically on equal terms with the boys. The developmental pattern of the teenage girl is such that she may compare favorably or even surpass the boys in fine muscle coordination, but she will be at a disadvantage in speed, reaction time, and, in particular, in strength. Compared with boys, girls have less heart capacity, a lower center of gravity, and minor though significant differences in the joints at the hip, shoulder, and elbow. Perhaps, because girls just cannot compete on equal physical terms with boys in sports, girls are less highly motivated toward highly competitive and extremely strenuous sports.

. . . .

> Man cannot live by bread alone. Nor can we justify a school sports program for girls solely on its contributions to their physical needs. Social needs and the expectancies and demands of the world in which we live are of equal importance to the meeting of physical needs.

. . . .

> It appears, then, that Eve just is not the same as Adam, albeit both are members of the human race. So, in evaluating a school sports program in terms of the needs of adolescent Eve, administrators might well consider that physical activity through sports is not an end in itself—rather, it is a means for a better life, present and future; that girls' needs for physical activity are, in part, the same as boys. But in many important areas they are unique. Therefore, a program based upon the needs of girls must consider both the social expectancy and the feminine self-concept.[14]

As stated by DGWS: "The one purpose of sports for girls and women is the good of those who play." Therefore, wholesale adoption of highly competitive programs has been limited in comparison to the developments for men. The instructional program and the intramural program are considered basic with interscholastic pro-

[14] Frances Todd, "Is the Sports Program Designed To Meet the Needs of Girls?" in Elmon L. Vernier (ed.), *Current Administrative Problems in Athletics, Health Education, Physical Education, and Recreation* (Washington, D.C.: AAHPER, 1960), pp. 133–38.

grams available when staff, facilities, and equipment permit these without curtailment of activities for all skill levels. Sports days (team identification), play days (mixed source teams), and telegraphic meets in such sports as archery, riflery, and bowling have been the practice. "It should be obvious . . . that no one type of competition is considered best for all situations; the primary intent has been to provide the greatest good for the greatest number of girls and women. On this basis, DGWS has emphasized programs in this order of importance: (1) instructional program, (2) intramurals, (3) sports days and play days, (4) extramural competition for those girls whose needs are not met in the first three." [15] Invitational games or even short schedules for track and swimming meets are now being established with due emphasis given to the social aspects of contacts with other schools and colleges and the use of women officials for such events. There are not enough of these officials, and there are not enough women now prepared for advanced coaching. This is an administrative problem, particularly since there is a short supply of women to teach physical education. To the author, it seems wisest to make haste slowly in this competitive program lest the pressures of speed force our women educators and our participants into problems that the men have not been able to solve completely.

COLLEGE PROGRAMS

The administration of college programs in physical education requires consideration of many complex factors. The approaches used in presenting and maintaining physical education programs on many campuses are diverse and include ideas that attack the problems from several angles. Moreover, the administrator of college programs faces several parallel responsibilities: the service or program for the general college student, and the professional education program at both the undergraduate and the graduate levels.

THE GENERAL PROGRAM

The college program in physical education has traditionally been a required subject-matter area, ranging in length from one to four years and in credit from one-half to two credits per semester. As emphasis has increased in subject areas heavily oriented to lan-

---

[15] Katherine Ley and Sara Staff Jernigan, "The Roots and the Trees: A History and Interpretation of the Philosophy of DGWS," *Journal of Health, Physical Education, and Recreation,* XXXIII (September, 1962), 36.

guage, science, and mathematics, and as secondary school physical education programs have improved in quality, there has been some tendency toward elective programs in physical education at the college level. Operative also is the philosophy that "requirements" in a democratically oriented society may be distasteful. The author firmly believes in a required program from the following standpoints. Our highly geared and highly automated society constantly leads us toward a more sedentary pattern of living to the neglect of maintenance of our cardiovascular needs for exercise. Day by day, we are exploring new ways to reduce our working hours, with a resultant increase in leisure time that we must learn to use wisely. Skills learned in physical education certainly should claim a share in the ratio of time assigned to leisure activities—and not the least of these skills are those related to personal safety. The structure of a democratic society, as pointed out in a recent article, contains elements of "essentials that may be required" within its basic philosophy of freedom of choice.[16] The required program should contain elective activities in order to satisfy the needs, interests, and abilities of students. Finally, we are facing crowded conditions in our colleges—smaller dormitory rooms, fewer recreational facilities in dormitory life, more pressure to attain higher academic standings, and more physical, mental, and social stress in the completion of the academic degree. A balance of learning is needed in education today. The student who wishes to prepare for family and community living as well as high specialization of a vocational nature needs to learn the values of an activity program.

Based upon the above discussion, the administrator of the general college physical education program is faced with several considerations that are curricular in connotation. Administratively, we are concerned that the college student be challenged by the college program and that it avoid repetition of the secondary school experience. The physical education program for the general college student may be structured with a core course as its base. Across the country, such a course operates under various names; it may be called body mechanics, fundamentals of movement, body dynamics, principles of movement, or any number of variations upon this theme. The purpose of such a course is to present vividly the "why" and "how" of movement or activity. This core becomes the springboard for choice on the student's part of other activity areas. Scheduling for depth of skill in one or two activities rather than

[16] Warren P. Fraleigh and William F. Gustafson, "Can We Defend Required Programs?" *Journal of Health, Physical Education, and Recreation*, XXXV (February, 1964), 32.

sampling bits of many skills is one route that may be followed. Using a problem approach based upon creativity and invention in movement education as an outgrowth of the "core" course is another possibility. Introduction of activities with which the student is unfamiliar is another administrative possibility. Physical education for the general college student should develop the content phases of physical education, bringing to the skills lesson the knowledges and background materials from anatomy, physiology, anthropology, psychology, and sociology, and presenting these coherently and succinctly.

Administration of the college program carries the same problems as the secondary school in terms of faculty load, staff selection, and provision of equipment and facilities. It moves ahead, however, in demanding superior teaching and superior preparation if the college student is to be challenged. The general college student deserves the opportunity to be taught by our best personnel. It is a sad practice to use only graduate assistants and beginning instructors for this important orientation of our future publics. The outstanding problem of administration of general college programs lies in the leadership role. A dynamic, forceful personality is needed who can present departmental needs and problems in a manner to gain the attention and the support of higher administrative officials, command the respect of departmental and college staff, and convince students of the values of an activity program within an academically oriented situation. The administrator focuses the emphasis in the general college physical education program upon fine instruction in an effort to establish a basis for intelligent selection among the many alternatives possible. It is hoped that the value structure of physical education will be emphasized, the content and knowledge phases stressed, and the potential of each individual given an outlet so that movement patterns and habits of participation will carry over into adult leisure time.

PROFESSIONAL EDUCATION

The professional education program has two main facets: the undergraduate program leading to the baccalaureate degree and the graduate program leading to a variety of degrees—some traditional such as the M.A., M.S., and Ph.D., and some professional in name such as M.P.E., M.Ed., and Ed.D. General factors such as staffing for competency; development of policies and practices to facilitate planning the programs; reviewing, revising, and improving curriculums; and evaluating progress toward the specific degree are common to both levels. Adherence to professional standards and to general college procedures such as admissions, routines of registration, and assignment of staff to administrative or teaching functions are usually premised upon an institution-wide pattern. Differences between undergraduate and graduate programs and the resultant administrative problems will be discussed briefly.

Undergraduate Professional Preparation. Programs at the undergraduate level carry the basic premise that a major in physical education needs a broad general education upon which the background sciences, the professional education needed for state certification, the skill learnings, and the theoretical structure of physical education may be based. Administration of this program imposes responsibility for planning an undergraduate professional curriculum that meets all the requirements for general education at a specific institution and for state certification. Because of the mobility of the population in this country, the administrator who is concerned with the future of professional students looks beyond his state borders and attempts to develop patterns that will facilitate transfer from one section of the country to another locale both in professional education courses and in physical education per se. Details of this program have been well documented in numerous texts on curriculum and, therefore, will not be repeated in this volume. The comprehensive statement presented by the Professional Preparation Conference of 1962 spells out the current thinking relative to professional curriculums.[17] The reader is urged to study the conference report.

Recruitment of superior major students is a universal administrative problem. This is a problem that has assumed major proportions in the last few years when women teachers of physical education have been in high demand. A brief discussion of certain techniques that have been successful may be pertinent. An attractive brochure giving both a picture story and a narrative digest of the preparation and possible future of women in physical education should be prepared and should be revised before either the pictures or the narrative are outdated. Many letters expressing an interest in physical education as a career are received from students who are still in junior or senior high school. A carefully composed form letter (to be typed individually) should be prepared with at least one paragraph added that states the adminis-

[17] American Association for Health, Physical Education, and Recreation, *Professional Preparation in Health Education, Physical Education, and Recreation* (Washington, D.C.: AAHPER, 1962). Report of a National Conference.

trator's appreciation of the problems faced by the specific student. One of the best recruitment devices known to the author is a scholarship for a freshman woman. This is difficult to handle; selection is one problem, and adherence to the original major course is another. Screening of candidates is feasible by means of the general scholarship requirements of the institution, with final selection by a staff committee. The use of the scholarship may be protected by a signed statement setting forth the rationale of the situation (see Appendix No. 3). Finally, recruitment is forwarded by personal letters to all scholarship applicants expressing appreciation for their interest in the field and the hope that their plans for college entrance will materialize.

Retention of students is a two-edged sword. There are students who enter college with uncertainties about their initial choice of major. Some of these students enter other fields, but some of these students need encouragement in physical education. The other edge of the sword cuts across the students who have decided upon physical education but who either do not have the requisite academic ability or who have personality or even physical difficulties that will mitigate against their success in this field. Careful staff appraisal techniques (see Appendix No. 4), sound medical advice, and careful advising are concerns of the physical education administrator. The staff members who act as advisers are the keys to this puzzle. Advisers must know the details of the curriculum and must be able to help the student plan a four-year program that will meet the criteria of teacher certification, general education, preparation in physical education, and still take into cognizance the interests and needs of the individual student. The administrator's responsibility lies in judicious selection of advisers, "advice and consent" relationships, and the morale factor of supportive procedures.

The physical educational major today may be offered in a coeducational department. Many theory courses are feasible under this administrative setup, such as, Introduction to Physical Education, History and Principles of Physical Education, Philosophy of Physical Education, Adaptives, Recreation Leadership, Camping, and Physical Education in the Elementary School. However, if courses such as Methods or Kinesiology are to be adequately covered, the differences in emphasis should be acknowledged by joint staffing of a man and a woman. Most dance courses and individual and dual sports can be offered in coeducational classes. Combatives, contact team sports, fundamentals of movement, body conditioning, and gymnastics demand separate classes for men and women because of the differing emphases.

Some of the gravest problems in the administration of the professional program in physical education are found in the conduct of student teaching. If a college laboratory school is available, the channels are well marked. If students are placed with cooperative teachers in public school systems, definitive channels of responsibility need to be established. Moreover, college supervisors must be assigned who are prepared to carry on liaison functions with these cooperating teachers. Standards of planning, scheduling of conferences, and evaluation techniques are matters for joint decisions on the part of the cooperating teachers and the college supervisors. The administrator of physical education has a responsibility for analysis of difficult situations and often finds himself called upon to resolve difficulties, with both the interest of the student in mind and support of the professional ethics involved. Student teaching caps the preprofessional experience of the college student; therefore, the problems associated with its best functioning should be of primary importance to the department.

A course in administration of physical education is usually offered in the undergraduate curriculum. In a book concerned with administration of physical education, it may be pertinent to suggest one way that has proved its practical value in teaching such a course (see Appendix No. 5).

Graduate Professional Preparation. General standards for professional preparation in physical education have been carefully and clearly outlined in the report of the Pere Marquette Conference.[18] Graduate study demands excellent preparation at the undergraduate level since graduate study aims to prepare specialists and to give depth to the study of the problems facing the profession. To a great extent, programs are tailor-made for graduate students in order to insure competence on the part of the individual student. Each graduate department sets up admission standards and qualifying examinations and spells out the means by which a graduate student becomes a candidate for an advanced degree. Progress toward the degree, comprehensive examinations, oral examinations, and filing of theses or dissertations are matters of concern at each institution.[19]

The administrator of physical education is concerned with mechanics, student progress, and, most important, the support of high

[18] American Association for Health, Physical Education, and Recreation, *Graduate Study in Health Education, Physical Education, and Recreation* (Washington, D.C.: AAHPER, 1950). Report of a National Conference.

[19] American Association for Health, Physical Education, and Recreation, *Graduate Education in Health Education, Physical Education, Recreation Education, Safety Education, and Dance* (Washington, D.C.: AAHPER, 1967). Report of a National Conference.

standards at each of the above steps toward the graduate degree. Staffing for graduate-level work is not a light responsibility. Often, the staffing for the professional program at the undergraduate level is combined with that for the graduate level. The larger staffs of the country are usually able to support specialists in swimming, dance, adaptives, and general sports areas who are then able to assist with research studies in these areas. Excellent preparation, sound experience, and superlative teaching ability are needed to instruct the theory courses in philosophy, curriculum, measurement and evaluation, administrative problems, adaptives, research literature, and research techniques at the graduate level. It takes sympathetic understanding of the student's problem plus courage to state the issues in the advising of graduate students. The staff must also be able to direct research. The involvement of graduate staff in group or individual research often sets the pace for the graduate student's interest and attainment in this phase of the work.

Several specific administrative functions need emphasis. Provision of facilities for research plus study and laboratory space for both the staff and the graduate students will enhance the value of the program. The research function of the graduate program is fostered by an atmosphere of interest, appreciation, and support. Although provision should be made for the terminal Master's degree without thesis research, departments that move steadily toward this pattern close the door to exploration of research possibilities and development of research potentials.

In a volume devoted to administration, it seems fitting that a paragraph should present the thinking with regard to instruction in administration at the graduate level. It is presumed that mechanical details such as purchasing standards and routines, sizes of classes, and student loads would be covered at the undergraduate level as well as the details of program planning and basic elements of space and facilities. Graduate level courses should be concerned with principles of administration, problem areas such as public relations, legal liability, and evaluation of staff and program. The intricacies of personnel selection, staff psychology, and the liaison that should exist between the department and other administrative units should be stressed. Long-range planning for facilities and studies of equipment under working conditions set up values for future use. The study of administration at the graduate level should take cognizance of such trends in physical education as team teaching, flexible scheduling, and use of mass media, movement education, stress on principles of movement, and academic content areas.

ADMINISTRATION OF CURRICULAR CHANGES

Unless the entire school or college has embarked upon curricular change, the administrative adjustments for pilot studies and establishment of new patterns are departmental responsibilities. Curricular changes involve careful planning, staff orientation, consideration of the techniques to use, and the implementation of such changes. If feasible, additional staffing will facilitate released time for personnel experienced in the situation to concentrate on planning and expediting these changes.

The administrator is expected to give careful and thoughtful leadership to such changes. The initial step in this planning is to consider the current program. Are the current objectives being met? Do new or enriched possibilities exist in the situation? If changes are made, how feasible are these in terms of current staff competencies? To what extent is the staff ready to involve itself in curricular change? Often, a survey of student reactions to a current program along with a survey of similar situations (geographically distributed) will reveal cues for the initiation of the curricular change.

Staff orientation and staff involvement in curricular changes offer a definite challenge to the administrator. One must consider both staff backgrounds and staff personalities. Among the staff, who is professionally prepared in the area under consideration? Which staff members can profit by in-service education in the area of change? What biases in attitude exist? How far will members of the staff go in involving themselves in the necessary study? What resistance may be faced from school principals or parents? How will the staff react to all these factors? Having analyzed these factors, the administrator must decide whether or not the climate is favorable for action. It takes patience to wait for the propitious moment.

Having decided that change is feasible, the administrator sets up conference periods for staff discussions. These cannot be hurried; again, there is a psychological moment when the staff is ready to move. Many changes are best initiated by a pilot project. For example, a new approach or a new activity may be introduced for one class on the college level or at one public school. The project is carefully planned, critically observed, and objectively evaluated. Success in the pilot project points the way for introduction of the change in all similar situations within the educational unit.

As implied in the preceding discussion, curricular change involves administrative concern. In addition to the staff orientation and staff involvement, there are tangible problems to be solved. Schedules, work stations, and staff loads often need to be modified. If new or additional equipment is necessary, these items become part of the budget problems. Consultant services, unless locally available, must be planned and budgeted. The curriculum should remain constantly under evaluation. In this process and in the process of curricular change, gaps in departmental planning or future needs may be revealed. Thus, the cycle renews its demands and the process is repeated.

SUMMARY

This chapter has presented the administrative problems of the physical education program as differentiated from problems of a curricular or philosophical nature. For the elementary school, administrative patterns to facilitate the teaching of physical education in the self-contained classroom as well as the use of a specialist have been discussed. The traditional games-dance-posture-exercise approach has been contrasted with the movement education approach in their respective administrative demands. The administrative details for noon-hour, special events, and intramural programs have been discussed.

The continuum of junior high and senior high has been developed in establishing administrative guidelines for the secondary school. Experiences in class and extra-class activities such as intramurals, interscholastic sports, pep clubs, and cheerleading have been presented with due reference to balance of the total program. The exploratory function of the junior high program with its lead into (for many students) the final education experiences in the senior high program form the framework for the administrative guides developed in this chapter. Team teaching, flexible scheduling, and use of TV and programmed instruction are the basis for additional administrative problems. The needs of the exceptional child demand administrative action.

Intramurals and interscholastic sports have certain common administrative demands, such as space, leadership, equipment, and scheduling. The problems in both these types of competition are augmented by the need for standards for physical protection and personal conduct, officiating competencies, travel limitations, legal liability factors, and the extent of the competitive seasons.

The college program in physical education operates with similar overall administrative procedures for the general and the professional programs. The advisability of requirements, core courses, or free electives requires administrative decisions. Questions of admission, retention, content of the major program, and student teaching are important administrative considerations. Graduate professional preparation includes the above factors plus the need to plan for research projects.

Germane to all the above considerations is the constant need to administer curricular changes.

PROBLEMS

1. Upon what criteria should an administrator base his program planning for physical education in the elementary school? Secondary school? General college program?

2. Outline and justify briefly the various phases of a physical education program for undergraduate majors (example, basic sciences). What administrative liaison functions may be involved in carrying out such a program?

3. What is the administrator's responsibility in upholding standards for graduate work in physical education? Liaison functions?

4. Coordination of extra-class activities is often a major responsibility for the administrator of physical education. How may assignments be spaced and division of labor arranged for seasonal intramurals and sponsorship of pep clubs, cheerleading groups, or sports clubs?

5. What is the role of the administrator in establishing values for the program of extra-class activities? How may these value standards be implemented?

6. How may the administrator develop interest in newer developments in curricular programming such as the use of "cores," educational TV, movement education, and programmed learning?

7. Plan a series of staff meetings for in-service education in the use of culminating events. State the educational level under consideration and cite briefly specific types of activities that could be considered.

8. Varsity athletics involve much detailed administrative work. Name a sport and set up the following forms:

   a) Inventory and check-out—uniforms
   b) Inventory and check-out—game supplies
   c) Conduct code for players
   d) Travel regulations for players
   e) Regulations and contract items for officials
   f) A guide to improved scheduling

9. Outline briefly the duties of an administrator in expediting a curricular change.

3

Organizational Procedures

Physical education is one unit in an educational structure. As such, we need to understand its relationships and its coordination with other units in the educational structure. We also need to understand its organization within its own scope to the end that the goals of physical education may be accomplished.

EDUCATIONAL STRUCTURES

In school districts, we often find the term "consultant" used to describe a director of physical education. Dependent upon the size of the district, there may or may not be assistants for secondary or elementary levels or for girls and boys. The responsibility for instituting and carrying out the program of physical education is assigned to these persons. Working in conjunction with school principals, the consultant sets up lines of communication with the teachers of physical education and coaches assigned to the various schools. He reports his activities and crystallizes his plans in cooperative endeavor with assistant superintendents, directors of curriculums, the personnel director, the superintendent, and eventually the school board. The consultant has organizational and coordination functions with the school psychologist, school health services, and the business or managerial personnel in the system. Charted, this may appear as shown in Fig. 3–1.

Variations upon this pattern will certainly be found since school districts differ in type, size, and internal structure. The administrator needs to know the organization of authority and responsibility within his own structure. He needs to be able to make the necessary contacts for cooperative effort in order to forward his goals. Physical educators too frequently ignore the larger efforts

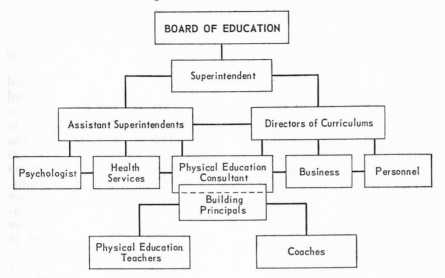

Fig. 3–1. Sample organizational chart for a school district. This chart indicates the overlap in authority between building principals (supervisory) and the physical education consultant.

of the school system and concentrate exclusively upon their own objectives. This is the wheel that may dig a rut rather than blaze a trail. A neophyte teacher with ideas is liable to announce that he wants a position where he can "do as he pleases." The young administrator or even the experienced administrator may decide that his authority should be final. It often is and often should be in matters *within* the *department,* but no one is a free agent in a large organization. The authority goes full circle from the people (in election of the school board) back to the people as students mature and become the people.

The reverse side of this coin must be examined. If responsibility for a program or a policy is passed via the channels from person to person, a stalemate is reached. Therefore, specific responsibilities with resultant action or authority are assigned to a central person. Cooperative endeavor is apparent as this person clears with other individuals of similar authority and with individuals higher on the scale. Thus, development of curriculums is a departmental matter that is later endorsed by principals, directors of curriculums, the superintendent, and, in some cases, the school board. After facilities are established, their assignment for use is a departmental matter. Coordination must occur if progress is to be made.

Many of the above factors operate in the college organizational structure. We wish to call particular attention to the liaison and communicative functions at each level of administrative organization in the college situation. Departments located in separate buildings with highly specialized functions are the order of the day in the college setting. Unless liaison plus communication are practiced and coordination takes place, each of these may become a unit divorced from the rest rather than one of many units. Whether or not Health, Physical Education, and Recreation are one unit or separate units is a matter of the local institutional pattern. There are advantages in streamlining by combining these departments to form college or school status. Separate college budgets, combined staff assignments, and fewer administrative stations have been cited as advantages. On the other hand, the highly specialized department focuses its attention, energy, and finances toward one goal. The chart in Fig. 3–2 is designed for the separate department status.

In small colleges, several of these "steps to the top" may be omitted, and a chairman of a department may find himself directly responsible to the president. By the same token, in a smaller institution, the chairman may not be given certain phases of authority, such as selection of staff.

INTERRELATIONSHIPS

The relationships that are developed by physical educators within the college or school are highly important in maintaining departmental status. Some of these relationships are concerned with other departments, while others are strictly internal. The business of unifying departmental efforts and coordinating the contributions of staff members demands time, tact, patience, and understanding of the various elements, the personalities, and all the local ramifications on the part of the administrator.

HEALTH EDUCATION

In the college setting, health services are generally housed in well-equipped functional units complete with limited hospital facilities and are manned by professionally trained personnel. A large secondary school usually maintains a well-equipped health service unit manned either by a health counselor or by a school nurse. In

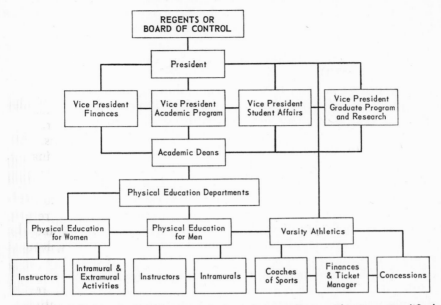

Fig. 3–2. Sample organizational chart for a college. This is a simplified chart. Colleges of Health, Physical Education, and Recreation will have additional cooperative relationships, and varsity athletics have many subdivisions that have not been indicated.

elementary schools in a large city or town, facilities for rest and emergency first aid are provided, with school nurses on duty a percentage of the time (shared between two or more schools). Whenever the school nurse is not available, the principal is expected to assume these responsibilities. Small schools and rural schools depend upon the teacher to observe deviations in health status and to take charge of emergencies.

The close relationship that should prevail between physical education and all phases of health education (services, environmental health, and class instruction) is reflected in the principle that physical education should always contribute to health, never detract from or injure health. This does not mean that either field is subservient. Each has specific contributions to make. When the full potential of each field is the objective, specialists in both health education and physical education should be employed. Both fields are interested in the development of the individual; in health practices that will enrich and prolong life; in clean, sanitary surroundings; and in developing attitudes that will enhance mental hygiene.

Health education and physical education need to stand shoulder to shoulder; neither should be the handmaiden of the other.

Coordination with health education takes several forms. Absolute adherence to the recommendations of the health examination (see Chapter 10) is basic to fine interrelationships. Cooperation with health services in follow-up procedures and in return to exercise programs after an illness or accident is necessary. In return, physical education may expect health services to emphasize the role of exercise in maintenance of health and to support physical education by careful analysis of requests for excuses from physical education. Closer interrelationships are indicated by the recent interest of the AMA in physical fitness and in exercise potentials.[1]

Finally, many schools and communities establish health councils to assist in thinking through specific health problems. Membership on these councils samples all agencies interested in health. In the school health council, home economics, safety or driver education, science, the students, interested parents, the school nurse, physical education, health education, and guidance counseling as well as administration would be represented. In a community health council, the municipal administration, the county medical association, parents, churches, community agencies, environmental health offices, the schools, and civic clubs would comprise the membership. The administrator of physical education may either serve on such a council or delegate this responsibility to a staff member.

OTHER DEPARTMENTS

There are physical education departments that pride themselves upon their self-sufficiency and their disregard of other faculty members. Such an attitude disgraces the profession and lends itself to bickering and disrespect. Sad but true, this situation may even exist in small or crowded schools where boys and girls must share facilities and equipment. The administrator of physical education should sit down with both parties and adjudicate this situation. Decisions on priorities and use of space may often be decided on a percentage basis. This percentage could be based on past participation statistics. At the same time, plans and space assignments can be made for coeducational activities. The competition is especially keen for space for interscholastic and intramural sports. Sometimes this problem can be settled by scheduling intramurals

[1] American Medical Association, *Physical Fitness* (Chicago: AMA, 1964), a brochure prepared by the Department of Community Health and Health Education; *Exercise and Health, A Point of View* (rev. 2d printing; Chicago: AMA, 1959), a brochure prepared by the Bureau of Health Education.

for an hour at the end of the school day and interscholastic sports later in the day. Another solution is scheduling intramural sports tournaments in off seasons, for example, intramural basketball in the fall. This is not an ideal solution, but when space is at a premium, this may be the only way out of the dilemma.

An administrator of physical education is faced with the problem of the time demands for extra-class activities upon his staff. These activities may conflict in their scheduling with staff or faculty meetings. Increasingly, faculty meetings are scheduled to avoid such conflicts. It is one of the administrator's duties to encourage staff attendance at all types of professional meetings. In the give-and-take of these meetings, the problems of physical education may be explained to other members of the faculty and one may gain an understanding of the problems of other departments. Mutual respect rests upon respect for competency, time needs, and scheduling. We must understand and respect the work of so-called academic areas if we expect consideration for our needs.

In colleges and universities, the situation is compounded by the autonomy of each college and by the irregular contacts campus-wide. Respect on the college campus is an administrative problem. Attendance at campus faculty or senate meetings will gradually give the physical education administrator an overview of the total situation. Publication, speaking at local and regional meetings, plus service on campus and other professional committees will assist in recognition. Not to be scorned is membership in the faculty club, participation as a sponsor of student organizations, and attendance at campus social affairs. The administrator of physical education not only should accept committee and sponsorship assignments but also should assist his staff to participate in all these phases of college life. Respect on any campus for a department is primarily based upon the professional integrity and fine educational standards of the department. We must also base our offerings and our policies upon the highest ideals and stick to these ideals in the face of pressures.

COMMUNITY RECREATION

The "lighted school house" epitomizes the concept of the school as the core or center of the community. Within the "lighted school house," adult education including recreation is conducted during off-school hours. Whether or not one is located in a community where this type of organization takes place, physical education departments are usually concerned with certain phases of community recreation. In some cities, the physical education admin-istrator supervises the recreation program presented in the schools. In other instances, close coordination takes place between the de-partment of recreation and the department of physical education. In the latter case, policies are established concerning the employ-ment of school personnel, the type of activity to be presented, and the expenses attached to the use of the facility (heat, light, cov-erage for breakage or damage, custodial services). Lines of re-sponsibility are drawn and schedules established. Certain of the problems faced in these interrelationships are spelled out in the following:

Assuming that each of our readers accepts the idea that your community is the basic recreational unit, let us think of your schools as a core or center for the planning or the programming of recreation. To do so, we must clear other possibilities. Why not use the luncheon-dinner service clubs as the clearing house for recreational activities? Each of these agencies is concerned to some degree with recreation. Each contributes time, energy, and/or money to pro-mote recreation. But each of these agencies, sincere and earnest in purpose, is hampered by the restricting factor of reaching only a few of the people part of the time. The help and the cooperation of every agency within the com-munity is certainly needed to make a recreation program function. The schools, acting as the core or center from which all interested persons function, has one very definite advantage. Every person at some time in his life crosses these portals—thereby being exposed, at least, to knowledges and attitudes that influ-ence his life patterns. In addition, the school enjoys an acknowledged place in the leadership patterns of your community, it receives your financial support in the form of taxes, and it serves as a pivot around which the many and varied self-directed recreational interests you have developed may be centered. Please note that you, as individuals, are the keystones in this structure. The school acts only as you take the responsibility for seeking its leadership.

. . . As voting members of your community you have established the school facilities. Perhaps, at the time that you made decisions with regard to school plants, playgrounds, parks and community shelters, you had not realized that the privilege you enjoy of determining your recreational outlets carries also the responsibility of providing support for the program.

. . . What about the financial resources in your community? Your service clubs will be interested in special projects but, generally speaking, they cannot carry the total expense of a recreation program. Your churches will also sponsor certain phases of the program but they cannot support all of it. You support your schools with a mill levy. This mill levy is based upon the economic factors represented by the real estate and/or intangibles upon which your community depends. What type of school you have depends upon your wishes. What type of recreation you have also depends upon your wishes. Yours is the re-sponsibility to utilize to the best advantage your school as the core center in your community.[2]

[2] Dudley Ashton, Wilma Gimmestad, and Janette Sayre, *The Community—The Basic Recreation Unit,* Nebraska Community Education Project, N. D., University of Nebraska, pp. 6, 7, 9, and 10.

LIAISON

The fact that interrelationships have been discussed indicates that the administrator of physical education is engaged in liaison. One could discuss this phase of administration as a factor in public relations or in personnel practices. Liaison, however, is concerned with coordination and relationships. Certainly, either good or poor public relations occur as a result of liaison functions. Since liaison concerns itself with bonds or connecting links, good or poor personnel practices could either forge or break these links. Liaison could, in fact, delve into any facet of administration and a case could be presented in its favor. Let us confine our remarks to its coordinating function. We may, perhaps, clarify these relationships by asking two questions and outlining the answers.

1. Where should liaison occur?
    a) College
        (1) Within the staff—new and old members
        (2) Staff—student
        (3) Department—college—university
        (4) Staff—department—other departments
        (5) Staff—department—community
        (6) Department—profession at large
    b) Public school
        (1) Board—superintendent
        (2) Board—community
        (3) Superintendent—coordinators—principals—teachers
        (4) Principal—teacher—pupil
        (5) Teacher—parent—pupil
2. How should liaison occur?
    a) Points of contact
    b) Lines of approach
    c) Lines of authority
    d) Guidance
    e) Ethics

If these liaison functions are to occur, the administrator of physical education needs background information and theoretical concepts for his thinking. He needs to understand that emotions are involved and that a goodly percentage of his time may be devoted to the study of staff psychology. How his staff adjusts to its specific environment and how they adjust to each other is important. How he, as the administrator, adjusts to other administrators is also an important factor. Careful analyzation of the reactions of a new dean or a new president is one phase of liaison. There are factors of stability needed in contacts between individuals; and, at the same time, no progress can be made unless changes occur. Changes in routine, in course content, and in reporting forms of grading systems tend to upset temporarily the balance of a department. The administrator then tries to understand and to estimate the effects of such changes and to restore the stability needed for establishing changes. Acting in his role of a practical psychologist, the administrator tries to find the key person or persons in a difficulty. He tries to guide the inexperienced or the inept in their relationships. He tries to identify their concerns, their motivations, and their pressures, and to resolve these. In so doing, he holds in respect the potentialities of each individual but never loses sight of the larger whole—the best interests of the department. In his liaison functions with other departments, in a college or school system, and with higher administrative channels, he tries to keep in focus the way in which his department fits into the total picture. He must demonstrate his ability and his will to fight for department needs; and, at the same time, he must use sound judgment and tact in knowing when to press forward and when to withdraw. Ability to think on one's feet and to speak in rebuttal is an asset in liaison. The concerns of liaison may be summed up by an analogy. Before an organist touches the keyboard, he sets a registration or an arrangement of instrumentation for his initial presentation. As his performance advances, he changes this registration in the interest of musical color or climax. His listeners are affected both intellectually and emotionally by this musical presentation. In liaison, members of a staff, administrative-channel officials, other departments, and the community react intellectually and, often, emotionally. It is the role of the administrator of physical education to realize the potentialities of all persons concerned and all the factors present and to use his instruments wisely.

DEPARTMENTAL ORGANIZATION

Departmental organization demands consideration of two phases: namely, staff organization and class organization. Many of the details of class organization are dependent upon the philosophy and policies adopted in staff organization. If the philosophy is based upon authoritative lines, details of class organization are liable to be inflexible. If the democratic philosophy is inaugurated, the decisions involved will tend toward more flexibility. Democratic philosophy and democratic practices do not preclude administrative decisions as necessitated by mandates from above or emergency situations. Power, however, is spread and many minds attack departmental problems.

STAFF ORGANIZATION

In most public schools, departmental organization is comparatively simple. The single teacher of physical education (man or woman) undertakes to coordinate his departmental offerings into the total school curriculum, places his own requests for equipment and supplies with his principal, decides lesser departmental policies, and interlocks his scheduling of extra-class activities with the total school picture. In fact, he runs a one-man operation. In medium-sized school systems where two or more persons are employed within a department, one person is designated, usually on the basis of length of service, as chairman of the department. In consultation with his peers, he makes certain decisions such as assignment of his teachers to specific activities or to specific grade levels plus the duties mentioned above. Large township, consolidated district, and metropolitan schools now have departmental organization based on specialization in teaching areas that is closely akin to that of large colleges and universities.

Two types of administrative leadership exist in departments of physical education. Each type has advantages and drawbacks. In some departments, there is a rotating chairman chosen by either election or selection from departmental ranks. This practice rests upon the premise that administration is not too different from the teaching function and may be assumed by experienced members of the staff. If the local situation is firmly established and the department has no local problems relative to repute, respect, or prestige, such an arrangement may have the following advantages. It may bring into focus new points of view, it may stimulate different personnel, and it offers incentive to more members of the department. On the other hand, there are a number of disadvantages. Departmental politics may rise to unpleasant heights, short tenure in the position leads to avoidance of administrative crises and power shifts up to higher echelons when staff needs are not pressed, there are degrees of fluctuation in carrying out long-range plans, and often policies are inconsistent. It should be pointed out, in closing this discussion, that tenure applies to employment but not to the type of position and that administration does not guarantee tenure in itself.

Authority and responsibility is centralized in the chairman or head of the department with division of labor and delegation of duties usually based upon specialization. The chairman of the department must keep time, strength, and energy for the larger issues and delegate many routine details to staff members. Thus, as indicated in Chapter 6, assignment to specific duties along with the authority to carry out these duties is one phase of staff organization.

At the same time integration is needed, sometimes within a designated phase of the work, sometimes within the department as a whole, and sometimes within the total institution. Here the goals of the department emerge to give common purpose and common direction to diverse interests and diverse capabilities. By mutual consent, the philosophy of the department is established, and the aims of its various programs agreed upon. Acceptance of and adherence to statements, such as the following, help to integrate the thinking and resultant action within a department.

Philosophy

We believe:

Our primary contribution, within the framework of a democratic society, is to aid each individual so that each may develop her own capacity to the fullest extent.

The specific contribution of physical education is to afford opportunities for the student to develop a realization and appreciation of the continuing need and value of physical activity. Believing in the worth of each individual, the program should be based on the needs and interests of the students and should be broad and varied in scope so that everyone may find satisfaction and success through participation.

We believe this implies:

A respect for a student as an individual
A concern for her happiness
A guidance toward appreciation and utilization of her own abilities as well as those of others
A realization and fulfillment of her own needs
An understanding and appreciation of the values of physical activity in daily living
A staff
Which reflects these beliefs in the presentation of a well-planned curriculum
Which keeps abreast of, and incorporates some of, the best and current trends of general education and physical education through membership in professional organizations, attendance at meetings, general reading, and advanced graduate study as needed
Which is aware of and operates within the expected standards and ethics of the teaching profession

The Professional Program

The professional program should provide a sound basis in scientific knowledge and educational techniques, a varied background of physical skills, and stimulate a continuing interest and desire to teach.

Objectives:

1. To help students acquire a sincere conviction that education is a potent force in American life with which they wish to ally themselves
2. To help students gain an appreciation of, an enthusiasm for, and a pride in the profession of physical education
3. To provide a sound basis in scientific knowledge
4. To encourage the acquisition of the specific knowledge of many and varied activities (rules, equipment, safety, etc.)
5. To apply the knowledges, skills, and techniques in a laboratory situation
6. To develop and improve those skills and techniques which will contribute to successful teaching
7. To develop inner security and emotional stability
8. To stimulate an intellectual curiosity toward all areas of learning
9. To help the students realize the importance of continued study and development

Service Program

The service program should stimulate an appreciation of physical education through a varied program of activities so students will find satisfaction through participation. This program should help students understand and realize the immediate and future values of participation in activity.

Objectives of the service program:

1. To provide an opportunity for each student to acquire skills in many and varied activities for her own recreational use
2. To encourage enjoyment and self-satisfaction through achievement in skill
3. To promote an understanding of the efficient use of the body in physical activity
4. To develop an understanding of the rules of safety
5. To develop an appreciation of the physical, mental, and social values of activity

Graduate Program

Objectives:

1. To improve the preparation of qualified individuals for teaching in schools and colleges
2. To stimulate specialization in one or more specific areas in the broad field of physical education
3. To introduce individuals to research in physical education
4. To improve the qualitative standards of teachers and/or administrators for positions requiring high professional competence and leadership
5. To encourage an awareness of and continued interest in current trends in education and physical education

Recreational Program

Objectives:

1. To promote sport and recreational interests for all women university students

2. To provide opportunities for women students to use skills and knowledges acquired in classes in a recreational situation
3. To encourage enjoyment and self-satisfaction through participation in many and varied activities
4. To develop an interest in activities which can be used after graduation
5. To provide opportunities for participation in co-recreational activities
6. To provide an opportunity to find social satisfactions
7. To encourage teamwork, cooperation, and sportsmanship
8. To provide opportunities for student leadership to help plan, conduct, and evaluate the recreational program

In a staff with only one or two dominant individuals, integration takes place by submission. This, however, is a questionable situation. Much to be preferred, although the path of the administrator is more rugged, is the staff with several individuals highly qualified in similar areas and several individuals highly qualified in specific "cutting-edge" areas. In such a situation, the specialists in dance, sports, aquatics, gymnastics, and fundamental movement consult, reach common agreements, and expect the administrator to help in integrating these interests. On the other hand, the persons concerned with curriculums, departmental evaluation techniques, and student teaching (either as cooperating teachers or as supervisors) cut across all the above interests, thereby achieving phases of cooperation and integration in the process.

The organizational pattern when staff committees function is approximately the same regardless of the activity. For example, a staff member is designated head of aquatics. All staff members who teach in this area become members of this committee. At the same time, one or more of these members may be heading another committee. The aquatics committee considers the content of its various courses, the standards set in these activities, and prepares skill and knowledge tests for the activity. Revision of course content results from observation and analysis of skill in the classes plus trends in the area. Item analyses of knowledge tests prepared by the departmental evaluation committee guide the aquatics committee in revision of knowledge tests. Thus, integration and coordination occur by virtue of both specialized and diversified interests. Integration of staff interests goes beyond the department in that the administrator must keep the staff aware of larger institutional interests, policies, decisions, and difficulties as they arise. By such communication, the department may contribute to these institutional aims and policies.

In coordinating the work of a department, one attempts to bring together the contributions of all members of a staff. Certain staff members have specific preparation in specific areas and these competencies must be respected. At the same time, all staff members must be given opportunity to develop new competencies. The answer may lie in multiple sections, when feasible, with in-service consultation for staff who are teaching these added sections. There are decisions in coordination of departmental work that move from staff member to staff member; there are other decisions that must move, either by advisement and counseling or by specialized function, up through the ranks to the chairman for arbitration. The chairman holds the responsibility for keeping the vistas wide and looking with depths of perception and perspective upon the total tasks of the department.

MEETINGS

We cannot leave departmental organization without discussing the need for two types of meetings: committee meetings and staff meetings. Within the compass of staff load, provision should be made for both these types of meetings. Staff members are frequently assigned reports, interim investigation or informal research, and reading materials that make demands upon their time. Only by such assignments may committee and staff meetings contribute to enrichment of the physical education program. Therefore, it seems wise to set aside a definite time for such meetings. One plan that has been used with success is the scheduling of committee and staff meetings on alternate weeks. When the entire staff is involved in study of a long-range problem such as preliminary statements for facilities, the preparation of a core course in physical education, or revision of a curriculum, committees would meet in a ratio of two or three times to one staff meeting. A schedule of such meetings for the semester should be prepared and a copy given to each staff member. In public school systems, general school staff meetings are regularly scheduled and should be attended faithfully by physical education personnel. It is also the practice in larger schools to schedule in a manner so that departmental meetings are possible. Increasingly, staff who are asked to serve on city-wide curricular projects are given released time to make their contributions more effective.

All meetings should be conducted so that time is not wasted and so that constructive results follow. To this end, the use of agenda setting forth items of business and distribution of minutes of the meeting are recommended. Staff should be encouraged to contribute to the agenda and to join in the discussions. Often, sharp differences of opinion arise. All sides should be heard and a decision reached, if only for an interim period. One thinks of the perennial discussions on grading and similar items. These are not repetitive; new conditions arise, new staff enter the picture; so, the issue must be resolved. There are two types of business that must be carried on in staff meeting: routine, and professional information and stimulation. Routines such as locker arrangements, safety reminders, equipment allocations, equipment needs, accident prevention, and roll book and other records are tedious but extremely necessary. Professional problems such as budget hearings in the legislature, reports from staff attending professional meetings, institutional procedural changes, and curricular decisions are items that stimulate the staff. A final word on staff meetings: start on time and end on time; hold the meeting to a feasible length of time and keep to the agenda. Finally, cancel a meeting if the business is trite and the time not warranted.

CURRICULAR ORGANIZATION

Two phases of curricular organization are pertinent to this discussion: short-range plans and long-range plans. Within an academic year, curricular organization is on the short-range basis. More and more elementary schools are organizing classes on a unit basis. Instead of the hit-and-miss lesson of a little of this and a little of that, well-coordinated units are planned. In the primary grades, two units may run simultaneously because of the shorter interest span of these children. Thus, a unit of games may be used two days a week, with a rhythmic or self-testing unit another two days, and a free choice of activity on the fifth day. It is quite feasible to use the movement education approach as well as the more traditional skills approach with this organization. As the interest span lengthens, the unit plan of organization extends. Units, at all educational levels, tend to follow a seasonal plan with emphasis upon fall sports at the beginning of the academic year and continuing across the sequence of team and individual sports. Winter brings stress on indoor activities such as dance, gymnastics, and stunts and tumbling. Swimming sequences are sequential in level, if possible, but are often dependent upon the availability of the facilities. Curricular guides are usually set up, keeping in mind the above general organization. Flexible scheduling, combined with team teaching, re-emphasizes attention to individual differences and individual accomplishment within the unit organization.

Many school systems and colleges develop long-range plans for curricular offerings. Lifting the sights a few years ahead (usually three or five) emphasizes the constant need to re-examine the curricular offerings and to move ahead with improvement. Administratively, this planning ties in with other considerations. Equipment budgets may be predicated upon a five-year span in an effort to increase the variety of activities in the program. Facility improvement may also be spread over a period of years. It is the administrator's task to coordinate these factors in long-range planning.

STUDENT LEADERS

Physical education has been named as a key place in which student leadership may be developed. It takes mature judgment and mature guidance on the part of the teaching personnel to distribute leadership opportunities justly and to guide student leaders wisely. How far the use of student leadership may be carried is dependent upon the age, experience, skill, and maturity of the students. Even in the elementary school, however, limited experiences are possible. Student leaders can be appointed by the teacher to secure equipment (a cardboard box of balls, etc.) from a central storage area and to collect and return it. Students may act (for a few days at a time) as scorers and referees for group games. This is a golden opportunity for *guidance* in fairness of decisions and honesty in tallies. Under close supervision, sixth-grade students who have proved themselves as responsible persons could lead small groups of lower-grade children in informal play and in simple games. At no time should complete responsibility be abrogated to student leaders. Emergency situations may arise. The necessity for teacher supervision of the inexperienced student is underlined by legal liability.

Student leadership opportunities in secondary schools and colleges occur in two situations: in class or in the sports program. In the class, this leadership may be highly structured or incidental. Use of students to demonstrate skills, team plays, and ways and means of "spotting" activities may be structured in the planning but occur incidentally as the lesson proceeds. Highly structured use of squad leaders or teacher aides may be evident with orientation and even prior instruction for these leaders. Certainly, at the secondary and college levels with the use of highly organized sports, scorers and referees and other officials should have received training and, if possible, ratings in officiating skills. Associate and intramural ratings in sports are now available for students and are a mark of prestige for those who qualify. In intramural sports, councils are formed consisting of sports heads (either appointed by the director of intramurals or selected by a sports board based upon interviews of candidates). These student sports heads are expected to arrange tournament play, keep the records in the sport, and represent the sport in business with the board. In varsity sports, student managers, particularly in smaller schools, act as hosts for visiting teams and officials, keep attendance rosters for practice sections, check on both game and personal equipment, and, in general, assist the coach with the details of the practice and game situation.

The administrator considers both the advantages and disadvantages of student leadership. From the utilitarian point of view, teaching time is saved by the use of student leaders and the teacher is freed to give more attention to individual needs. Students are given an opportunity to experience both the excitement of leading their peers and the responsibility incumbent upon the honor. Great care needs to be exercised to be sure that this opportunity is made available for all students. Herein lies the difficulty. Not all students emerge as fine leaders; therefore, the teacher using various devices rotates leadership, stresses the qualities needed to be both a good leader and a good follower, and constantly guides this experience. The administrator must help the teacher who fails to see the weak spots, needs counsel with regard to chronic difficulties, or views assignment of leadership roles as an avenue to personal popularity. Excellent judgment, careful supervision, and wise guidance offer unlimited challenge to both teacher and administrator in developing student leadership.

CLASS ORGANIZATION

All organizational procedures from the educational structures to the use of student leaders come into definite focus in the manner in which classes in physical education are conducted. Recreational opportunities abound in physical education, but the heart of the program is instruction. If the instructional class is short circuited, the entire program suffers. As might be expected, a number of administrative policies and procedures as well as the principles and philosophy affect the instructional aspects.

CLASSIFICATION

The most obvious and the simplest classification for physical education classes is that of grade level. In the elementary school, grade level is usually the basis for assignment to physical education with occasional seasonal combination of two grades at the upper levels. Such scheduling enables the boys to participate in contact sports based on football, while the girls play soccer. More and more attention is being focused on fine physical education programs for elementary school children. In keeping with the employment of specialists to teach physical education in the elementary school, classification groupings may occur within the class schedule. Thus, the class could be organized with groups for low- and high-skilled participants. Very few elementary schools use formal classification tests for grouping and assigning classes. In some states where physical fitness has developed local scores, the results may be the bases for classifications within the assignment. It is common practice to use height, weight, and age classifications for participation in track and field events.

The administrator of physical education on the secondary level faces quite a problem with regard to classification of students. With the increasing emphasis on individual needs and individual potential, classification of students would provide better groupings for optimum results. The practical fact, however, is that students may be assigned to physical education whenever a free period occurs upon their schedules. Ideally, as a required subject, physical education should be assigned first along with English and other basic courses. So, before considering heterogeneous grouping, we first need to establish homogeneous grade-level assignment. It is particularly important that seventh- and tenth-grade students be assigned separately to physical education without mixing in other class levels. As the students enter physical education at the junior high school level and again at the senior high school level, definite orientation helps them to adjust more easily to both the physical education and the general school program. There are arguments pro and con on homogeneous grouping. The pro side states that upper limits can be extended for highly skilled students and more individual attention given to students with poor skills. On the other side of the coin, heterogeneous grouping within grade levels is favored for the challenge and example that the more highly skilled offer their classmates and for the opportunity afforded to develop understanding and respect on the part of all students for the capabilities of others.

The general administrative climate of the college lends itself to classification groupings. It is possible to plan classes based upon levels of instruction. In limited situations, heterogeneous classification occurs and, thereby, restricts the progress of individual students. Increasingly, depth instruction offering beginning, intermediate, and advanced sections in specific activities is the order of the day. With the increase in leisure time, depth in skill is probably our best chance for adult participation in activity.

The administrator's concern in this problem is to provide for classification of the most refined type possible in a local situation. There are many classification devices discussed in test and measurement texts that may be used for the total school population or for structuring within the class assignment. Reduction of repetitive experiences together with optimum development for the individual student is the yardstick for use in each situation.

TIME AND SCHEDULE PROBLEMS

Time and schedule problems operate hand in hand. One cannot schedule without time allotments, and time allotments influence schedule decisions. Class size is often dependent upon facilities plus specialized needs in certain activities, resulting in additional scheduling decisions. The staff available as well as the number of teaching stations must also be considered.

Although state laws are in force in a number of states, the time allotment indicated is generally a minimal program rather than a program that meets exercise needs. It is hoped that intramurals, extramurals, and free play will help to meet the physiological needs of growing children. Stated time allotments range from twenty to thirty minutes a day to three hundred minutes per week. With such limited amounts of time, the physical education program necessarily should be devoted to the instructional phase.

Elementary school scheduling tends to follow the self-contained class pattern with class size so determined. Depending upon local conditions, it can be as little as twenty minutes or as high as forty-five or fifty minutes per day for upper elementary children. When an entire elementary school is sent to the playground at the same time, even with large areas, several safety problems occur. Older children in the excitement of play may invade the areas assigned to small children. Younger children may chase balls or other equipment across a group or team game of older children. Bodily collisions, aroused tempers, and similar incidents result. A solution is that of staggered scheduling—all the kindergartens or first grades assigned at one hour, second grades at another time, and so on up the ladder. Groups may then be separated by open spaces, and the possibility for spreading the running and chasing activities is increased. Staggered scheduling also contributes to better supervisory practices. Use of the mid to late morning and mid to late afternoon hours is the best practice for elementary school physical education scheduling.

In the secondary school, scheduling must follow the pattern of the general school day. Although an hour period each day is recommended, class periods may be as short as forty-five minutes. This leaves minimum time for activity after dressing and showering needs are set. When the same facilities must be used by boys and girls, the scheduled classes may be forced to meet Monday–Wednesday–Friday one week and Tuesday–Thursday the next, with alternation between the sexes on this schedule. A plan which takes into account coeducational units has girls scheduled Tuesday–Thursday–Friday and boys Monday–Wednesday–Friday, or vice versa. Friday then is kept open for coeducational activities. Class size ideally would vary with activities, but because of facilities and time demands, this is seldom possible. Probably the best maximum size is thirty-five. Team sports, aquatics, and gymnastic and body-building activities can be accommodated using this number. Careful planning will enable the teacher to conduct two individual sports or an individual sport plus body-building practices within a single class of this size. Classes that are enormous in size (sixty to ninety) should have two or three teachers assigned with adequate teaching stations. When one teacher must handle a large class, about all that is accomplished is some supervision of recreational activity. In order to provide adequate time for instruction, showering, and personal grooming, double periods have been scheduled fewer times per week. The few places fortunate enough to try this have found it to be an excellent solution. Team teaching with the use of flexible schedules (as high as three modules allowed for skill instruction; two modules for skill practice; and as low as one module for lecture, film, or demonstration) may also help in solving this problem.

In small colleges with only a service program to be accommodated, scheduling classes two or three times a week is a fairly routine procedure. Large college and university schedules are a different story. With constantly increasing college enrollments plus the trend toward more academic content as a basis for the physical education activity course and the trend toward depth in skill attainment, college schedule construction may be compared with puzzle-solving. More people must be accommodated often in the same space, yet classes cannot be heavily increased in size. Moreover, specific college facilities such as the number of tennis courts or bowling alleys limit the size of such classes. For large groups in body-building activities, the use of TV with several groups accommodated in the same large area has been one solution. Dovetailed scheduling with groups showering and dressing while other groups are using the activity areas is another solution. These two expedients are minor issues when one considers the factors involved in scheduling for large service departments plus undergraduate and graduate major programs. Equitable decisions must be made on the basis of available teaching stations, assignment of classes to staff members best prepared in specific areas, total number of staff available, total college scheduling regulations, and optimum size for specific activities. As staff morale is involved, it is a problem not to be lightly tossed aside as a mechanical detail. Every staff member deserves consideration with reference to the length of the teaching day. Therefore, some schedules will start late in the day and move into evening hours, while others will start early in the morning and terminate earlier. Blocking time for research and for preparation is appreciated by staff members.

Teacher load at any level is another facet of the time and schedule problem. It is difficult to make definite statements on teacher load because there are so many local factors operative. In the public schools, thirty hours per week (including extra activities) is the usual pattern. At the college level, loads vary from a basic assignment of twelve to sixteen academic hours per week. Various colleges have various ways of computing staff load. In some instances, an activity class is equated one and one-third hours to equal one academic three-credit course. In other cases, a total number of points or assignments are used as the base—such as seven or eight assignments. In this case, teaching a graduate course would be counted two or three assignments; theory courses for majors, one and one-half to two depending on the level of the course; activity courses, committees, and extra-class (sports, etc.) assignments as one point. This system is based on the amount of preparation needed. In all instances, an administrator works constantly to equate the teaching load. A word on overloading new staff members is pertinent. They are usually young, anxious, and willing, but inexperienced, and need to spend time in orientation and adjustment. Extremes in loads should be avoided either for the inexperienced or the highly capable.

CLASS ROUTINES

Substitutions and Excuses. The moment one starts to work with class routines, one is faced with the substitutions and excuses from physical education that have developed over the years. There are both historical and cultural implications in this situation. Historically and culturally, we are committed to religious freedom; this is a basic tenet and one that should be respected. Few religious beliefs ban exercise per se, but there are objections to dance which deserve respect. Substitution of another activity is possible in some programs, but in limited situations, it may be necessary to excuse a student for the duration of a dance unit with return to the program for the next activity implied. In the past, we have experienced substitution of ROTC (Reserve Officers' Training Corps) for physical education programs both in secondary schools and in colleges. This was based upon the belief that the laboratory exercises provided adequate physical activity. Another cultural substitute based upon heavy emphasis has been that of excusing athletes from physical education. Again, this is a case of ignoring the wide range of objectives in physical education. The girl who possesses high skill in a specific sport, especially a team sport, may be denied the opportunity for developing interest in an activity for use in adult leisure time. Far better is the practice of excusing the athlete, based on training or fatigue reasons, for the duration of a specific season but expecting her to return to the regular program at the end of the season. Only in this way may the athlete experience the benefits of a well-rounded program.

Substitution of cheerleading, baton twirling, and marching band for physical education is equally limited in outlook. In the words of a college committee considering the merits of physical education:

. . . The evidence seems to us to indicate that a certain type of physical education course may be justified on quite the same utilitarian grounds as that of English composition. The type of physical education course here envisioned is one which would provide the student with some basic knowledge of body mechanics, some basic knowledge of the relation of physical exercise of appropriate sort to physical well being, and an introduction to the rudiments of a number of widely utilized recreational sports. It would be hoped that the knowledge and skills imparted in this course would be useful during the college years, but in substantial measure would enable the person to adapt himself more easily and readily to personal needs which may arise after college days.

. . . Committee members are unanimous in their belief that there are no suitable alternates for the physical education requirement envisioned.

. . . The basic concept of the physical education requirement is that the physically educated person will not only have skills in several recreational activities but will also understand his physical self and his total exercise needs in relation to his life today and as an adult tomorrow.

. . . Evidence before the Committee indicates that the major goal of the proposed program concerns the development of concepts, habits, and skills which may well carry over into later life.

. . . In the judgment of all committee members a well-rounded university education dictates both knowledge and skill in the physical education area. And, as the Committee views the matter there are no valid alternate ways of insuring that this phase of education will be covered.[3]

There are two types of excuses from physical education: a single-day excuse from a temporary difficulty and a long-term medical excuse. The temporary difficulty is easy to handle. The local policy states who may authorize such an excuse and for what reason. When a school nurse or a health counselor is available, simple excuses because of a cold or some temporary incapacity are referred to that office. In like manner, short-term excuses or recommendations for light activity after an illness or as postoperative procedure are cleared by such an office. Short-term excuses and recommendations for placement in adaptive programs are approved only upon the advice of a physician. Valid excuses of this type should specify the length of time and should be reviewed at the close of this period. Permanent medical excuses are few and far between and are valid only under complete medical authority. The more excellent the program and the more it takes into account not only the growth and development factors but also the intrinsic activity interests of the students, the smaller is the demand and the feasibility for excuses.

Makeups. There are two schools of thought on this subject: (1) that all classes missed should be made up, and (2) that absence from physical education should be treated exactly like absence from any other class. Since physical education demands participation in activity, a policy on unexcused absences should be established. Beyond a reasonable limit, credit and grading should be affected by absenteeism. Unless absences because of illness are treated as such, some of the health factors in the program may be defeated. There is no value to student or program in participation merely for the sake of a body in activity too soon after illness or at the onset of illness. In such cases, the student needs help from the teacher in the skills and activities missed—a chance for practice if desired or a chance for deferred evaluation. Absence in physical education carries inherent penalties in lack of skill. If absences are made up hour for hour in any activity regardless of the student's original registration or crowded into short spans of time, the spaced activity and social-skill objectives of physical education are defeated. One might just as well set an electric timer and insist upon situps or even jumping in place until the buzzer sounds. In other

[3] Used by permission of the University of Nebraska. January, 1965.

words, there is an opportunity in absences to educate the student in the values of his program of physical education.

Roll Call. The question of absences brings into focus the question of recording attendance in physical education classes. There are many devices for calling roll. The pros and cons of these belong in a discussion on methods. We list briefly the following possibilities:

1. Oral roll call (time-consuming)
2. Numbers on the floor (check the vacant numbers)
3. Oral number call (note the numbers omitted)
4. Squad roll call
5. Assistant checks attendance in dressing room
6. Assistant checks attendance during class period
7. Use of tag board (remove tag and place in box)

Whatever device is used, roll call should not waste class time. The importance of accurate records is emphasized in all phases of administration by laws dealing with aid to education based on average daily attendance. Moreover, attendance in individual classes is emphasized by the concept of *in loco parentis*. Responsibility for the student is constant and may not vary from class to class. To this end, many schools require that attendance slips for each class be filled out, and these are collected and recorded in the main office period by period.

Costumes. One phase of class routine is that of checking costumes. It is customary in physical education classes to change from street clothing to washable basic costumes—either one-piece tunics, jumper costumes, or shirts and shorts (bermudas, jamaicas), socks, and tennis shoes. There are several reasons why a change in costume is needed: (1) Street clothes do not allow for freedom of movement and may be damaged in activity, (2) uniforms are attractive in appearance and establish equality in the class, (3) uniforms designed for activity make for safer practices, and (4) health practices may be emphasized since these costumes are laundered. Schedules should be established for laundering of costumes and checking students who are delinquent. Absurd penalties, such as a number of laps around the gymnasium, for late laundry duty should be avoided. If the program is attractive, the limited activity possible in street clothes plus its reflection in skill grading is penalty enough.

Laundry Problems. It has become common practice for schools and colleges to furnish clean towels at the end of each activity

period. This certainly is an improvement over the damp and mil-
dewed personal towel that defeated good health practices. Large
school systems and universities either arrange for commercial laundry service or operate their own laundry system. The laundering
of personal outfits is the student's responsibility as indicated in the
previous paragraph.

Lockers and Showers.   When clothes must be changed for activity,
storage space for street clothes and personal belongings is needed.
Assignment of lockers adjacent to showering facilities is usually
spaced to facilitate dressing. A locker is assigned, and several in
sequence are left empty for use by other classes before a locker is
assigned to the next class member. Depending on the type of
storage facility in use, locks and combinations and the use of the
small storage locker or basket in relation to full-length period use
lockers must be carefully explained. A short lesson on the use of
showers will obviate many minor difficulties and be a time saver.
Shower regulations, such as permission for a sponge-off during the
menstrual period and the use of plastic containers for shampoo
preparations, should be established and their use practiced. The
aesthetic and personal comfort resulting from showering is a matter
for educational comment.

Class Routine.   It pays to take the time to establish class routines
at the beginning of the school year and briefly when needed at the
beginning of a unit. Usually, five minutes is allowed for dressing
for activity and ten to twelve minutes for showering and dressing
in street clothes at the end. In situations where the length of the
period will justify a longer time at the end of the lesson, students
will be happier not to be so rushed and to have a chance for personal grooming.

A roll-call device follows dressing with the lesson proper using
as much time as feasible within the allotted class period. Within
the lesson, routines for the safety of students are needed. Routines
for use of equipment and return of equipment to storage areas both
protect the equipment and help to safeguard the student in action.

Records.   Accurate, time-saving ways of keeping class and school
records should be devised. Records of attendance and grades may
be recorded on class cards or in roll books. Absolute accuracy,
attention to neatness, and attention to details of date, time, place,
and activity are irksome details but details that are very important
both to the student and the school in later years. Health records
giving the status of all students in physical education must be main-

tained. Locker and basket assignments must be recorded. Promotion, final grade sheets, and summary of the year's work are constants. Careful analysis and recording of accidents are needed. Equipment records are kept both seasonally and yearly. Finally, most teachers keep an outline, a log, or a chart indicating their plans and outcomes for the physical education classes under their jurisdiction.

SUMMARY

This chapter has outlined the educational structures for physical education in school systems and in colleges. The interrelationships that are basically implied in these outlines have been discussed and the liaison functions of the administrator of physical education indicated. Growing out of liaison, staff organization is developed to foster integration as well as diffusion of the duties within a department. Where and how student leadership may assist with staff function as seasonal and even long-range plans are implemented have been questions of concern. Finally, the details of class organization spell out the organization procedures of the physical education program.

PROBLEMS

1. Chart the lines of authority in physical education for your school district or college situation.

2. In what ways may an administrator implement health practices within the physical education program?

3. Define the roles of the health education specialist and the physical education specialist in the schools.

4. Structure a health council for your school or community situation. Suggest three problems that may arise in a physical education program that might be brought to the attention of such a council.

5. Liaison helps maintain the delicate balance in departmental relationships. Illustrate this fact concretely from your own experience.

6. Set up the staff organization for a secondary school with a department of six teachers (men or women). Assign their teaching functions and structure their departmental duties.

7. Develop an organizational seasonal plan over a three-year spread for a junior high school enrolling approximately three hundred girls.

8. Chart the qualifications needed by students under consideration for a student leaders' club.

9. Plan a three-year cycle for alternation of seasonal physical education activities for a senior high school.

10. State the interrelationships among teacher, time allotment, sizes of classes, and scheduling in planning a physical education program.

11. You are asked to allow a talented girl to substitute voice lessons for physical education. The reason given is that such lessons will improve her breath control even as sports improve breathing capacity. State your answer and your reasons for it.

12. As a prospective teacher or administrator of physical education, what records would you set up and how would you handle these?

4

Public Relations

During the days of the great depression in this country, we acquired the habit of labeling organizations with cryptic initials; we had the WPA, PWA, NRA, and other similar designations. We, in physical education and allied fields, have our initials which are intelligible only to the initiate. We speak airily of AAHPER, ARFCW, NAPECW, NCAA,[1] and numerous other lettered combinations. We are the initiate and we understand these alphabetical puzzles. Because we like to streamline everything in American life, our culture lends itself to a chapter theme: P.R.—not P.S. At its end, we shall look forward to your being among the well informed as far as these initials go.

In the past decade, the public schools and the colleges of this country have been faced with stringent criticism—often of a destructive nature. This criticism, however, has been sincerely offered as constructive advice in the interest of the best possible education for every child. All phases of education, including physical education, have come in for a share of this questioning. Our athletic contests are understood by the general public in terms of prestige for a specific school, in terms of *what* athletic contest, *where* it will be held, *who* is playing, *what* the statistics on the players portend, *when* this contest will be held, and *how* the decisions will be made. Does the public know *why* these athletes are in action? They think they do—to decide a championship, and that is true. But there are reasons more fundamental and with deeper values that are bypassed. This is our fault; this is lack of communication. This is the P.R. phase—the public relations that we need to put into

[1] AAHPER—American Association for Health, Physical Education, and Recreation; ARFCW—Athletic and Recreation Federation of College Women; NAPECW—National Association for Physical Education of College Women; NCAA—National Collegiate Athletic Association.

practice so that the values of all phases of our physical education program will be clear and understood by our various publics.

> I keep six *honest* serving men,
> (They taught me all I knew)
> Their names are What and Why and When
> And How and Where and Who.[2]

In Kipling's time, the phrase "public relations" was expressed in the above quatrain. These "six honest serving men" are still the heart of public relations. All we need to do is to put them to work. But all six must work as a team if fine relations are to be established with our publics.

WHAT DO WE COMMUNICATE?

What does this term "public relations" mean? Are we concerned with propaganda in this instance? Do we attempt to propagate the principles of physical education as evidence of our professional zeal? This is only part of the intention of persons of integrity who interest themselves in the problems of public relations. The plural form used in the term implies the "give and take" so necessary on this two-way street. Physical education, as is true in other phases of education, must be supported by either tax funds or tuition fees. The public supplying these funds has a right to know where, how, and why this money is spent. These publics have a right to express their ideas, opinions, feelings, and judgments in regard to this program. Improvement of public reaction to the physical education program is one responsibility of an administrator, a staff, and a member of a school system. If better communication can improve attitudes and motivate our publics to favorable action, then one function of physical education has been realized. Are we talking about publicity? This, conceivably, could be a minor phase of a public relations program, but we would sell ourselves short to stop at this point. We are talking about confidence in a program built on confidence in persons. We are talking about communication between physical education personnel and their publics and the reverse of this equation. We are talking about establishing a climate in which common understandings may be fostered between the members of the community and the school or department. Having established such a climate, these channels for communication must be kept open, or the prestige that has been laboriously ac-

[2] From *Just So Stories* by Rudyard Kipling. Used by permission of Doubleday & Co., Inc., and Mrs. George Bambridge.

quired will slip away. One inadvertent word or one tactlessly handled situation may easily disturb this delicate relationship. Dichotomies exist in public relations. Public relations are complicated, and information offered to the public must be based on facts, yet the public may distort these facts in interpreting them. Public relations must present information objectively, yet the publics sometimes respond emotionally. In short, public relations weave a fabric that may be flimsy and easily torn, or, if properly loomed, a fabric whose tough fibers will stand the stress and strain of change as well as the passage of time.

WHY DO WE NEED PUBLIC RELATIONS?

Why do we believe that fine rapport with our publics is so important? Without communication among the numerous publics (students, staff itself, staff to staff within a given situation, other departments, other phases of administration, ancillary staff, parents, the people of the community, and others), misunderstandings, frictions, and even total ignorance of the physical education program can lead to unnecessary disunity and loss of goodwill. Communication, or the lack of it, is one of our keystones. Communication within the staff may definitely affect staff morale. This being true, the effect of communication upon our publics is amplified. Griffiths in discussing these problems has called communication "a verbal science." Within this science, Griffiths identifies three factors: talking, listening, and writing.[3] We talk to and with many publics under circumstances where the choice of a word or a phrase may change the entire perspective of the field of physical education. Very definitely, we need to talk, to explain our offerings, to introduce our audience to new developments, and, sad but true, to assure our publics that we have the ability to converse, discuss, and make formal presentations. The author agrees with Griffiths that we need to listen. One wonders, sometimes, if this is not a lost art. Many frictions occur, particularly among staff members, because of a closed mind unwilling to listen to what is being said. We need, as administrators and as staff members, to listen to the words being used in the community as they refer to our field, to listen to the overtones and the nuances of the voice, to weigh and measure and hold our reactions until we have heard all sides of an issue. To answer too soon is often to court disaster. We need to

[3] Daniel E. Griffiths, *Human Relations in School Administration* (New York: Appleton-Century-Crofts, Inc., 1956), p. 18 and chapter on Communication.

write to inform our publics and each other of the why of our actions. What we write and how we write will be discussed later in this chapter. Suffice to say, at this point, that these communications must be based on fact and clearly stated. Why is communication so important in public relations in physical education? One reason may be that the professional physical educator who is able to talk well, to listen wisely, and to write clearly is in a position to destroy a stereotype that has existed for too many years. This stereotype takes several forms: (1) that physical education and varsity athletics are synonymous, thereby concentrating attention on the skilled player; (2) that physical educators just throw out a ball and thus discard the teaching action; (3) that physical educators are slovenly and, in the case of women, masculine in appearance; (4) that physical educators have little or no ability to speak or write intelligently. Yes, communication is indeed a keystone. How else can we convince our publics that we are sincerely interested in all our students, that we value the factors in the teaching act that make learning a challenging experience, that the physical educator today reflects the culture in which he finds himself by making an appropriate appearance suited to the occasion, and that he desires to hear the public reaction and to speak and write intelligently in response. Communication spells interaction: talking, listening, writing.

WHEN SHOULD WE BE ACTIVE?

When are we engaged in a program of publicity for physical education? It is certainly true that upon the advent of some special event such as a championship game, a city-wide demonstration, or a professional conference, we engage in specific publicity. This accelerated effort, however, should be our change in pace and not "crash" tactics or "a flash in a pan." To be effective, public relations must be continuous as well as consistent. If public relations are to function as a means of evaluation, then the questioning attitude of "what progress are we making," "how are we serving our publics," and "in what ways may we improve" needs to be constantly on the professional agenda. Every teacher thus becomes an agent for fine (or poor) physical education as he faces a class. Every custodian, matron, and secretary is engaged in public relations as he or she answers questions, relays information, and either complains about or agrees with school policies. There is no "Golden Age" in public relations, but there are "golden moments"—every moment of every day. We need to seize every chance we encounter and "tell and share" the values of physical education with each and every public. Only in this way may we correct misconceptions, modify prejudices, and present the image of physical education in its best possible role to our publics. We have a number of stereo-types in image and in idea that need our attention. Among these we find the idea that every boy should be an athlete, that women who teach physical education are poorly groomed, that athletics and physical education are one and the same, that an adolescent who happens to be a fine athlete should be exploited, that all children enjoy highly organized physical activities, and that physical education instructors do not need academic ability. Spasmodic efforts with highly concentrated propaganda will not erase these images. Consistent, constant attention to fine programs of physical education and well-prepared personnel coupled with cognizance of the effect of both chance remarks and formal presentations may well pay public relations dividends.

HOW DO WE COMMUNICATE?

How do we communicate in order to establish this rapport with our publics? In the words of our folklore, "What you are speaks so loudly that I cannot hear what you say!" This being the case, all contacts that we make must be geared to an affirmative response. We are living in a remarkable age to which we may react either with cynicism or with hope. In this century, we have seen vast technical advances that have raised the standards of civilization beyond expectation. We have seen the power that development of hydroelectric complexes has brought into our homes. We have become accustomed to the automobile and to the jet plane. We are seeing the initial phases of atomic energy and its possible effect upon our daily lives. We have witnessed the pioneering probes into space, and we realize that a new day may well bring us into close contact with other planets in the solar system. No phase of our civilization can escape the impact of these developments. The gadgets available have triggered an increase in sedentary patterns of living. The startling demands for immediate know-how have caused an emphasis to be placed on languages, mathematics, and the sciences in our school systems. Suddenly, parents, who were content ten years ago to let the content in education amble along, want to be sure that their children have the background that will enable them to compete effectively in tomorrow's world. What has been the impact of these forces upon physical education? Two of the great leaders of this country, realizing the swing toward sedentary patterns and knowing the need of strong, able citizens, have initiated and implemented the physical fitness movement. Both President Dwight D. Eisenhower and President John F. Kennedy were motivated by economic demands as well as efficient military personnel, if necessary. Both men were aware of the tendency in our culture to swing to extremes—in this case, heavy emphasis upon mental development at the expense of physical, social, and spiritual needs. Culture, in this country, is not a simple living routine. At the same time that we were developing our mechanized society, we were increasing our emphasis upon varsity sports (frequently placing these adult concepts in children's play) until we currently have school and college athletic programs that verge upon the professional concept. How do we meet these impacts in a public relations program? Some of us are beset with grave anxieties—will the economy of the country be able to cope with these advances in the face of world demands upon our natural (both animate and inanimate) resources? What is happening to our young people that they give evidence of such deep-seated unrest and discontent? Will the fitness program and semiprofessionalized school athletics overshadow a program for full physical development for all youth regardless of skill level, physique, race, or sex? What are these cultural factors doing to us who are engaged in physical education? How are we reacting to these forces? This is public relations in physical education. Is fear of the atomic future destroying our joy in movement? Is fatalism leading us to a "don't care" attitude? Are we judging current programs in physical education upon the basis of our experiences in dictated exercise series in the elementary and high schools of this land at the turn of the century? These are negative reactions at a time when we need positive thinking. Only a public relations program geared to the positive values of physical education in life today can hope to be effective. We must stress the values of each phase of the program. We must see that the program is wide enough and varied enough to elicit interest and participation from the unskilled to the highly skilled person, from the physically handicapped to the physically endowed, and from the baby to the oldster. To do this, our public relations must take a positive approach, acknowledging any limitations openly, but, at the same time, pointing up the contributions in the various forms of play, the physiological values of stress in movement, the psychological release of change in pace, and the socialization opportunities that may occur within a well-conceived and well-conducted program of physical education.

To number four of our "serving men," *how*, we also assign the role of the media used in public relations. All of us are familiar with the demands of the public press for news releases. Too often, these releases have been devoted to the cause of varsity athletics. No one disputes the need for publicity in this area; the argument, however, is premised on the possibilities in additional areas. In all cases of news releases, the "six honest serving men"—what, why, when, how, where, and who—must give their respective bits of information and the release must carry a date for its use. News releases written in simple, clear, layman's language will be welcomed by the press. To be worthy of inclusion in daily, weekly, or monthly publications, such articles must be timely and of specific interest. Therefore, an account of a school assembly would be appropriate for a school paper, whereas the information on a city-wide demonstration would be of interest to both parents and the citizens of a community. Examples of articles of interest to both these publics are a series of articles on safety precautions used in physical education activities, articles on the planning and development of physical education facilities for a specific situation, or articles on the ways in which new equipment, such as apparatus, is being used. Exercising good taste in the type of materials presented and presenting curricular improvements carefully and clearly will result in publicity that adds value to the physical education program.

Bulletins must be prepared for the use of both staff and the general public. Criteria to be used are the same as for press releases. If this material takes the form of a "flyer," the standards for good posters are involved. These include a single bit of subject matter, attractive spacing, and attractive colors employed to bring into significance some device that attracts attention. A "flyer" for intramural badminton might carry the heading, "Birds in Flight." Brochures are often prepared for informational purposes and for recruitment of either staff or students. Excellent picture stories are the heart of such publications. It is well to remember that offset printing is a better medium to use than mimeographing and that a good quality paper is good economy in this instance. Ideas for these publications cannot be conjured up at will. It is wise to maintain a file of current pictures of departmental activities and to jot down unusual devices that one uses subconsciously.

Currently, radio programs are not as frequently used as television. There is some use of informational programs in which the principles of presentation for either radio or television are identical. It would be well to "tape" one's voice and to study the results before appearing on either medium. One must speak more slowly, more distinctly, and be acutely conscious of the tone of voice in use to avoid nasal transmission, monotony, or disturbing hesitations. For both radio and television, more than one voice is a relief to the audience. Therefore, panel discussions or interviews are to be preferred to speeches. As we use television more and more as a teaching aid as well as for the information of the public, we need to study the preparation of the telescript and the use of movement in front of the camera. The camera reflects what is done; therefore, poorly executed movement, poorly planned sequences, or too many people moving too fast will not help our programs. A single bit of information per program, carefully presented, might well be the goal. Excellent programs have been presented by school systems to inform the public of the goals and progress of various subject-matter areas including physical education. There is a fine opportunity for educating many publics when a college staff cooperatively prepares a series of televised sports lessons or a series of dance lecture-demonstrations.

Another medium that may be used has been labeled "exhibits" by the author. Included in this category one may find bulletin boards. Attractive devices, use of color, and clearly stated items are the rule for bulletin boards as well as for posters. One must be sure that a bulletin board carries a message. In like manner, exhibits of course offerings, layouts for playgrounds, sports diagrams, and complete departmental offerings are other avenues to use. Film strips and even full-length film presentations are used as exhibits of correct ways of performing motor skills, subject matter to be included in units of study, and the presentation of the principles, practices, and procedures in physical education.

Departmental reports and letters are also media for public relations. All reports should be accurately and neatly prepared and expressed in clear-cut terms. Reports that meet deadlines carry positive connotations for the department. "Hearings" before authoritative committees, if handled well, become a medium of communication for the department. Letters should be answered promptly. This statement should not be taken as a demand for an answer by return mail or on the same day that a letter is received. There are letters that have been answered in haste with resulting poor public relations. Many times, it is better to sleep on a decision and thereby avoid confusing an issue. It is a sad state of affairs, however, to find a department or an individual with the reputation of neglecting routine mail.

Demonstrations or public performances of any kind are a potent means of public relations. Numerous articles and books have been written on the preparation, staging, and evaluation of public performances. Discussion of these phases is unnecessary here, but several of the principles involved should be mentioned in the interest of public relations. Any type of performance or athletic event for which admission is charged has a number of responsibilities to the public. First, these events should be carefully timed to last approximately one to two hours, and they should start and stop on the dot. Second, admission fees, even if nominal, impose standards of perfection upon the presentation. Third, a higher degree of skill, adequate technical arrangements, and adequate spectator space are additional standards that must be met. Demonstrations use the standard of length and starting and stopping on time. A demonstration, by its very name, indicates varying degrees of skill and the inclusion of all students in some capacity. Technical facilities such as lighting, costuming, and scenic backgrounds are much simpler, if not omitted, for demonstrations. The emphasis in the demonstration is put on a learning situation for the audience; and, although the demonstration must be carefully prepared and all performers skilled in specific events, the total presentation is more informal in nature. Our culture is eye-minded as well as ear-minded, and it is vitally interested in the activities of its young people. Therefore, demonstrations that represent the culmination of a fine physical education program are excellent media in public relations.

Another *how* is community services. Administration of physical education, particularly at the college level and increasingly at the secondary level, is involved in providing certain community services. It is an axiom that the needs of the physical education school program must receive first consideration, but departments are committed, by virtue of their support, to community services. The administrator of physical education finds that guidance is necessary for staff members who become so dedicated to the "extras" of either the total community or the school community that fundamental duties become secondary. The matter of use of facilities and equipment will be discussed later.

There are some fine lines of demarcation to be drawn in public relations. When may the school or college offer services without disturbing the balance of private agencies? In many cases, this line is drawn by stating that these services are open only to faculty and faculty families. Recreational evenings, individual sports tournaments, and swimming and dance for children fall into this category. Other services such as town and gown classes, square dance clubs, and open gymnasium hours might be made available for the total community. It would be impossible to state exact activity assignments or exact participation lines, as these would depend upon the local situation. Suffice it to state that these services are fine provided that they are in addition to, not instead of, the instructional program.

State-supported colleges have another responsibility for programmed services which is sometimes treated too lightly. Communities often request consultant services to help in planning curricular revisions, recreation for youth, summer playground programs, and similar needs. It takes time to answer these calls and to arrange travel and personnel, but it pays rich dividends in the understanding of physical education.

WHERE DO WE COMMUNICATE?

It is obvious that we cannot discuss any one of the "six serving men" as an entity; therefore, we have, in part, implied where we engage in public relations. Surely, by this time, we know that every person-to-person contact reaps its harvest of either bitter resentment, utter indifference, simulated interest, or sincere support. We engage in person-to-person public relations when we talk among ourselves as staff members. If such discussions are professionally constructive, we have reinforced the positive values we will stress when we face a larger public. If these discussions become internecine warfare based on personal insecurity, jealousy, or bigotry, we may reflect these attitudes to the detriment of the profession. Constant alertness is the watchword of the truly professional person.

Public relations are built from group to group but remain dependent upon confidence in individuals and in the programs they sponsor. The reactions of a physical education staff to proposals within a larger faculty may be either positive or negative. If a staff can discuss options objectively and make concrete suggestions of merit, their opinions are liable to be held in esteem. But if a staff derides changes of shifts in emphasis without cause and in a biased fashion, public relations between these two groups will become strained. Additional group-to-group relationships could be cited, such as teachers as a group in relationship to administrators as a group, or parents as related to teachers. But the point is reiterated that group-to-group relations depend upon individuals within the group.

Another phase of this group relation is that of a specific physical education group with the general public. The classic example is the varsity athletic setup. In large colleges and universities and the larger school systems, the formal publicity necessary to the conduct of the varsity athletic program is distributed through established channels. In smaller institutions, this publicity must be handled by administrators, teachers, or coaches. Media that may be used have been discussed in this chapter. Our concern, at this point, is that interaction does occur between institutional personnel and the general public and that, because of the inherently high interest in athletics, pressures may exist that may place false values on the program. Solving the problem of establishing the fine values that may accrue from varsity athletics without antagonizing local pressure groups often places public relations in the category of a fine art.

In similar fashion, the interactions between groups of parents, groups of teachers, and community groups must stand the test of sound public relations—relations that are based upon fact, upon consideration of the rights of all individuals involved, and upon value systems that are complimentary rather than derogatory.

The question of *where* can again be asked relative to one's activities in daily contacts. Sound public relations are a function of daily living patterns—in the classroom, in the barber shop, in the grocery store, in the beauty shop, at church, at bridge parties, at the backyard barbecue, on the playground, in the pool, in the gymnasium. One cannot afford to forget the results of one's words, attitudes, and actions upon other persons or other groups.

WHO ARE OUR PUBLICS?

Who are these persons to whom we communicate and from whom we expect interaction on a positive plane? The administrators of either a college or a public school system who are concerned with physical education have a primary responsibility to meet the demands of public relations in a constructive way. Such an administrator should not take lightly the responsibility of setting up channels of communication, of meeting emergencies calmly, and of daily contacts with staff, students, and the general public. His reactions to small details have ramifications far beyond his immediate bailiwick. Thus, he must preserve equanimity in the face of major and minor crises. He must be prepared with the answers to the important and also the nagging questions. He must, with sincerity, evidence his confidence in his field, in all members of his staff, and in his students and their parents.

Second, all members of the staff should have shared in departmental affairs so that they are prepared to answer both the casual and the pointed question. There is an *esprit de corps* that can be established in which pride and loyalty are carefully compounded to form a base for operations. Not only should the professional staff acquire this sense of cohesion to fine standards, but also the ancillary staff. It takes patience and training to impress upon a student clerk that the telephone is one key to public reaction. But if she can realize that stature is gained by answering "Physical Education for Women" rather than a brusque "Phys Ed" or "P.E.," then one contact has been bettered. Details of taking messages correctly, answering routine inquiries, and making appointments can be handled in the same way. Matrons and custodians, if carefully supervised, will also acquire a measure of pride and pleasure in the contributions that their efforts in keeping the working areas clean and in order add to the program. The pride in accomplishment that one would expect from the professional members of the staff is too obvious to need discussion.

We are only beginning to realize that our students comprise a power echelon whose potential in public relations has not been fully tapped. Students who understand why physical education is a part of the school curriculum, who know what learnings are possible within the area, who value participation in activity as a way of living, and who are well informed on the value systems inherent in physical education are sources of widespread, fine relations. By the same token, the indifferent and misinformed student becomes a hazard. We are becoming more concerned in our curricular offerings that we teach why and how activities occur. This is well and good, but our primary concern should be so fine a program that it will sell itself to our students. There can be no substitution for excellent teaching. This is probably the soundest foundation for a good public relations program.

Who are the publics to whom we are addressing our public relations? The groups discussed above operate in a dual capacity—as recipients and as dispensers in our field. Three additional groups are worthy of comment. We are deeply concerned that the staff members of the college or public school system who are not affiliated with the department understand physical education. This may be a difficult assignment, as prejudices derived from poor programs, personal disadvantages in a past experience, or the discipline of a specific subject area may cause negative reactions to physical education. Many of these situations are remedied better by informal, personal contact than by propaganda campaigns. To this end, attendance at staff and faculty meetings and functions plus participation on faculty committees become a "must." Second, parents form another public. Some of the same factors just mentioned may operate in this case. In addition, a parent resents any humiliation, unnecessary embarrassment, or slurring reference to his child. Minor incidents, then, should be settled without flurry and with due consideration of cause and effect, yet with respect to the principles involved if public relations are to remain stable. Finally, the community, in general, is another public that must be given deep thought and due consideration. The ethnic composition of the community deserves attention. Are there persons of Finnish blood who will revel in the great runners of that nation? Can the Mexican children show us the steps of the provincial dances? Should we not be interested in the patterns that arose in the ghettos of Europe? How fleet are the Negro children in our midst? Another phase of community public relations is that of consideration of the economic status of the town, county, or city. Every member of every community wants the best possible education for his children, but physical education is expensive, and we have sometimes demanded too much and too elaborate equipment and facilities. The question of the ideal beggars this point when elaborate facilities lie unused because of inadequate or poorly planned programs. Finally, the moral and spiritual values that are possible in physical education can best be reached by support of the clergy and churches within a community. Anyone interested in fine public relations in physical education should give this concept some thought.

The "serving men" of public relations may alter their roles in obedience to the interpretation of the individual using them. We have indicated our interpretation of their various roles as well as some cross-currents that exist in public relations.

The professional responsibilities that one is called to assume contribute either positively or negatively to public relations. As a member of a profession, one learns to serve professional organizations at local, state, and national levels. Services that are performed range from membership on minor committees to the presidency of a national organization. As one grows in professional reputation, appearances at conferences as a panelist or as a speaker become the order of the day. As professional stature begins to emerge, authorship of articles and books enters the picture. To engage in such activities, an individual must be willing to budget time, give up leisure to the cause of "midnight oil," and plan deliberately and carefully to avoid jeopardizing one's basic teaching responsibilities. These professional responsibilities will reflect credit and add prestige to the individual and the department if handled well.

POSTSCRIPTS

It has been said that battles are won by the army that "gets there firstest with the mostest." We began, in this century, to realize that this neatly packaged thought has more to it than arms and men when we faced some of the cultural problems of World War II and the Korean War. We realized that matériel was needed to win battles, but liaison among groups was even more important. Matériel in war is worthless if human resources and abilities are neglected or ignored. So it is with public relations if media are used abundantly but human errors, human prejudices, and biases mar the picture.

SOME POSTSCRIPTS

"Sorry you aren't here." These are the people whose interests we have not reached. These are the "dubs" who are afraid to participate because only "stars" are welcome. These are the oldsters who can no longer play team sports but who would welcome a chance for modified individual or dual sports. These are the academically minded whom we have antagonized by emphasizing our physical activities without pointing to their academic roots. These are the parents whose children feel the brunt of peer disdain from lack of the teaching of skills. These are the young staff members who seem to find no toe holds on the prestige ladder.

"Wish you could join us." These are the untapped sources in our communities that we have not bothered to unearth. These are the alienated souls who do not understand our goals and whom we have not bothered to educate. These are the young professional people in our midst to whom we have given no helping hand. These are the administrators whom we "talk about" rather than "talk with."

"Wish I could have done something about that." These are the accident situations we did not foresee. These are the poor contacts we sometimes make with students. These are the antipathies we arouse by dogmatic demands upon reluctant administrators. These are the emotionally overstimulated and physically overtired boys and girls who have been pushed beyond their maturity levels by our ambitions.

The above postscripts are the negative side of public relations. "Come on in, the water's fine" is a positive postscript and one that could be profitably applied to public relations. There is a great deal of foresight, sound philosophy, and alert administration in a good program of public relations. For the administrator of physical education who is keenly aware of the import of his program on his many publics, the motto should be "Public Relations—Not Postscripts."

SUMMARY

Public relations are what we tell our publics, when we tell them and why we inform them, how and where we conduct our contacts with them, and to whom we speak. Our publics are manifold, extending from our neighbors, our students, and our fellow teachers to top administrative personnel and community leaders. Communication and rapport with our publics are constant necessities in physical education. Our daily class materials as well as our special events hold great interest for the layman. Moreover, our close contacts with our pupils and athletes offer ideal chances for fine public relations rather than questionable postscripts.

PROBLEMS

1. What is the difference between propaganda and public relations? Cite a satisfactory example of each in physical education.

2. State three mass media that could be used in forwarding physical education in a public school situation. Outline briefly four standards to be observed in using *each* of these.

3. In preparing a recruitment pamphlet for use in a college department, list the criteria of excellence to be observed. State the case of a picture story versus a prose presentation.

4. Name five *publics* touched by any physical education department. Suggest liaison channels and types of information that should be available for each public.

5. Discuss the public relations role of prior preparation and of personality traits usually found in each of the following physical education agents:

  a) Superintendent of schools

b) Director of physical education
c) Teacher of physical education
d) Athletic trainer
e) Matron in a girls' locker room

6. Discuss the public relations aspects of the use of school gymnasiums or play fields by recreational groups.

7. What standards should be used in preparing and presenting a demonstration in physical education for a local community? State the reason for each standard that you name.

5

Legal Factors

There is no doubt that teachers, coaches, and administrators of physical education are well aware of their moral responsibilities for the best possible development and education of the student. Moral responsibility for the safety of the student is also well recognized. The shadow area comes into focus when some form of legal involvement occurs in specific cases. This chapter will highlight the legal factors in physical education. Necessarily, the laws and their interpretation become matters for investigation in specific communities.

GOVERNMENTAL LINES

Within the past decade, we have become increasingly concerned with the possibilities of federal aid for education. Legislation (permissive, mandatory, or enabling) has been established and is in the process of hearings, floor debates, and final decisions at both federal and state levels. Our professional organizations are concerned that the members of this profession keep abreast of these developments and understand the impact of these laws upon the profession. In the near future, federal funds may be available for research (particularly upon an interdisciplinary approach), for development of recreational areas adjacent to or contingent upon water conservation projects, for highly specialized personnel, and for provisions for youth rehabilitation. Whether or not these possibilities become mixed blessings remains to be seen.

A second phase of federal legislation with which administrators need to be familiar is the Constitution with its various amendments and the Bill of Rights of the United States of America. The Constitution does provide certain liberties. Violations, particularly of religious freedom, can be a source of negative community reaction as well as legal action.

State legislatures, by state constitutional intention, exercise control over educational law and function in the various states. Statutes are passed by state legislatures setting up school codes. Under these codes, provisions are made for the educational leadership in the state. State departments of education then function under the state superintendent of public instruction or a state commission of education. State boards of education that act in supervisory or advisory capacities may be either appointed by the governor or elected by the people. In like manner, boards of education and/or control or boards of regents are responsible for institutions of higher education that receive state support. State departments of education may or may not include personnel whose specific assignment is the advancement of physical education within the state. Shortly after World War I, there appeared upon the law books of numerous states additional legislation that set forth the requirements by time allotment or by credit for physical education. Unfortunately, those laws that were marginal in this respect were often considered as the maximum requirement for physical education in the schools. The same was true of the preparation of teachers. A second unfortunate outcome was the fact that these legislated requirements became targets when financial support or educational stresses were in question. Therefore, we point to the axiom that it is wise to educate the public as well as to legislate if physical education is to receive full support. In those states where the leadership of physical education, health education, and recreation was and is guided by well-prepared, fully experienced personnel held responsible for these programs, excellent progress has been made. Certification of teachers may be coded by state legislatures, or this responsibility may be assigned to the state department of education. In either case, careful lines of communication are needed that are three dimensional in nature. Teacher education institutions, state departments of education, and administrative personnel in the schools need intercommunication to serve the best interests of education. Physical education is affected by certification codes in its own right and in its service functions to departments such as elementary education.

Local option in education is a prerogative held in esteem by local communities. School districts operating under the broad powers delegated by the several states elect boards of education which in turn hire superintendents, teachers, and other personnel to conduct the educational pursuits and the business of the school system.

Edwards reports certain local powers relative to the administration of physical education. These are:

1. Authority to require physical examinations
2. Authority to employ nurses, dentists, and physicians
3. Authority to provide *first aid* to injured pupils
4. Authority to provide athletic facilities and make profits from athletic contests
5. Authority to establish and maintain camps for school pupils
6. Authority to insure school property and teachers
7. Authority to permit practice teaching in the schools
8. Authority to contract [1]

Acting under the authority granted to boards of education, local systems formulate rules and regulations designed to best advance education in that specific situation. Tax levies, curricular offerings, provision for facilities and equipment, and all details of the organization of the school district or system are under the jurisdiction of the board of education, which duly delegates authority to administrative personnel.

We are concerned with the differentiations in local, state, and federal authority beyond the point of status information. Currently, there are federal aid to education proposals in process that we hope will aid physical education by providing funds to improve leadership at both state and local levels. Often, permissive legislation is needed to enable more than one governmental unit to combine forces to improve a recreational situation. LB 756 passed in 1963 by the Nebraska Unicameral is such a law. This is an enabling statute stating that more than one town or county could combine forces and finances to provide recreational facilities and opportunities. In states with rural populations, an enabling act of this type is or will be well received.

PROBLEM AREAS

It is obvious that, by virtue of the nature of physical activity, physical education is open to hazardous situations. There is no need to push the panic button, but there is need to identify our problem areas and to conduct the program as carefully as possible. All forms of physical activity have potentially dangerous moments. Our first problem area is that of the thoughtless instructor. Legal opinions tell us that we are expected to exercise foresight in relation to the conduct of the activity. For the administrator, this

[1] Newton Edwards (ed.), *The Courts and the Public Schools* (Chicago: University of Chicago Press, 1955), pp. 150–71.

means careful teacher selection to secure mature, well-prepared, and conscientious instructors. Instructors of this type will realize the value of teaching skills and of selecting activities suited to the age and maturation level of the students. They will understand that students need warnings regarding their own safety before they start certain activities, that students need to be taught the correct way to use equipment (from balls to parallel bars), and that students need disciplined reaction to many physical education situations; for example, the safety codes that elementary school children may develop for their free-play periods. Teachers of this type understand the necessity for close supervision of every phase of the program.

We mention three especially vulnerable facility spots: playgrounds or playing fields, swimming pools, and locker rooms. Several outdoor situations that seem to have accident potential are placing game areas so that they overlap, student infringement on the rights of others (bullying, horseplay), uneven play surfaces or holes in the surface, and poor placement of the play area in relation to community traffic. Swimming pools must be carefully supervised from two standpoints: sanitation and safety. If a school system or college employs a sanitary engineer, he checks on pool temperature and bacteria count. The cleaning standards are phases of his responsibility. Both the sanitation and safety are the responsibilities of all instructors, since reports on these conditions are in order. Regulations regarding the use of the pool should be carefully written and rigidly followed (see Appendix No. 6 and Appendix No. 7). Buoys, ropes, and other protective equipment should be provided, and a qualified lifeguard should be on duty whenever a pool is in use. Pools must be kept locked when not in use. It is also wise to use electric-release locks operated by the teacher or matron so that keys may not be misplaced or duplicated. Locker rooms should be carefully planned for traffic flow and for ease in supervision. Checking locker rooms at the end of each class period and at the end of the activity day is a fine procedure.

There are a few especially vulnerable spots, also, in the curriculum. Use of all forms of apparatus must be carefully taught, and students must be restrained from attempting performances that may appear spectacular but may be beyond the skill of the learner. Two other factors with regard to apparatus that need constant checking are the correct use of spotting and the correct placement of mats under and around apparatus. All types of apparatus must be inspected for safety at regular intervals and immediately preceding class use.

In the stunts and tumbling unit, great care must also be exercised in the teaching program. Tumbling must be taught with careful progression; protective equipment and spotting are needed. There are elements of fear on the part of certain students that may result in tension and/or questionable incidents. Unreasonable demands within a required program can lead to trouble. Certainly, teachers trying to teach this phase of physical education should have received careful preparation.

The role of conditioning for participation is receiving more and more attention as our activities are stepped up and as the physiological demands of these activities increase. Adequate conditioning is demanded by endurance swimming, certain fitness tests, team and individual sports, tumbling and gymnastics, and vigorous forms of dance. Not only is performance enhanced by conditioning, but also the health and safety of the student comes into focus. It is obvious that health examinations should precede all phases of physical activity.

Interscholastic and intercollegiate athletics have problems that are emphasized by their popularity and prominence in the culture today. Because of this emphasis, we often find more attention paid to the health and safety of varsity participants than to those in intramural athletics and the regular class offerings. Standard practice for varsity sports includes a medical examination for the specific sport. In addition, either by contract or by volunteer agreement, physicians are in attendance at most varsity events. The protective equipment for contact sports is carefully selected for and individually fitted to the athlete. The codes in use by the National Collegiate Athletic Association and the State Athletic Activities Associations help to control factors of overplay as well as eligibility. With the trend toward interscholastic sports for women, The Division for Girls and Women's Sports has set up standards and is currently studying needed controls. In sports for both sexes, at all ages, more scientific information is needed regarding physiological reactions to intensive activity and the psychological effects of the emotional overtones under stress.

Transportation of teams is a problem in many schools. If at all possible, bonded public common carriers should be used. There are liability problems related to requests for return from the contests with relatives or friends, problems related to the use of private cars for either class or team transportation, and problems related to the driving of privately owned cars by students.

Another problem is the safe seating of audiences at athletic contests. This is a matter for thoughtful consideration. When seating is permanent, safety building codes generally take care of the situation. When folding bleachers that can be stored against the wall are available, their construction is more solid. When temporary bleachers are used, their construction is a matter of concern. Moreover the use of bleachers raises the question of safety during regular physical education classes and, also, the question of adequate spectator distance from the sport in action.

In the total physical education curriculum, there is the question of procedure when an accident occurs. In the case of elementary or secondary school students, routines should have been established for reporting accidents immediately to the school nurse or the principal. Adequate facilities and supplies for emergency first-aid measures should be available. The school should possess a file of names and addresses of persons to be notified in case of illness or accidents (parents or other relatives and, if the parents are willing, the family physician). For indigent students or for use in extreme emergencies, a file of physicians available for call should be maintained. A cardinal rule is that a student who is ill or who has been hurt should never be sent home alone. If the parents cannot come to the school, a responsible adult should accompany the child, both for his safety and to explain the circumstances to the parents. In case of accident, first aid should be administered by qualified persons. This means that teachers of physical education and coaches should be certified in first-aid procedures. First aid is just what it says; it is not diagnosis, nor is it medical treatment. Such phases of assistance are the prerogative of the physician. In colleges, the same general principles are true except that Student Health Services are notified. In turn, if indicated by the condition, Student Health will notify the housing unit, the Office of Student Affairs, and the parents. A complete record of every accident should be kept on file; copies should be made for the teacher, the school or department, and the doctor or medical services. Figure 5–1 is a sample form that has been used successfully. In addition, The National Safety Council School Accident form is available.

The fact that accidents do occur brings us to the problems involved with insurance. Shall the schools and colleges provide for all students in physical education and sports? Shall the institution provide contact (group insurance opportunity) for option at personal expense? Does the athletic department carry insurance coverage for all athletes in all sports? Are teachers and coaches covered by liability insurance? These questions as well as those in the above problem areas will be discussed in the remaining

```
┌─────────────────────────────────────────────────────────────┐
│                  INDIVIDUAL ACCIDENT REPORT                   │
│                                                               │
│  Name of Student_____ Date_____  │
│  Address_____ Age_____   │
│                                        Telephone_____   │
│                                                               │
│  Activity, at time of accident_____ │
│  _____ │
│  _____ │
│                                                               │
│  Place and time of accident_____ │
│  _____ │
│  Describe fully how accident occurred_____ │
│  _____ │
│  _____ │
│                                                               │
│  What was done about it?_____ │
│  _____ │
│  _____ │
│                                                               │
│  Name and address of witnesses_____ │
│  _____ │
│  _____ │
│                                                               │
│  Was the accident due in any way to defective                 │
│  equipment or neglect of University personnel?_____  │
│                                                               │
│  Signature of staff in charge _____   │
└─────────────────────────────────────────────────────────────┘
```

Fig. 5–1. Sample individual accident report.

sections of this chapter. (For a detailed description of various state laws pertaining to liability, see Appendix No. 8.)

TERMS

In order to realize how legal questions are resolved, it is necessary to follow the lines of authority higher up or down the line. School boards establish rules and regulations designed to order the administration of schools in a uniform way under specific local conditions. Generally, school boards operate under enabling as well as mandatory legislation (laws). When an altercation occurs that is carried into court, a decision is necessary. Precedents established in previous cases of a similar nature are consulted. When needed, the attorney general may be asked for opinions or legal interpretations of the laws.

Shroyer points out that legal ignorance does not excuse a teacher from liability.[2] Immediately, one is faced with the definitions of liability.[3] Liability infers that one has an obligation to carry out. Failure to fulfill obligations may result in law suits based on negligence. On the other hand, commission of an act that is judged unreasonable in nature may also be labeled as liability. Leibee identifies the elements for successful maintenance of such a suit as:

(1) Duty to conform to a standard of behaviour which will not subject others to an unreasonable risk of injury.
(2) Breach of that duty—failure to exercise due care.
(3) A sufficiently close causal connection between the conduct or behaviour and the resulting injury.
(4) Damage or injury resulting to the rights or interests of another.

(The term "negligence" refers to the presence of ALL FOUR of the elements above mentioned although it is sometimes used to refer only to breach of duty.) [4]

It is presumed that a reasonably prudent man would recognize the possibilities of danger in a situation and would act to avoid it. Negligence, as indicated above, has a passive element when omission of a duty might result in injury. The classic example of this type of negligence is the withdrawal of a physical education teacher from a supervisory duty with a class or any informal play situation. Since one standard commonly held by boards of education is that of the teacher being held responsible for the conduct of the pupil *in loco parentis* (in place of the parent), the importance of supervisory responsibilities is obvious. The presence of an excessively aggressive pupil in an informal, unsupervised play situation or even in the class situation may result in injury to another child by unnecessary contact. Such a situation may be called negligence, and, if so, such negligence must be established in court. The party or parties held responsible for such situations bring us to our next point. Sovereign immunity operates in certain states. This is the concept that "the king can do no wrong"; i.e., the common-law inference that governments cannot be sued without their consent.

[2] George Shroyer, "Personal Liabilities of a Secondary School Physical Educator," *The Physical Educator*, XXI (May, 1964), 55.
[3] For detailed legal definitions, see Appendix No. 9.
[4] Howard C. Leibee, *Tort Liability for Injuries to Pupils* (Ann Arbor: Campus Publishers, 1965), pp. 8 and 9.

Thus, the school board or school district is protected but not the teacher, who may be sued on the grounds of personal liability. When the school board or school district by law may be held liable for torts (legal wrongs) of employees at work, this is called vicarious liability or the respondent superior.

A few more concepts are needed to understand administrative and teaching responsibilities with regard to legal liability. An adult is expected to realize that a child is irresponsible, but as maturity increases, there are certain immunities that may apply. Such an instance is contributory negligence when carelessness or rejection of the standards that have been set are ignored by the plaintiff (student). A second immunity can be found in the term "assumption of the risk." Spectators at an athletic event have assumed the risk of watching either fast or proximal action. School districts, as well as householders, have been sued for having an attractive nuisance on the premises. During vacation periods, playground equipment is often partially dismantled in order to make it unusable. This practice is to avoid, as far as is feasible, legal action based on an attractive nuisance. A nuisance is said to be an item that has an inherent danger (for example, trees and fences). An attractive nuisance is considered to be an item that has allure for children but is inherently dangerous to them. Thus, apparatus of a swinging type on an elementary school playground under supervision could be used with due regard to safety. Adequate sandpits under fixed apparatus plus correct installation will cut the hazards. But swings, seesaws, and items of this type are frequently dismantled over vacation periods. The final legal term that we shall discuss is proprietary function. When fees are charged for participation in physical education or recreation activities and a profit results, the authorities involved are serving a proprietary function. Depending upon the statutes of the time and place, they may or may not be held liable in cases presented before the courts.

ADMINISTRATIVE IMPLICATIONS

We have discussed some of the problem areas in physical education and then indicated the legal terms, thereby implying the possibility of legal recourse in the event of accidents or negligence. The matter of legal liability is one of the tightropes of administration. An administrator needs to exercise eternal vigilance if adequate safety measures and due caution are to be observed by the total staff. On the other hand, fear of activities could prove to be a detriment to both staff and students. The answer lies in safety precautions plus safety awareness combined with careful management of the many factors of the total program.

SUPERVISORY PROBLEMS

Policy statements and definite procedures for supervision of all types of activities are the joint responsibility of the administrator and his staff. Policies with regard to gymnasiums, pools, fields, and other facilities used by outside groups or by informal groups are necessary. Such statements outline priorities for use, determine ways and means of securing permission for use, and definitely set the lines of responsibility in such use. There is a trend in physical education toward open gymnasiums for informal use. Under all such circumstances, it is wise to have a permanent staff member in charge. Immediately, this poses budgetary considerations, but, if play areas are to be used to the fullest extent, the public should be prepared to meet the expense. Swimming pools, as stated earlier, must have lifeguards on duty, a staff in charge, and matrons and cage men available for the dressing rooms.

Many school systems have regulations that demand the presence of the teacher in dressing rooms before and after class sessions and in play areas whenever these are in use. Equipment, such as trampolines, should be closed and locked when not in use under direct supervision. Other types of apparatus should be placed, if possible, in large storage areas. Even small equipment, such as a ball, can be a hazard when left available without supervision.

Matrons and custodial help should be aware of hazards with which they may come in contact. These persons should be asked to report electrical difficulties, slick floors, loosened boards, broken locker doors, and other items of this type.

One phase of supervision that is imperative is the filing of an accident report immediately. Staff should be encouraged to report the most minor of incidents as well as any major accidents. Follow-up of any incident is needed to be sure that the student has reached the school nurse or the principal or the college health service. Inquiry and observation of students returning to activity after an incident is the final phase of this supervisory duty.

Supervision should be active in nature and should stress safety. Students need to be taught skills carefully and need to practice safe ways of participating in activity. The overly daring student should be cautioned, and the overly active student should be watched for signs of fatigue. High standards of skill contribute both to better performance and to greater safety in action. Careful attention to the skill level of each student is necessary.

Finally, supervision includes inspection of all equipment. Not only is equipment inspected to assure that it is safe but any defects should be reported in writing. The placement of apparatus (for example, mats for tumbling) in relation to the organization of the class should be watched. Overcrowding, too close proximity of students waiting to perform, and too few mats are signs of danger.

The administrator of a physical education program is concerned that the above supervisory practices are matters of common action on the part of all teachers and coaches. Foresight is needed to avoid legal liability. A reasonable man is presumed to exercise due caution particularly if his responsibility involves children. The standard set is that of complete adherence to supervisory duties at all times and in all places.

WAIVERS

A waiver is a statement by the parents that they will not hold the school responsible in case of accident (usually used for trips or athletic participation). These have no legal validity since a parent cannot waive a claim for his child. Permission slips are used, however, as one means of being sure that the parents are aware of the activities in which the student is participating. It is very important in structuring sports participation for girls that this type of permission has been granted.

TRANSPORTATION

In the past, problems associated with transportation have been largely confined to varsity sports. Today, we have need to transport classes to highly specialized facilities such as golf courses and lakes for canoeing, scuba diving, and other aquatic sports; outdoor education project groups to camps or woods sites; dance groups to symposiums; as well as various teams to competitive events. Forensic groups must be taken to meetings, music groups to festivals and symposiums; classes need to visit art and historical museums; and science classes need to visit laboratories of various types. Transportation, therefore, is no longer a physical education problem per se; it is an institution-wide problem. The administrator of physical education should investigate policies and procedures set up by the school district or institution before planning transportation programs. Usually, forms are available for recording needs and arrangements for these trips. The use of common carriers with bonded drivers or school buses operating under board of education regulations is recommended. If private cars must be used, adult drivers are a "must"; filing evidence of the insurability of the driver and the car is customary, and student riders should be covered by accident insurance. Many institutions maintain group and accident coverage within which a student may be insured for one or more days or for a sports season at a very nominal fee. Another factor in transportation is the adult supervision provided on various kinds of trips. When elementary school children go on field trips or to another school for an invitational game, it is customary for the "room mothers" to assist the teacher. The many problems of such trips thus are brought to the attention of the mothers. In the case of older students, it is difficult sometimes for the parents to realize all the problems. Returning to the school in the same car and under the same supervision is a primary problem. One of the administrative duties of a coach or supervisor is to help students set up standards of conduct that will represent the school to advantage and also be a factor in safety when large groups travel together. The source of payment for travel also has legal implications. Athletic teams, supported by entrance fees, generally enter into contracts with common carriers or agreements with the board of education with regard to the use of school buses. If the parent or student pays individuals for the use of private transportation, the legality of these fees in relation to the insurance of the vehicles in use should be established.

INSURANCE

Most college varsity programs carry accident insurance plans to meet the expense of injuries and illnesses resulting from varsity participation. In secondary schools, the pattern is varied. If the school district as a governmental agency has immunity from suits, claims on this insurance carried by the board of education are a moot question. An interesting question under such circumstances is: "Does purchase of insurance against tort liability waive common law immunity?" Shapiro discusses this, saying: "The view is that governmental immunity is a historical anachronism; that it is legally unsound and unjust and has no place in modern day society, especially since liability insurance is universally available to provide against the dissipation of the public treasury." She points to the 1963 session of the Minnesota legislature restoration of the "rule in actions against school districts," but a provision was also enacted that "school districts procuring liability insurance become subject to the newly created statutory provisions relating to tort liability of municipalities for the duration and extent of the coverage." [5] This moot question is further clarified by the following discussion.

Legal Precedents.[6] At this time, there has not been any substantial litigation on the question, "Does purchase of insurance against tort liability waive common law immunity?" to predict any definite trends. As long ago as 1943, it had been frequently argued on behalf of the pupil injured in the negligent operation of a school bus that the immunity of a school district from a suit in tort should be held to be waived when the district carries liability insurance. This argument has not prevailed in the absence of statutory regulation. In *Ayers* v. *Hartford Accident and Indemnity Co.*, 106 F.2d 958 (CCA, 5th 1939), it was held that the injured party could not have the advantages of the liability insurance although the school district had paid a substantial sum in premiums to the insurer. However, the doctrine of immunity from tort for the acts of the servants of a quasi-municipal corporation (school district) has, in recent years, been forced to yield to the paramount desire to provide protection for the injured person. Hence, in 1940, a statute was adopted in Kentucky making school districts liable in tort to the amount of the insurance carried. This statute was passed after a pupil was killed by the operation of a school bus in 1938. The administrator of the pupil killed was not allowed to recover, although the school district carried liability insurance.

Another significant and leading decision in this area was the decision rendered in the case of *Thomas* v. *Broadlands Community Consolidated School District*, 348 Ill. App. 567, 109 N.E.2d 636 (1953). In this case, two questions were presented: (1) Was the defendant immune from suit? (2) If immune, did the carrying of liability insurance operate to remove the immunity either completely or partially to the extent of such insurance? In answer to these questions, the court held that the defendant, a public school district, was not liable for injuries resulting from a tort; but, to the extent it had provided insurance coverage, it had waived its immunity to suit.

Finally, the basis for this line of decisions, stating an affirmative answer to the question, seems to extend from an enlightened trend in some states toward elimination of the doctrine of sovereign immunity. A prime example is the state of Oregon where a court reasoned in *Vendrell* v. *School District*, 226 Or. 263, 360 P.2d 282

---

[5] Frieda S. Shapiro, "Your Liability for Student Accidents," *NEA Journal*, March, 1965, p. 47.

[6] Prepared by William Barret Schenk, student in law.

(1961) that, since the legislature knew of the rulings, school districts could perform only governmental actions, and still authorized actions and suits to be maintained against them for injuries arising from some acts or omissions—Or. Rev. Stat. sec. 30. 320 (1961) read with sec. 30. 310 (1961)—and provided for the purchase of liability insurance—Or. Rev. Stat. sec. 332. 180 (1961)—then it must have been the legislative intent to lift the immunity to the extent of the insurance *actually* purchased. In the *Vendrell Case*, the plaintiff was fifteen years of age and enrolled as a freshman in a high school in the defendant school district. There, playing football against a rival high school, he was tackled very hard and suffered a broken neck and permanent injury to his spinal cord, resulting in paraplegia. The court held that a school district which does not purchase liability insurance is immune from liability, and that its immunity is lifted only to the extent that it is *authorized* to purchase and *in fact has obtained* insurance covering the activities in question.

In summary then, a few courts have gone along with the lifting of immunity, but they are definitely in the minority. The courts that have gone along with this have done so only *if the purchase of insurance is authorized by statute,* and *only to the extent that the insurance has in fact been purchased.* The situation as it now stands would seem to require legislative modification. Based on the above cases, in a narrow perspective, it could be stated that the purchase of insurance against tort liability does waive common law immunity. However, this does not mean that a particular court will adhere to the above mentioned enlightenment. For such a case, the court may choose to (1) completely abolish the immunity doctrine, (2) completely reaffirm the doctrine by overruling the above cases, or (3) acknowledge the partial "lifting" of immunity coupled with, let us say, a mandatory requirement of liability insurance for all school districts.

The state high school athletic (activities) associations have developed group accident insurance plans that are used in many states. In plans such as these, parents are given the opportunity to carry such insurance under reasonable premiums. Probably the best known of these plans is that of Wisconsin with its option of group (total pupil participation) or individual plan. In some of these insurance plans, all phases of competitive sports plus the regular physical education program are covered. In other plans, varsity athletics only, or specifics such as football only, constitute the coverage. Administrators and coaches must be alert to the implications in various types of insurance coverage and should offer information to the general public regarding the possibilities for such coverage as far as local rulings make this action feasible. If the insurance program is subscribed to through school auspices, applications, premium collection, and accident claims must be processed and machinery set in motion to care for the details. George and Lehmann point out that many plans are not insurance but benefit plans that provide substantial financial assistance in relation to their cost. As such, it becomes the moral obligation of the school to secure the cooperation of local physicians relative to the medical fees involved in the claims filed.[7]

Another type of insurance coverage is a general student accident policy. Whether school accident insurance or student accident insurance is in use, safety education and integrity in the reporting of claims are necessary. Unnecessary or casual use of claims may tend, in the long run, to nullify the protection that insurance affords.[8]

Although every teacher senses his moral responsibility for the health and welfare of pupils when an unfortunate incident occurs, it is possible that the teacher may be held legally liable. Individual liability insurance is often carried by the instructor as protection against damages that could well go beyond his financial resources. In some cases where an instructor has heavy responsibility for physical education activities and others of a similar nature, the premiums are high. In states where group coverage is permitted by law, various educational organizations offer their memberships liability coverage while engaged in professional duties. Usually, a nominal premium of $1 per year provides liability protection up to $10,000.[9] It is also possible to secure an occupational liability rider, at economical cost, if one carries a blanket policy on property. Administrators need to inform younger staff members of their liability and of these means of coverage that help to insure peace of mind.

SUMMARY

Legal liability poses many problems for the conduct of physical education activities. This chapter has outlined the authoritative channels for laws and regulations relating to education and physi-

[7] Jack F. George and Harry A. Lehmann, *School Athletic Administration* (New York: Harper and Row, Inc., 1966), pp. 140–45.

[8] Roger C. Wiley, "Student Accident Insurance in the Public Schools," *The Physical Educator*, XX (May, 1963), 74, 75.

[9] Carl A. Troester, Jr., "New Service for AAHPER Members," *Journal of Health, Physical Education, and Recreation*, XXX (December, 1959), 12.

cal education. (See also Appendix No. 8.) Some of the problem areas of physical education have been indicated together with the legal implications concerning these. Administrative implications have then been drawn. In the end, as in the beginning, the problem is moral as well as legal. It is basically a case of the use of sound personal judgment. It is a case for common-sense decisions backed by conscientious, dedicated teachers and coaches who keep the best interest of the individual student foremost in their thinking.

PROBLEMS

1. Differentiate between the moral and the legal responsibilities of a teacher of physical education.

2. Set up a plan justifying legally the inclusion of physical education in federal aid for a state department of education.

3. Cite permissive, mandatory, and enabling legislation with reference to physical education that has been enacted in your state.

4. Discuss three or more hazardous areas in physical education with regard to legal liability.

5. Write safety codes for the use of three types of gymnasium apparatus.

6. Debate this statement: "Resolved that 'vicarious liability' should take precedence over 'personal liability' in cases of negligence."

7. Discuss several phases of supervision of physical education activities that may be related to legal liability.

8. Make a table of possible insurance coverages for physical education and athletic activities feasible in your state.

9. As a supervisor of physical education in a school district, prepare a brief digest of all the legal factors needed by teachers under your jurisdiction.

6

Personnel Problems

Of all the problems that confront any administrator, the manifold and multilateral problems of personnel are the most demanding in terms of judgment, finesse in human relations, and import on the morale of the staff. Only a few of these problems deal with tangibles such as salary scales, leaves of absence, insurance benefits, and similar matters. The majority of these problems deal with the intangibles of human reactions as men and women work with their fellow human beings.

THE ADMINISTRATOR AND THE STAFF

What kind of person should this individual be who administers the program of physical education? Because the physical education program is so varied and touches upon so many phases of community effort, the administrator of this program must realize that the patience of Job and the stamina of an Atlas are needed. First, such an administrator must be endowed with fine physical and mental health. The hours that must be covered are long, and one must meet each moment with the stamina and the vitality that either supervision of established activity or suddenly needed decisions happen to demand. Knowing your own work capacity, sensing your own weaknesses (from avoidance of major decisions to abhorrence of the details of scheduling), and stressing your own strengths (as counselor, teacher, or public relations agent) will result in more efficient operation on the job. It is necessary to maintain a sensible, stable point of view. Self-control, tempered by the humor woven into most petty irritants, will help to keep the administrator on an even keel. Self-control is a major by-product of sound mental health. An administrator must enjoy his work and must display his reactions. In this way, he may build his ability to

121

take the stress of reverses and the tensions of the problems that arise. Finally, in this review of personal characteristics of the administrator, we emphasize his value system. Does he possess such high integrity that his staff believes firmly in his purposes, his reactions, and his decisions? Is he fair to all members of the staff in listening to needs or grievances? Does he avoid carrying grudges? Does he weigh and measure the many factors in each problem before he reaches a decision? Is he available for personal problem conferences as well as professional, and does he respect the confidential nature of many of these problems? No man can be all these things all the time. But he can be constantly aware of the admonition: "To thine own self be true, thou cans't not then be false to any man."

Professionally, an administrator of physical education must be well prepared. This criterion demands a well-rounded major in both the undergraduate and graduate degrees. In many states, the standard of preparation for teaching physical education is rising; therefore, it is imperative that an administrator of physical education have, at least, the master's degree. For reasons of status as well as the breadth of preparation, administrators of physical education at the college level should have a doctoral degree. If an administrator decides that a doctoral degree is terminal as far as professional preparation is concerned, he is selling himself and his department short. Constant study of professional literature and attendance at workshops, clinics, and professional meetings are necessary to keep ahead of the developments in the field. A second aspect of the preparation needed for administration in physical education is experience. Without teaching experience at all levels (elementary, secondary, and college), the administrator has little basis for many of his decisions. This point is particularly true in teacher education and graduate work. Furthermore, preparation plus experience should result in a more mature point of view. Finally, an administrator must be willing and able to support physical education by contributing to the work of professional committees, professional organizations, and professional meetings.

Although an administrator has to develop skill in a number of detailed operations such as purchasing, budget classifications, and scheduling, these are concrete matters that are learned by precept and by practice. Of far greater importance are the skills in human relations that must be mastered. Working with a staff involves an attempt to understand the individuals involved. No administrator can alter completely the behavior of a staff member who enters a new situation with a negative attitude. This person is ready to criticize, in an attempt to rationalize his own reactions, everything from living conditions in the community to departmental policies. Under these circumstances, as well as more favorable ones, the administrator tries to create an atmosphere of acceptance of the individual and approval of all actions which do not jeopardize the work and standards of the department. There is much to be said for both the administrator and the subordinate who face daily problems with a positive attitude. Adaptation to local conditions has been an important means of progress from the beginning of recorded history. Realizing that grievances often arise in the department from problems of personal insecurity, lack of preparation, or in adaptation to differing departmental mores; from family responsibilities; from financial needs; from lack of personal acceptance by other staff members; and from personality traits, an administrator spends part of every day advising and counseling staff members. These are daily problems of leadership, but the administrator must look beyond this point to the future. Many of these personnel problems must be decided in terms of what is best for the department in its total relationship. An administrator must be willing to deny the whims of the moment out of respect for the best functioning of the future. For example, a staff member who cannot say "No" to outside requests for self-satisfying activities must be warned that energies are drained and department objectives suffer from such overparticipation. This is not to state that the physical education staff should not be encouraged to sponsor college or community groups, but it is to state that this staff activity should reach a happy medium—neither too little nor too much. The above problem may become a source of minor friction. A major problem with potentials for the future can be cited in failure on the part of an administration to select key staff members in terms of their probable ability to project departmental progress in terms of curricular change and/or research. Thus, the administrator needs skill in daily staff contact and in relating this contact to future departmental development.

Years ago, staff members strove to reach a point in their professional careers where an administrative post would be achieved. This concept of administration, per se, being the pinnacle of professional achievement is no longer operative. We are aware today that certain individuals make their best professional contributions in teaching or research, while others make their best contributions in administration. The administrator, then, is both the leader of the team and a member of it. In this dual capacity, he must forecast the needs of the department, set a climate in which advancement in thinking may be put into practice, and, in general, exercise his capacity as a leader. At the same time, he must contribute his share of the spadework in any project undertaken and be available to iron out any details in coordination that might add to smoother departmental teamwork. If an administrator considers himself to be a machine that tools the paper work of the department, a status quo will probably result. He must be willing to accept his leadership role, and he must develop creative thinking if a department is to move ahead by "sinking its teeth" into current and future projects.

How may we structure these personnel relationships within the department in cross-departmental and higher echelon relationships? There are established channeling lines that must be maintained in these structures. There are parallel lines that run from staff member to staff member and department to department. As long as these lines are horizontal, as indication of equal status, very little friction occurs. But individuals with high ability soon pull these lines to diagonal relationships, and, human nature being as it is, minor misunderstandings may then occur. There are vertical lines also representing relationships from staff member to staff member as is the case in staff committee chairmanships. Here, responsibility and resultant authority are vested in a staff member, for example, a departmental activity committee or a departmental testing committee. The total staff receives recommendations from a testing committee, and after due consultation, a consensus is reached. At this point, the testing committee chairman has the authority to carry out the recommendations of the committee. An isolated staff member may not always agree with the final decision, but he disciplines himself to accept the decision of the majority. This is democracy in action. As Griffiths so aptly states, "recognition of authority is different from imposition of authority." [1] In this connotation, also, one may consider the line and staff relationships from chairman or supervisor to staff member. Here, the teacher recognizes the necessity for centralized authority in order that the work at hand may be expedited. The chairman or supervisor recognizes the expediency of the authority of the dean or assistant superintendent of a school system, and so this structured authority moves up to the top administrative officer who in turn completes this cycle by consultation with his board of regents or board of education representing the will of the population. It can readily be seen that, if these lines of authority are ethically valued and if each individual who shares in this authority considers this a moral as well as a con-

[1] Daniel E. Griffiths, *Human Relations in School Administration* (New York: Appleton-Century-Crofts, Inc., 1956), p. 309.

crete responsibility, the judgments that result will be shared and better understood by all concerned.

A potent factor in the mesh of relationships existing between the administrator and the staff is that of the manner in which decisions are accepted. We have a trite saying in administration that it is the decisions that get you down! There are moments when a split-second decision must be made. The administrator, at this point, calls upon his past experiences and his knowledge of how this decision may affect the closely woven mesh of interdepartmental relationships, and he relies upon the confidence of the staff in his ability. If a decision can be based upon consultations with staff, with higher administration authorities, and often with students, the fact that more persons may exercise judgment increases the base for acceptance. There are many factors in all staff decisions: total staff adjustment, legal and moral authoritative rights, known and unknown factors of a specific problem, and the time limits imposed by the circumstances. It is wise not to make hasty decisions, and it is also wise to avoid raising issues unduly. In the final analysis, the administrator of a department of physical education carries the responsibility for all phases of departmental contact, procedures, and development. In response to this responsibility, the administrator may have to refuse permission for certain activities and to take the initiative on other decisions.

Administrators in physical education, in common with all administrators, face a number of problems in human relations. What does the staff member specializing in sports, dance, or swimming expect in the way of opportunity for his activity? How does this specialist adjust to other specialists and their demands within a department? How does the teacher of physical education in an elementary or secondary school see his role in relation to that of his fellow teachers? Does the staff member regard progress on the part of another staff member as a threat to his security or as advancement for the department? How well can the individual stand the stress of departmental competition and still cooperate in departmental projects? What about the administrator? Does he use his knowledge of staff personalities to establish domination over the situation by means of fear and even the derisive sarcastic comment? In other words, tolerance, mutual respect, and mutual confidence are needed. Man is able to extend loyalty to a cause or a person, to think creatively, and to judge objectively. The well of human resources has barely been tapped. It will overflow under fine conditions, but it will recede if the climate is one of bias, prejudice, or punitive action. The administrator and his staff—does the behavior on each side of the weighted scale balance to foster fine staff relationships?

STAFFING

Professional preparation in physical education has made great strides in this century, including graduate study at both the master's and the doctoral levels. A neophyte teacher is expected to have a bachelor's degree and, shortly thereafter, graduate study in progress. In spite of this advance in terms of formal preparation, staffing remains a problem. Selection, after locating candidates, is difficult, and retention poses its problems sparked by our restless generation. Few young teachers come to departments or schools with the maturity or the experience to handle all situations that may arise. As an introduction to the discussion of staff problems, the following quotation is appropriate:

Personnel policies should include selecting the competent, training the inexperienced, eliminating the incompetent, and providing incentives for all members of the organization. Even informal organizations such as street gangs follow these procedures. Personnel policies in formal groups such as school faculties should be clearly defined. Selecting the competent is essential to recruiting potentially effective group members. Training the inexperienced is essential to obtaining maximum productivity from individual members of the group. Eliminating the incompetent is essential to maintaining the integrity and cohesiveness of the group. Providing incentives by meeting the individual needs of group members is essential to maintaining group morale and assuring maximum productivity.[2]

SELECTION

The concept of selection of staff carries with it a number of responsibilities. First, the administrator must know what type of work he expects the candidate to undertake. Is he searching for a teacher of elementary school physical education, or a junior high or senior high school specialist? Does he want a combination of teacher at the secondary school level and consultant for the classroom teachers in the elementary school? At the college level, does he need a specialist in sports, dance, or swimming? In teacher education, does he need a specialist in the areas related to the scientific background of physical education—kinesiology and physiology of exercise? Does he need a person with experience as well as preparation in elementary and secondary physical education to

[2] Edgar L. Morphet, Roe L. Johns, and Theodore L. Reller, *Educational Administration* (Englewood Cliffs, N.J.: Prentice-Hall, Inc., 1959), pp. 57–58. By permission of Prentice-Hall, Inc.

supervise student teaching or present methods? In all cases, it would be well to prepare a job analysis and, in so doing, review the capabilities of other staff members before launching a search for personnel. By conference with respected colleagues, by inquiry to teacher placement bureaus, or by personal contact, credentials of candidates interested in such openings may be gathered. The reading and analysis of credentials is serious business. Few people ask for recommendations from persons with whom they may have been in conflict. Therefore, one must learn to read between the lines, checking such items as sequences and length of experience, omitted references from a stated teaching situation, and ambiguous cover-all statements in such papers. The policy of asking experienced staff members to read credentials and to share in staff selection is to be commended. A staff member may focus attention upon an item that the administrator reading from another point of view may have missed. Having so shared in this selection, they have a responsibility to help this new staff member in his initial contacts within the situation. There is a morale factor, also, in being included in the selection process of one's colleagues. A personal interview is highly desirable for purposes of assessing how the candidate faces a professional colleague, to evaluate personality traits, and to gain some information on the candidate's general philosophy and professional outlook. As indicated by Castner and Ashton,[3] a time lag may nullify all these standards. If the administrator fails to follow up by contact and by the appointment of a promising candidate, or if the candidate fails to answer inquiries promptly, the selection process grinds to a halt.

RETENTION OF STAFF

Retention of a balanced staff is exceedingly difficult in this era of school systems and departments in competition for needed personnel. A basic factor, in this problem, is that of staff morale. A more complete discussion of this vital area comprises another section of this chapter. A number of factors operate in retention of staff. The first of these is the prestige of the department within the school system or college. Although departments with a limited staff experience frequent turnover as the younger staff gain in professional competence and advance to more challenging opportunities, a small department with an excellent reputation holds many advantages and often retains outstanding personnel. The use of

3 Lillian Castner and Dudley Ashton, "Wanted: College Teachers," *The Physical Educator*, XVIII (December, 1961), 129.

salary scales is conducive to a feeling of security on the part of personnel. Most public school systems have developed excellent instruments of this kind, and there seems to be a trend toward salary floors at the various academic levels in college teaching. Tenure, wisely used, is also a factor in retention of staff. The availability of fringe benefits such as life insurance, sick leaves, accident and disability insurance plus actuarially sound retirement systems add to the attractiveness of any teaching position.

Although retention of staff is a stabilizing agent in any department of physical education, there are times when the distasteful responsibility of eliminating the incompetent must be assumed. Several phases of incompetency should be indicated. Among beginning teachers, there will always be a few persons who are unable to adapt materials to local needs. It may be that a change in locale and type of situation will solve this problem. With experienced teachers, indifference to assigned responsibilities, personality conflicts, and failure to maintain social distance, particularly since physical education lends itself to informal teacher-pupil contacts, may be causes of incompetency. Any one of these situations must be firmly but tactfully handled both for the sake of the morale of the individual and of the department.

SPECIALISTS

With the wide range of activities covered by the term "physical education," large secondary school and college departments are finding it necessary to provide specialists in such areas as dance, aquatics, specific team and individual sports, and gymnastics. Specialists as consultants are also needed in supervisory roles for elementary and secondary schools. The administration of physical education has become so complex that this area in the larger situations demands a specialist. Moreover, as graduate study increases, the younger people entering the profession are planning their professional careers more wisely and projecting their future attainments. As a result, they plan specific levels in preparation for supervisory duties or teacher education, and they concentrate their graduate study around clusters of course content. Such professional planning is excellent and should lead to increased staff competence and higher levels of professional relationships. Administratively, two problems are created by this trend. The first of these is to avoid overspecialization on the part of staff members. Certainly, every staff member has specific skills and interests, but one must be alert to the dancer, the swimmer, or the sport enthusiast who does not appear to be aware of the cohesiveness of the total field. This is one of the gray areas of administration in which an administrator carefully analyzes the situation and coordinates solutions in the best interest of the personalities and the needs of the department. There is a second staffing problem—that of knowing where to recruit personnel for specific areas. To this end, the administrator attempts to keep up-to-date lists of institutions that prepare dance or swimming specialists, to watch the progress of young teachers who have identified their goals, and to maintain professional contacts that lend themselves to open appraisal of potential personnel.

ANCILLARY PERSONNEL

In physical education, the ancillary personnel constitute a vital link in the working chain. Unless the secretary functions well, the myriad details associated with the program are often abrasive in nature. If an administrator carries ancillary personnel on the departmental budget, he is in a position to assign work and set the standards more advantageously than if the schedules come from a third person. Secretaries, custodians, and matrons will be more interested in service to an institution where fringe benefits such as social security, sick leave, insurance, and retirement are available and where the staff, students, and ancillary personnel operate in a climate of mutual respect. It well behooves the administrator to support these auxiliary benefits and to spend the time to explain carefully the benefits that may be accrued through such programs.

The climate established by the secretary in charge of a departmental office has implications for public relations both within the department and with wider publics. The usual competencies in secretarial skills are needed, but beyond this, a secretary in physical education needs much patience and know-how in personal relationships. The wide variety of activities results in a wide variety of technical preparation with which the staff expects help. A physical education department usually spans several programs, such as the general instruction program, the professional program, intramurals, clubs, and graduate work. All of these channels bring many individuals to the office with inquiries, materials, and personal problems. Often, the reputation of the department, with regard to consideration of individuals, rests on the friendliness or antagonism set up by the secretary.

If the work schedules for specific areas are planned and checked by a custodial supervisor, cooperation can be secured by conferences to define the unique needs in a physical education program. Types of work schedules will be discussed later. With respect to the necessary housekeeping in any gymnasium, the author believes that gymnasiums, pools, dressing and shower rooms, and offices should be spotlessly clean. Yeoman service can be rendered by the teaching staff in reporting needed services and in complimenting excellent work.

Finally, there is the climate of mutual respect among staff, students, and ancillary personnel. Matrons and custodians should be oriented upon induction into the job on such matters as the responsibility of the staff for classes and class procedures. They should be apprised of policies with regard to the use of surnames for staff. Students, when necessary, should be made aware of the contributions of ancillary staff to their welfare. As is true in so many instances, an example of courtesy and consideration is contagious in these relationships.

FORECASTING PERSONNEL NEEDS

A major problem that all administrators face today is that of constantly increasing enrollments. Because of the tax base, few top administrators are willing to forecast specific increases in enrollment and to authorize additional staff before the students are actually in class. Many times, the statement is made that additional staff is possible if the students have materialized. Under these circumstances, an administrator needs a reserve list of persons who are willing to accept emergency appointments. This is often feasible in a large city, but seldom feasible in a small town. Whenever advance registration techniques are in use, the disadvantages of these conditions are somewhat alleviated. A device that may be used, as well as the statistics in the national picture, is a chart for a specific locale showing increases in enrollments over a period of years. See Table 6–1.

Besides verifying the need for additional staff based upon increased numbers, it is necessary for the administrator of an educational system or institution to be able to pay for additional services. Therefore, it is wise to forecast such needs in asking budgets. Unless such long-range planning has been feasible, it is quite likely that funds may not be available. It is also necessary to know where personnel can be secured. This problem was briefly mentioned relative to securing specialists. The department or school system

Table 6–1

Increases in Enrollment

Years	Freshmen		Sophomores		Major Theory and Practical; Electives; PE. 154		Total Number of Students		Staff Increase
	1st Sem.	2d Sem.	1st Sem.	2d Sem.	1st Sem.	2d Sem.	1st Sem.	2d Sem.	
1965–66	1,397	1,221	505	476	490	539	2,392	2,236	1
1964–65	1,215	1,110	516	419	426	495	2,155	2,024	2
1963–64	987	907	491	434	234	355	1,712	1,696	1
1962–63	894	842	455	406	217	211	1,566	1,459	½
1961–62	782	715	387	351	210	217	1,379	1,383	–
1960–61	708	643	427	383	188	230	1,323	1,256	–
1959–60	594	554	434	395	160	198	1,188	1,147	–
1958–59	573	511	408	398	155	228	1,136	1,137	–
1957–58	530	490	368	352	186	164	1,084	1,006	–

that has a reputation for outstanding service in the field, for due consideration in terms of fair employment practices, and for creating opportunities to forward the advancement of younger personnel will find itself in an advantageous position to attract fine staff members. Recruitment of personnel cannot be left to the day of need. An administrator needs to meet and to know the young people in the field, to watch their progress, and to anticipate the professional direction that seems to be in process. If and when this individual is ready for a change and has so informed his own administration, the lanes are clear for contact and for possible orientation in a new direction. As staffing, because of increased enrollments plus higher standards of preparation, becomes increasingly difficult, the wisdom of long-range planning in terms of both finance and personnel becomes a clear directive.

STAFF INFORMATION

A major administrative problem in personnel work is that of keeping a staff informed. There are numerous devices that are used to accomplish this task. In spite of care and attention to the many lines of communication that we shall discuss in this section, there are occasions when communication breaks down. The human element is operative at both ends of any continuum. Smooth operation of a department depends upon an informed staff; therefore, let us explain some of the ways that may be used to reach this end.

Orientation to a new position, or induction as this process is sometimes named, is our initial line of communication. All letters written to incoming staff must state clearly the responsibilities of the position, the plans for opening the academic year, and information regarding possible housing. A note of welcome in these letters helps to alleviate the uncertainties that may be troubling a new staff person. It is always necessary that the work assignment must be undertaken immediately. Time should be scheduled for a conference in which some of the business details, the departmental organization, and the functions of the specific assignment are clarified. Staff meetings are fine, but newcomers are sometimes overwhelmed by the self-assurance of their colleagues. The more friendly and more relaxed the atmosphere, the better the chance that the newcomer will be able to feel at ease and to find a place in the total staff pattern. Experience has proved that the moment one becomes involved in the work of any organization, one's interest and ability to contribute rises. An administrator should never employ a person whose ability to take responsibility may be in question. Induction, then, includes taking over responsibilities and settling into the working patterns and personal relationship patterns best suited to a particular staff situation. The administrator sets the stage for this process through careful orientation, judicious assignment, and creation of an atmosphere of goodwill.

Most school systems have developed handbooks for teachers in which certain policies and procedures are spelled out. Such an instrument is a definite need in large secondary school and college departments of physical education. A handbook serves a dual purpose—orientation for new staff and a frame of reference for both old and new staff. If the handbook merely gives information of a routine nature, then a well-informed administrator can easily develop it. If the handbook represents staff decisions for those parts of the program under its jurisdiction, then the materials should be based upon conferences and group decisions, and revisions will of necessity take place as the specific situation changes. Working cooperatively, a staff may develop the philosophy and principles, statements of the curriculums in operation, and policies with resultant procedures. Many technical details may be spelled out in such a handbook, thereby saving time for more important matters. Handbooks are timesavers, but like all other lines of communication, the staff must become aware of their importance and use them.

Numerous items of information originate on or cross the desk of the administrator. Some of these items should be communicated up or down the lines of authority. An administrator passes on to the staff statements of policy or procedure, standards to be followed, and scheduling or classification details; and to the channels up the line, he conveys such information as professional contributions of a staff member, recommendations for promotion, budget requests, and reports or documents that represent professional thinking. The administrator also must function as liaison officer among members of the staff. Thus, the administrator stands at a crucial point in this web of cross-information. He must understand and assist with the need for communication across the staff line, while, at the same time, he must furnish information to those in higher administrative roles and channel other information down to his staff colleagues. It well behooves the administrator to assimilate carefully all written communications that come to his attention, to listen with concentrated attention to the problems and comments presented to him. An experienced administrator listens also for what is not said and pays a lot of attention to nuances and tone of voice. Griffiths has identified listening as a cue device in fine personnel administration. He notes the blocks to good listening as (1) preoccupation, (2) emotion blocks, (3) use of stereotypes, and (4) two-valued thinking—the "for-against" attitude.[4] So this matter of communication is concerned with three points of view: first, "What are you saying?" second, "Are you being heard?" and third, "Are you listening?"

Bulletins may be used as a means of communication. One often wonders, however, if just the appearance of a mimeographed page does not produce a negative reaction. There is no way out of this dilemma. Procedures such as travel authorizations, insurance and retirement benefits, as well as incidental notices on changes in schedule, calls for meetings, and similar details must be placed in writing and must reach the hands of all personnel.

Staff meetings offer another outlet for communication. There are two types of staff meetings that are needed in the administration of physical education. Because physical education has so varied a program and deals with many areas in which detailed organization and coordination must take place, certain staff meetings must be devoted to these routines. If all staff meetings are concerned with routine, an indifferent attitude may develop. Staff meetings should generate professional enthusiasm. Discussions of current professional problems, seminars to develop new course

---

[4] Griffiths, *op. cit.*, p. 87.

materials, and reports of professional meetings should be included in the layout of staff planning. Routines are important, but so is staff motivation.

We shall discuss staff morale in the next section of this chapter, but there are items concerned with fringe benefits and staff status upon which the staff needs information. Morale is often affected by a lack of this information. All staff should be informed of group accident and group life insurance benefits if these have been made available by the institution. Practically every school system and college has a retirement plan of some type, and we find that social security benefits by referendum of specific groups are also provided in a number of instances. The more mature individuals on a staff who are closer to facing the reality of the close of a teaching career will make an effort to secure such information, but younger staff members need to understand why age thirty or a tenure of years may be designated as eligibility requirements. The staff needs information on leaves of absence; what happens in case of illness, or death in a family; and time released for purposes of advanced study or attendance at professional meetings. Staff members need to be told the bases for promotion, what the opportunities for advancement are, and how salary increments are determined. Although all these material benefits are desirable, the status of physical education in the school or the college is the crucial issue. The staff needs to be well informed on this point so that the supportive influence of excellent status may be reflected in the work of the department.

Information in a department of physical education may be represented by a cross, with the administrator placed at the transept. The staff line up on the arms of the cross channeling information to the administrator and receiving information from him. On the vertical bar of the cross, the administrator receives and channels information both up and down the lines of authority. Breakdowns in information occur when either the staff or the administrator fails to pass along needed facts or decisions or fails to listen to instructions, organizational details, or problems.

ESPRIT DE CORPS AND ETHICS

Esprit de corps is a nebulous state. On the one hand, a problem of grave concern serves to unite a staff; on the other hand, such a problem may create the tensions that split or divide the staff. Not only are we concerned with problems, but many daily contacts and interactions among staff members affect the situation. Let us look at some of the behaviors involved.

The climate in which one works has a great deal to do with one's reactions. If a staff member feels that he is accepted by the administration and by his colleagues, he acquires a sense of security, both socially and professionally. If the climate is permissive, he will feel encouraged to launch into new ventures in teaching techniques, in course content, and in research. Creativity and invention may grow and mature in a permissive climate, particularly if the staff climate acknowledges the accomplishments of each individual staff member. A domineering, authoritative climate stifles the creative urge while, at the same time, it lends support only to those members of the staff who are willing to subjugate themselves within a defined hierarchy. Professionally, it is possible to define the permissive climate, but socially, this is difficult. Far too many professional persons expect to find their social outlets within the circle of the staff. Such a practice limits the acquaintance and frequently results in a buzz session and discussion of departmental business that would be better left at the offices. As one phase of *esprit de corps*, it is wise to encourage the staff to find interests and friends outside as well as inside the department. When all friendships are centered within the staff, newcomers find it difficult to join such a charmed circle. There are other components of departmental climate that will be discussed as this section is developed.

There are two phases of staff selection directly related to *esprit de corps*. Definite standards of preparation are usually in use in most school systems and college departments. Minimum preparation in physical education is the baccalaureate degree with more advanced degrees demanded for staff positions requiring heavy or specific responsibilities. Maintenance of this standard is needed, and necessary deviations, because of timing of staff vacancies or a shortage of personnel, must be talked out with the staff. The second phase is the selection of excellent personnel—in preparation, in experience, and in personal qualities for positions of staff leadership. Responsibilities that cut across all staff functioning such as departmental testing is an example. The staff must be able to develop confidence in this leadership. Another phase is that of selection in a change of administrators for a staff. A voice in setting up the standards to be used as the guidelines and a chance to talk with candidates are prerequisite to acceptance of new leadership by a staff. Selection is a delicate task; the staff wants balance in competence maintained, improvement over past performance, and a personality that will lend itself to harmony and fine adjustment. In short, a staff is a team with duties defined for each member. It is hoped that the quarterback will call the signals wisely and that the line will be able to attack each new problem supported by a backfield of staff cohesiveness.

If a staff is to work as a team, it must participate and share in certain of the decisions as well as the responsibilities for carrying out these decisions. When reports are in preparation that affect the total staff, this must be a shared result. It is well to involve the staff in decisions on anticipated building needs, policies relative to curricular offerings, evaluation procedures, changes in use of space, resolution of scheduling conflicts, and other policy-procedure matters where administrative decision is not mandatory. The practice of limiting staff participation in decisions to senior staff members soon engenders a sense of frustration on the part of younger staff members. A climate of attention to opinions of the entire staff lends itself to more constructive participation and to better teamwork.

Frictions may develop in a department when assignments are vague or overlap. No two human beings view the same piece of work in exactly the same manner. It is difficult in physical education to clarify the relationships existing in certain phases of the curriculum; for example, where will we include a course in sports management, in teaching techniques of sports, in methods, or in officiating? Staff conferences of the personnel concerned usually clarify such points. Clarity in assignment to areas is a definite administrative need. Most large departments assign the function of heading up specific sports, dance, aquatics, and gymnastics to specific instructors. (See Appendix No. 10.) The administrator must then function to keep these lines clear and to channel requests from each subchairman to the proper authorities. Assignments of this type should definitely be related to the preparation and experience of the instructor. When the responsibility to function as a subhead is delegated to an individual, then the commensurate amount of authority to carry out this function must also be delegated. Castetter has stated the problem of assignment clearly in discussing some of the human complications in this problem:

1) Lack of clarity in lines of responsibility and authority
2) Assumption of line functions by staff personnel
3) Excessive levels of authority
4) Dual or multiple jurisdiction
5) Lack of understanding of organizational relationships
6) Lack of coordination [5]

[5] William B. Castetter, *Administering the School Personnel Program* (New York: The Macmillan Co., 1962), p. 74.

A well-accepted administrative policy is that of the "open door." To an administrator's door come staff members with both personal and professional problems. Grievances are aired, leaves are adjusted to cover personal emergencies, and professional guidance may be either sought or offered. The conflicting values held by staff members are talked out; the younger members are cautioned to be patient for results, while the older members are urged to try newer ideas; specialists are urged to consider the total needs of the department, and generalists are counseled to respect the expertness of the specialists; the skill enthusiast and the academician are brought together to face each other's point of view. The "open door" policy serves as the entrée needed to implement staff advising.

In the process of staff advising, an administrator becomes aware of staff jealousies (often asides in the conversation) and thus is enabled to set up channels to establish social cooperation that may offset some difficulties. There must be a great deal of "give and take" in staff relations. Professional maturity develops over the years as one gains in competence and in faith and in respect for another person's ability to do a job. As the staff matures professionally, one finds that understanding and awareness of the needs and interests of other staff members increase. Hand in hand with this process of maturation on the part of the staff is the administrator's sensitiveness to individual staff characteristics and reactions. Stereotyping individuals as a sports person per se, a dancer, a conservative, a "diehard," or indifferent, and similar categories, must be avoided. If the staff realizes that professional opportunities serve as vehicles for developing professional maturity, staff members can be expected to put a shoulder to the wheel. With attractive teaching conditions and adequate salary scales, the staff may be relatively content to postpone additional graduate study or attendance at professional seminars. Advanced graduate study and post doctoral study and/or research should be urged. Minor frictions between individuals, misunderstandings with regard to assignments, and problems related to student progress are phases of staff advising that are needed from day to day.

Cohesiveness exemplifies one of the qualities that may be described as loyalty. Blind adherence to policies or blind devotion to personalities certainly would be objectionable. We are hearing, however, of the need in all organizations to develop loyalty. There are several avenues that may be explored in this attempt. Integrity on the part of the staff in supporting established principles and policies and integrity on the part of the administrator in avoiding promises that cannot be kept, reporting faithfully line decisions with their accompanying reasons, and treating each staff member fairly in relation to all others contribute to the value structure that gives rise to loyalty. Pride in the record of a fine department and in the accomplishments of its graduates moves ahead into pride in one's profession. Other cohesive factors that should be mentioned are pride in the accomplishments of fellow staff members and firm, intelligently directed belief in the benefits that accrue from physical education.

Every word that has been stated in this section has its relative value in a discussion of morale. Staff participation in departmental affairs, professional maturation, the climate in which one works, advising staff, and staff interactions are all contributing facets of morale. This is similar to the law that the whole is greater than the sum of its parts. Morale has a plus factor. Perhaps it is the ability to keep trying in the face of obstacles; perhaps it is the sense of teamwork or unity that pervades staff thinking; perhaps it is that high plus factor—an unselfish professional attitude. There are staff securities that must be present for fine morale. Every staff member must know his status on the staff and must feel reasonably secure that he is being fairly treated as to teaching load, salary increments, opportunities for advancement, and recognition of his contributions. An atmosphere of respect for the leadership at both the peer and higher administrative levels must be apparent. There must be consistency in administrative acceptance; the staff member wants appreciation of his skills, abilities, and progress in professional undertakings but not at the price of momentary enthusiasm. Morale dips into community mores—are teachers accepted as contributing citizens or are they considered outsiders? Conversely, does the teacher resent the community in which he has decided to work and condemn it in terms of his past experiences? The department or the school system has certain rights that must be observed, such as coordinating and channeling the efforts of all personnel toward the greatest good for the greatest number of students. Frictions may arise when an individual desires a personal release that nullifies the above principle. Adaptive behavior on the part of the teacher and the administrator then occurs, with morale hanging in the balance between hostility and acceptable mature reactions. Thus, with high morale, we would expect fairly stable staff reactions even under emotional stress, reduction of hostility between individuals, and cooperative working agreements.

Esprit de corps presumes a condition of professional awareness that lends itself to the development of fine practitioners. That being the case, physical education along with education in general must exemplify the traits of a profession. The professional preparation previously mentioned is the initial level of attainment, practicing those parts of the profession for which one is most adequately prepared is another level, and willingness to serve beyond specified assignments with emphasis on the ideals of the profession rather than personal gain bring one to the top step. Professions usually organize their ideals into a body of beliefs upon which practice should be based. Such a document is known as a code of ethics. A number of years ago, the American Association for Health, Physical Education, and Recreation developed a code of ethics that has been operative to date. Originally, this code was based, in part, on the principles of the code of ethics of the National Education Association. Because of the amplification of the NEA code and the excellent organization of its thinking, we now quote this code as adopted by the NEA Representative Assembly, Detroit, Michigan, July, 1963.

CODE OF ETHICS OF THE EDUCATION PROFESSION [6]

PREAMBLE

We, professional educators of the United States of America, affirm our belief in the worth and dignity of man. We recognize the supreme importance of the pursuit of truth, the encouragement of scholarship, and the promotion of democratic citizenship. We regard as essential to these goals the protection of freedom to learn and to teach and the guarantee of equal educational opportunity for all. We affirm and accept our responsibility to practice our profession according to the highest ethical standards.

We acknowledge the magnitude of the profession we have chosen, and engage ourselves, individually and collectively, to judge our colleagues and to be judged by them in accordance with the applicable provisions of this code.

PRINCIPLE I

Commitment to the Student

We measure success by the progress of each student toward achievement of his maximum potential. We therefore work to stimulate the spirit of inquiry, the acquisition of knowledge and understanding, and the thoughtful formulation of worthy goals. We recognize the importance of cooperative relationships with other community institutions, especially the home.

In fulfilling the obligations to the student, we—

1. Deal justly and considerately with each student.
2. Encourage the student to study varying points of view and respect his right to form his own judgment.
3. Withhold confidential information about a student or his home unless we deem that its release serves professional purposes, benefits the student, or is required by law.

[6] Quoted by permission of the National Education Association.

4. Make discreet use of available information about the student.
5. Conduct conferences with or concerning students in an appropriate place and manner.
6. Refrain from commenting unprofessionally about a student or his home.
7. Avoid exploiting our professional relationship with any student.
8. Tutor only in accordance with officially approved policies.
9. Inform appropriate individuals and agencies of the student's educational needs and assist in providing an understanding of his educational experiences.
10. Seek constantly to improve learning facilities and opportunities.

PRINCIPLE II

Commitment to the Community

We believe that patriotism in its highest form requires dedication to the principles of our democratic heritage. We share with all other citizens the responsibility for the development of sound public policy. As educators, we are particularly accountable for participating in the development of educational programs and policies and for interpreting them to the public.

In fulfilling our obligations to the community, we—

1. Share the responsibility for improving the educational opportunities for all.
2. Recognize that each educational institution may have a person authorized to interpret its official policies.
3. Acknowledge the right and responsibility of the public to participate in the formulation of educational policy.
4. Evaluate through appropriate professional procedures conditions within a district or institution of learning, make known serious deficiencies, and take any action deemed necessary and proper.
5. Use educational facilities for intended purposes consistent with applicable policy, law, and regulation.
6. Assume full political and citizenship responsibilities, but refrain from exploiting the institutional privileges of our professional positions to promote political candidates or partisan activities.
7. Protect the educational program against undesirable infringement.

PRINCIPLE III

Commitment to the Profession

We believe that the quality of the services of the education profession directly influences the future of the nation and its citizens. We therefore exert every effort to raise educational standards, to improve our service, to promote a climate in which the exercise of professional judgment is encouraged, and to achieve conditions which attract persons worthy of the trust to careers in education. Aware of the value of united effort, we contribute actively to the support, planning, and programs of our professional organizations.

In fulfilling our obligations to the profession, we—

1. Recognize that a profession must accept responsibility for the conduct of its members and understand that our own conduct may be regarded as representative.
2. Participate and conduct ourselves in a responsible manner in the development and implementation of policies affecting education.

3. Cooperate in the selective recruitment of prospective teachers and in the orientation of student teachers, interns, and those colleagues new to their positions.
4. Accord just and equitable treatment to all members of the profession in the exercise of their professional rights and responsibilities, and support them when unjustly accused or mistreated.
5. Refrain from assigning professional duties to non-professional personnel when such assignment is not in the best interest of the student.
6. Provide, upon request, a statement of specific reason for administrative recommendations that lead to the denial of increments, significant changes in employment, or termination of employment.
7. Refrain from exerting undue influence based on the authority of our positions in the determination of professional decisions by colleagues.
8. Keep the trust under which confidential information is exchanged.
9. Make appropriate use of time granted for professional purposes.
10. Interpret and use the writings of others and the findings of educational research with intellectual honesty.
11. Maintain our integrity when dissenting by basing our public criticism of education on valid assumptions as established by careful evaluation of facts or hypotheses.
12. Represent honestly our professional qualifications and identify ourselves only with reputable educational institutions.
13. Respond accurately to requests for evaluations of colleagues seeking professional positions.
14. Provide applicants seeking information about a position with an honest description of the assignment, the conditions of work, and related matters.

Principle IV

Commitment to Professional Employment Practices

We regard the employment agreement as a solemn pledge to be executed both in spirit and in fact in a manner consistent with the highest ideals of professional service. Sound professional personnel relationships with governing boards are built upon personal integrity, dignity, and mutual respect.

In fulfilling our obligations to professional employment practices, we—

1. Apply for or offer a position on the basis of professional and legal qualifications.
2. Apply for a specific position only when it is known to be vacant and refrain from such practices as underbidding or commenting adversely about other candidates.
3. Fill no vacancy except where the terms, conditions, policies, and practices permit the exercise of our professional judgment and skill, and where a climate conducive to professional service exists.
4. Adhere to the conditions of a contract or to the terms of an appointment until either has been terminated legally or by mutual consent.
5. Give prompt notice of any change in availability of service, in status of applications, or in change in position.
6. Conduct professional business through the recognized educational and professional channels.
7. Accept no gratuities or gifts of significance that might influence our judgment in the exercise of our professional duties.

8. Engage in no outside employment that will impair the effectiveness of our professional service and permit no commercial exploitation of our professional position.

This brief discussion has defined *esprit de corps* as a nebulous state. No one can predict the exact reaction of another human being. Environmental hazards, personality traits, and school and community mores influence *esprit de corps*. It should be the responsibility of every instructor and every administrator to think carefully about both individual and chain reactions if staff personnel are to work together productively and harmoniously.

LEADERSHIP

The leadership role in a school system or college department is generally assigned to the administrator. A leader who maintains high standards in coordination of effort, in curricular content, in appraisal techniques, and in departmental advancements sets a challenging pace. Leadership in a department should be geared to providing both followership and structured leadership roles for members of the staff. Structuring leadership roles is not to be interpreted as manipulation but rather as a coordinating function of the administrator. The administrator, knowing the interests and potential abilities of staff members, assigns activity heads, research and testing chairmanships, student advising, and even departmental social leadership with some insight into the possible results. The administrator's role is leadership, but it also encompasses the recognition of initiative and ability of fellow staff members. If an administrator expects his staff to stick to the job, he must set the example. Structured leadership assignments are futile if the staff feels "put upon" and believes that the administrator is handing out work that should begin at home. There are morale factors as well as professionalization factors in the leadership role.

The development of staff leadership is a pressing problem. Unless an administrator is willing to have leadership roles assumed by staff members, the more capable persons experience a sense of frustration in trying to assist with staff projects. On the other hand, careful guidance is needed to insure correct channeling of any decisions. One of the most difficult tasks in the development of leadership is that of encouraging quiet, retiring staff members to enter leadership roles. All of us are human; therefore, staff members are reluctant to undertake such responsibilities unless they are sure that the administration will support their efforts. Leadership can only be developed by experience. Repeating the experience of the experienced may be pleasantly easy, but it will not forward the professionalization of the total staff. Identification of leadership traits may help the administrator in making specific assignments. Individuals selected to lead a staff committee should have both knowledge and experience in that area, should understand the relationship of the area to the total curricular pattern, should be alert to new ideas and developments, and should be able to sense the reactions that are taking shape.

It has been said that there are three types of administrative leadership: laissez-faire, autocratic, and democratic. Under the laissez-faire philosophy, the staff members go their separate ways with little or no coordinated effort. The result may be a loss of morale because of the insecurities and the cross-purposes that develop. On the surface, an autocratic administration may appear to be highly successful. Things get done expeditiously, and there are individuals who enjoy the release from responsibility that a dictated regime represents. Democratic administration has been misconstrued and misinterpreted. It is sometimes conceived as administration in which a staff makes all final decisions and the administrator becomes a figurehead. This is not feasible nor is it responsible behavior either in government or in educational institutions. There are decisions that an administrator must make himself. Some of these are channeled directives; some are made to preserve staff cohesion. The art lies in sensing the moment when the supportive positive "No" is needed. Democratic leadership takes time. There is a lag in understanding and acceptance of alternative decisions by individuals. Authority is given to the administration along with the responsibility of the job. Therefore, when immediate decisions are needed in a democratic setup, the administrator must make them. A parallel case would be the role of the President of the United States in time of war. The fine line between license and the freedom to act as an individual, to contribute one's competencies, and to develop one's abilities is carefully drawn in democratic administration. As Tead succinctly states: "Democracy is the ordering of a given society in order to control personal power in the interest of freedom, and by the same token to channel personal power in the interests of public service." [7]

A prime leadership responsibility is motivation of the staff. In many school systems, the policies and practices included in salary schedules, service credits, and professional advancement activities

[7] Ordway Tead, *Art Of Administration* (New York: McGraw-Hill Book Co., 1951), p. 69.

serve as more or less mechanical motivation devices. In colleges, the same is true with regard to promotion (rank) policies. Professionally oriented motivation, however, has more personal implications. The administrator must be concerned that those who are dilatory in carrying out details realize the importance of these in total staff functioning. But more important is motivation of staff to move forward into advanced graduate study, into research, and into professional activities such as committee and organizational work, both local and national in scope. Conflicts in values of a personal nature may retard this process. Self-image is a contributing factor. What outside recognition do you expect, or is the boost to your self-respect and your pleasure in your work enough motivation? What general avenues of growth are you following? As an administrator, can you raise the objectives of the staff so that growth occurs in personality adjustments, in teaching ability, in breadth of interests, and in community and professional contributions?

Leadership on a staff, consciously or unconsciously, utilizes appraisal of staff members. Human effort is a consistent variable. Whenever a goal of any type is set, then the organization, the procedures, and its attainment may be modified by the reactions (positive or negative) of the persons concerned. As a result, judgments occur that in turn modify future leadership responsibilities. The controlled balance that is exemplified in healthy attitudes toward staff work often uncovers latent leadership abilities. The reverse of the coin, appraisal that is bickering in type or that is operative upon different criteria for different persons or purposes, undermines objectivity in appraising leadership. Tact, kindliness, and insight into other people's personality problems as well as competency in the field must be considered in developing staff leaders.

The administrator is the key to leadership on a staff, but he must be concerned with unlocking opportunities and thereby widening professional horizons for other members of the staff.

IN-SERVICE EDUCATION

There is only one reason for in-service education, namely, the improvement of instruction in physical education. There are morale advantages in in-service education. Individuals becoming involved in group projects discover new interests and begin to explore these. There is a sense of putting one's shoulder to the wheel in staff study groups that helps in setting group thinking and raising professional standards. This is definitely a way to improve our programs and one that must be explored and encouraged particularly with younger staff members. An attitude of willingness to learn and to adopt new developments to current needs lends itself to increased professional awareness. We have often thought only of upgrading curricular offerings in terms of taking advanced graduate work.

Among suggestions made for in-service education is that of constant attention to professional reading. Current professional periodicals and the numerous books and pamphlets published every year provide ample reading material. If the administrator reads widely and is able to recommend specific materials in specific areas, the staff profits from the stimulus of example. From time to time, controversial issues arise in education as well as in physical education that are worthy of staff discussion. In similar manner, when excellent films are scheduled for classes, a staff seminar to review and discuss applications of these materials adds to instructional techniques.

Another method of in-service education particularly needed for multiple-section courses is that of auditing as a learner-teacher the presentation of a course by a senior staff member. This must be a mutually acceptable arrangement, but it offers many chances for the engendering of mutual respect among staff members.

Conferences and consultation by all staff members concerned with an area, for example, supervision of student teaching, affords another way to offer in-service education. The leaders of such conferences grow in ability to understand and to handle the intricate personnel problems of student teaching, while the participants share this experience as well as learn new ways to approach teaching problems.

Research, professional committee work, and the writing of professional articles or books are other avenues that serve dual roles. They make a contribution to the profession and, at the same time, add to the professional stature of the individual.

There is a morale factor in all phases of in-service education. None of us like to be bypassed when the accolades are being handed out. Credit where credit is due in the form of publicity and congratulations as well as more material forms of professional advancement should be the rule if one expects a staff to remain alert and eager for professional advancement.

SUMMARY

This chapter has been concerned with personnel problems in physical education, ranging from the administrator through the staff and on to ancillary personnel. We have pointed out material aspects affecting this situation, such as means of communication, fringe benefits, and established procedures. We have been gravely concerned with interaction and judgments that are intangible. Morale, leadership, and professional status have cast their votes and been counted. Finally, we emphasize that personnel problems are never solved completely. The same problems recur and new answers must be found. Personnel relationship is an administrator's heavy responsibility and one that is never static.

PROBLEMS

1. State your theory of good human relations.

2. What role does motivation play in the behavior of an administrator? Describe one or more problems that have occurred because of the difference in values between staff and administrator.

3. Communication is a "must" for administrators. How would you deal with

   a) A parent exploiting a major student's ability in golf?
   b) A fellow teacher who undercuts your contributions in the department?
   c) A staff member who is silent at all staff meetings?
   d) An angry matron who claims students have "high-hatted" her?
   e) A custodian who anticipates reprimand by vocalizing his overworked condition?

4. How can authority be delegated along with responsibility and yet maintain the line and staff concept?

5. List morale factors present in any educational setup. List morale factors present in your educational setup.

6. Who do you believe should make the decisions in your staff situation? Why? What kinds of decisions are operative?

7. Leadership is necessary in administration. What are some of the problems faced by leaders in developing fine human relations within a staff? How do specialists or consultants fit into this picture?

8. List factors that the administrator should be aware of in developing fine human relations. List factors that the staff member should be aware of in maintaining fine human relations.

7

Facilities

The development and maintenance of facilities constitute a constant problem for the administrator of physical education. As a result of experience, consultation with architects, and various professional conferences, standards for facilities have been established. Before discussing specifics, we shall review these standards.

STANDARDS

INDOOR

Facilities should be planned with due regard to the community needs as well as the needs of the educational unit in question. Disregard of either phase of this situation may result in disadvantages for either program with resulting friction. However, the purposes for multiple use within an educational structure of a single unit are in question. At the elementary school level, a combination lunchroom-gymnasium is open to healthful environment problems plus inadequate use by either program before, during, and after the noon hour. In like manner, a functional multipurpose room that is overscheduled with competition among Parent-Teacher Association groups, music, certain phases of art, audio-visual offerings, and physical education inhibits the elementary school physical education program. A multiple-purpose room that is too decorative, for example, a fireplace, Philippine mahogany walls, and draped floor-to-ceiling windows, retards the elementary school program for active play. At the secondary school level, the combination auditorium-gymnasium has several disadvantages: (1) the loss of time for activity before and after the use of the facility as an auditorium in placing and then storing temporary seating units, (2) the inherent danger at the edge of the stage if permanent seating occupies the floor and the curtailment of certain activities when the stage area is small, (3) the constant friction when two departments try to carry on well-designed curricular offerings using the same space. Most college physical education facilities are used constantly for activity. In small colleges, there may be use of physical education space at the registration intervals. If so, due regard for the well-finished gymnasium floors and a prompt exodus, so that the time for classes is not infringed upon, are in order. Thus, the standard is established that indoor facilities for physical education should be planned specifically for this use. Administratively, if so planned, these facilities under careful regulation and supervision may also be used during non-school hours and during vacation for community recreation.

The total facility (school or college building) should harmonize with other buildings in the vicinity as far as architectural characteristics are concerned.

Recognition of the economic resources of the community is entailed in the type of facilities provided. An elaborate facility requiring heavy upkeep is a waste of funds when a functional facility could be better supported by the community.

A physical education building on a college campus needs to be located near the classroom and dormitory complex so that students may reach classes easily and so that recreational interests may be well served. In an elementary school or a secondary school, indoor physical education facilities are usually placed in a wing of the building or even in a separate structure. With such planning, the noise factor present in wholesome participation does not disturb the academic classes. See Fig. 7–1.

Teaching stations should be supplied to cover the enrollment needs of the specific situation. These stations (a unit of space in which the teacher may conduct a class) should be adequate in number and varied in type so that a well-rounded program of physical education may be offered. Maximum space should be allocated to activity areas. Offices, service areas, corridors, and foyer are figured as a part of tare.[1]

Building codes, sanitation codes, and legal requirements of the state must be observed. Construction, functional use of the facility, and the program offered are affected by these codes. Administration of the environment in which physical education takes place

---

[1] Tare—an architectural term derived from gross weight or gross square feet. Various formulas are used, but tare (walls, halls, offices, service areas, dressing and locker rooms) is figured at a percentage of the square feet planned for activity.

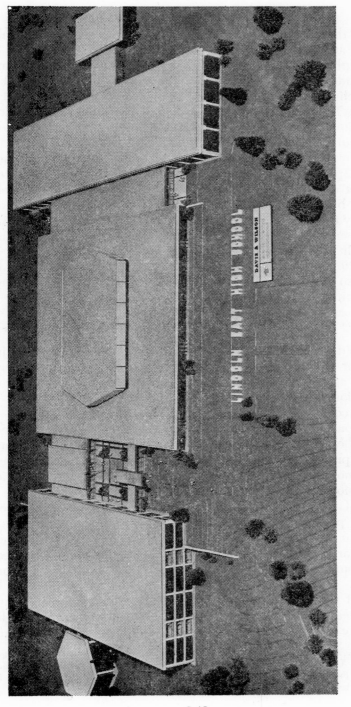

Fig. 7–1. Architect's model of a well-planned high school complex. (Used by permission of the Lincoln Public Schools, Lincoln, Nebraska.)

is one of the grave responsibilities in this field. Excellent health standards are mandatory.

Geographic and climatic conditions demand attention in standards for indoor activity. Play sheds for rainy days are excellent in southern climates but are not practical in regions that are subject to blizzards. The amount and kind of indoor space is also dependent on the climate. Indoor pools are more practical in cold regions since an outdoor pool may be used so few months in the year.

In renovation of existing facilities or in the planning for new facilities, specialists in physical education should be consulted. The needs of a specific physical education program are thereby presented by persons aware of the specialized activity areas demanded by the program. Professional architects and structural and landscape engineers may then weld these needs into a design that meets both legal and educational requirements.

Population trends and school enrollment predictions should be analyzed so that renovations and additional facilities are planned flexibly to meet future needs.

OUTDOOR

To avoid repetition of the general items needed in planning grounds for outdoor activities, we shall discuss these first. Regardless of the age level to be accommodated for activity, the following considerations are operative:

1. The contour of the land must be considered in selection. Is it level enough to accommodate the large-size sports areas needed? On the other hand, is it too low to drain well? Sufficient acreage should be provided to enable the program to be pursued with ease, to accommodate multiple use by the community, and to provide for expansion.[2] Courts for outdoor sports should be oriented to the path of the sun in a given locale. The long axis of play (generally, the path of the ball) should be at 90° to the sun's rays at mid or late afternoon. Protection of the player's eyes and safety of other participants are factors in sun glare. In many instances, playing courts are simply oriented north and south on the long dimension.

2. What types of natural landscaping can be saved in developing the area? Is there a grove of trees that can be utilized for shade? Are there isolated trees whose locations are advantageous?

---

[2] James L. Taylor, *School Sites, Selection, Development and Utilization* (Washington, D.C.: U.S. Department of Health, Education, and Welfare, Office of Education, Special Publication No. 7, Government Printing Office, 1958), pp. 37–39. Information on recommended sizes of school sites state by state.

Are there any rolling slopes in northern climates that could be used for ski instruction? Is there a pond that could be incorporated into the landscaping and used for winter skating? If no natural materials are at hand, can this area be landscaped without undue expense? The topography of the land should be used to increase the beauty of the setting. Preservation of shade trees and natural water facilities whenever possible is recommended. Provision for level play areas in uneven locations by means of rock-retaining walls to avoid erosion enables the planners to consider rolling land. Use of climatic conditions, such as frozen shallow ponds for ice skating and low hills for ski instruction in the north, and natural water resources for water sports and small craft in the south, adds to the enrichment possibilities of the program.

3. Drainage is necessary if the area is to be kept free of standing water. On the other hand, a watering system is needed to preserve turf. Preplanning for installation of tile drainage and, at the same time, water lines with convenient outlets will prove economical in the long run. Land should be selected that can be adequately drained (elevation and contour) and where the water table is not a factor in development of the locale. On slopes, drainage should occur at the top of the slope.

4. Selection of a site for new facilities that avoids industrial areas, railroad tracks, heavily traveled highways, and air traffic is advisable. Fencing with border plantings of shrubs and hardy flowers will add to the safety of an area and also to its beauty. Fencing is also necessary to protect surfaces and equipment and to safeguard persons at play. Heavy duty chain link fencing with the posts set in concrete gives excellent service. It is expensive. Therefore, if it must be supplied in units, fencing of the boundary where there is heavy traffic should receive priority. Areas such as tennis courts and kindergarten or tot lots need fencing, but a less-expensive type will suffice.

5. With the increase in leisure time, play areas are greatly needed for night use. Wherever neighborhood or community groups as well as school events are under consideration, initial planning for outdoor lighting is advised. Location of power lines, light poles, and switchboards as well as candlepower and shadow problems are part of the total problem. Utilities should be available and at a reasonable cost.

6. Provision for various surfacings to accommodate multiple purposes makes for better use of the area. Play area layouts and surfacing suggestions will be described later in the chapter. For an analysis of playground surfacing, see Table 7–1.

Table 7–1

An Analysis of Playground Surfacing

Surfaces	Year-Round Utility Use	Multiple Use	Dustless	Fine-Grained Non-Absorbent	Durable	Resilient	All-Weather Footing	Reasonable Cost	Low Maintenance	Pleasing Appearance
							Qualities			
Earth	—	x	—	x	x	x	—	x	—	x
Turf	—	x	x	x	—	x	—	x	—	x
Aggregate	x	—	—	—	x	—	x	x	x	—
Bitumen	x	x	x	x	x	x	x	x	x	x
Concrete	x	—	—	—	x	—	x	x	x	—
Masonry	x	x	—	—	x	—	x	x	x	—
Miscellaneous *	x	x	—	—	—	x	—	x	x	—

* Miscellaneous: tanbark, sawdust, cottonmeal, rubber, plastics and vinyls, asbestos, cement, boards, wood.

SOURCE: Adapted from James L. Taylor, *School Sites, Selection, Development and Utilization* (Washington, D.C.: U.S. Department of Health, Education, and Welfare, Office of Education, Special Publication No. 7, Government Printing Office), p. 47.

Elementary Schools. Provision of at least 5 acres of play area plus 1 acre for each one hundred students enrolled in an elementary school has been the standard over a number of years. In communities where park-schools are planned, 15 acres are needed to accommodate the adult activities that are added to those of the children. Elementary schools built years ago or built in crowded urban areas seldom have this much space. Often, the school was placed in the center of a square, thus effectively eliminating wide play areas. The placement of the building along one side or at the corner of the play area releases more space for play. The area provided should be planned for functional use. Smaller children need an area restricted to their use for protection purposes and for developmental play. They need soft surfaces (sawdust, tanbark, or sand) under the apparatus provided for them. They need some hard surface upon which to run bicycles, tricycles, wagons, and roller skates. If possible, a wading pool may be used to advantage; and, of course, they need grass for both formal and informal play. Shaded areas for quiet activities add enrichment to the program.

As elementary schools advance in grade level, they need hard surfaces laid out for court games and turf surfaces of larger areas for lead-up games and modified team sports. Running surfaces and jumping sites for track and field events are also needed.

Secondary Schools. Acreage recommended for junior high schools varies from 10 to 25 acres, while that for senior high schools is placed at 25 to 40 acres. With increased emphasis on campus-type secondary school planning, this space is not unrealistic; if anything, it is too limited. Provision must be made for seasonal team games, individual sports, track and field events, and for accommodation of spectators (plus parking) if interscholastic sports are part of the program. Official-size fields and courts (usually minimum size) are used. The ground selected must be adaptable to these activities, and their placement in a safe manner must be feasible. Most of the time, outdoor areas are shared by boys and girls or the playing areas are adjacent. This practice lends itself to wide spaces and to dual use of the facilities when necessary. Part of the area should be hard surfaced for tennis, handball, basketball and volleyball. Track is increasing in importance for girls. More jumping pits and provision for running events plus open turf areas for field events will probably be seen in the future. For area dimensions, see Table 7–2.

Layouts of playing areas generally make use of the same area for two or more activities. Softball and soccer, speedball or speed-a-way, and hockey or lacrosse can be planned for multiple use of space. Basketball, volleyball, shuffleboard, and paddle tennis can be superimposed on tennis courts to provide multiple use of hard-surfaced areas. Beauty in landscaping and some shade are needed at the secondary school level as well as at the elementary school level.

Rural Consolidated K–12 School. With the constant increase in consolidation of schools, it seems wise to consider the play area for such a school. Since both elementary and secondary activities must occur at the same time, an area of 40–50 acres is advised. A sample plat for an outdoors area is given in Fig. 7–2.

Colleges. Older colleges and small colleges frequently find themselves hemmed in by town or urban growth with no funds available for expansion of the playing areas. More and more cars are crowding the campuses; and, as students and staff demand parking space, there is real danger to the few open fields in evidence. Fortunate, indeed, is the college with a new campus and adequate acreage for play areas. If 40 to 50 acres are recommended for high schools, then that for colleges should be in multiples of 100. This acreage should probably be split up with certain areas planned within the dormitory complex for informal use, such as hard surfaces for volleyball, basketball, and general recreation. Areas close to

Table 7–2

Recommended Dimensions for Game Areas *

Games	Elementary School	Junior High School	High School (adults)	Area Size (including buffer space)
Basketball	40' × 60'	50' × 84'	50' × 84'	7,200 sq. ft.
Basketball (college)			50' × 94'	8,000
Volleyball	25' × 50'	25' × 50'	30' × 60'	2,800
Badminton			20' × 44'	1,800
Paddle tennis			20' × 44'	1,800
Deck tennis			18' × 40'	1,250
Tennis		36' × 78'	26' × 78'	6,500
Ice hockey			85' × 200'	17,000
Field hockey			180' × 300'	64,000
Horseshoes		10' × 40'	10' × 50'	1,000
Shuffleboard			6' × 52'	640
Lawn bowling			14' × 110'	1,800
Boccie			15' × 75'	1,950
Tetherball	10' circle	12' circle	12' circle	400
Croquet	38' × 60'	38' × 60'	38' × 60'	2,200
Roque			30' × 60'	2,400
Handball (single-wall)	18' × 26'	18' × 26'	20' × 40'	1,200
Handball (four-wall)			23' × 46'	1,058
Baseball	210' × 210'	300' × 300'	400' × 400'	160,000
Archery		50' × 150'	50' × 300'	20,000
Softball (12" ball) †	150' × 150'	200' × 200'	275' × 275'	75,000
Football			160' × 360'	80,000
Touch football		120' × 300'	160' × 360'	80,000
Six-Man Football			120' × 300'	54,000
Soccer (men):				
Minimum			165' × 300'	65,000
Maximum			240' × 360'	105,000
Soccer (women)			120' × 240'	40,000

* Table covers a single unit; many of above can be combined.

† Dimensions vary with size of ball used.

Source: Adapted from *Planning Facilities for Health, Physical Education and Recreation* (rev. ed.; Chicago: The Athletic Institute, 1965), p. 18.

the dormitory complex but located in conjunction with physical education facilities would provide fields for seasonal team and individual sports both as class activity and as intramurals. A golf range and, if possible, a golf course is advantageous to the total program. Archery ranges and banks of tennis courts (the standard is one court to every fifty students enrolled) invite participation, especially if they are lighted for night use. If the college can afford only one pool, then an indoor facility is advised. But, if finances

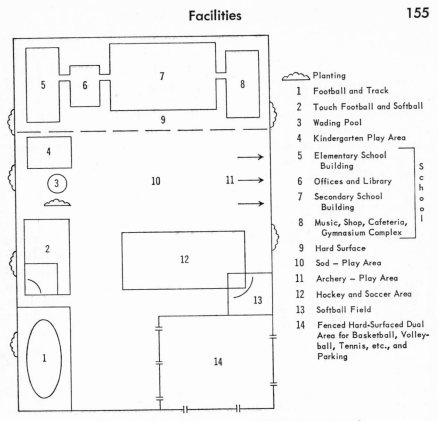

Fig. 7–2. Sample diagram of a K–12 school complex.

permit, an outdoor pool, with adjacent areas to be used for outdoor cooking and informal social group gatherings, is desirable. Students should be taught how to handle small craft safely and to observe all safety precautions in surfboard riding, scuba diving, and other aquatic activities. Stadiums will not be discussed because it would require a volume to cover the subject. Outdoor facilities in colleges should be attractive to the student and should encourage activity on his part. Students are young adults whose life patterns are taking shape. The skills and interests of the college years will be reflected in the habits of recreation of these young people as they enter the working world.

UPKEEP OF GROUNDS

Most colleges and a great many public school systems maintain grounds crews who move from one area to another, trimming trees and shrubs, and cutting, watering, and maintaining lawns. Fields, under properly rotated use, benefit from such care. Cooperative planning for special events is possible when grass fields need to be clipped short. In certain climates, watering is a necessity and becomes a problem in the use of fields. Cooperation in the way of weekend watering schedules often solves this problem. It is the responsibility of the physical education administrator to see that fields are correctly laid out and marked for sports participation. Careful inspection of fields is needed to locate areas that suddenly sink or holes that form. These should be reported to the grounds crew for filling and tamping.

OUTDOOR TRAFFIC FLOW

No general regulations can be laid down with regard to traffic flow since every layout of grounds for activity differs. One, however, has only to notice the muddy tracks and eventual paths that cross playing areas to realize that short cuts will always be taken if possible. It follows, then, that a study of the "paths" of least resistance is in order. The use of hard-surfaced paths cuts down erosion. It is obvious that paths should be kept to a minimum.

Areas that are a potential danger to pedestrians should be screened off from the total play area either by fencing or by trees and shrubbery. Thus, swings and other play equipment that move in space should be placed near the edges of the area and duly protected. Archery and golf ranges should be planned for directional flight of arrows and balls toward the edges of an area.

In our mobile society, provision must be made for parking cars both for participants and for spectators. Parking areas should be located at the edges of the playing areas and must be fenced off from the turf surfaces. Open parking areas are an invitation, under crowded conditions or even for personal convenience, to use turf surfaces. Curbs, lanes, and other traffic controls are necessary unless parking occurs under the direction of an attendant.

Due consideration of the density and flow of traffic on adjacent streets tends to increase safety of the players. It is sometimes necessary, because of population distribution, to locate a school near heavy industry or on heavily traveled main roads. In such cases, location of the play areas back of the school and away from the heaviest general traffic flow is advisable. Scheduling intramurals or extramurals with regard to the hours when the traffic flow is low is also a safety device. Termination of activities fifteen to thirty minutes before or after the heavy traffic hours helps to decrease the safety hazards for students.

SHORT- VS. LONG-RANGE PLANS

Administrators of physical education face constant problems relative to both long- and short-range plans for facilities. If long-range plans have been adequately developed and if funds have been made available, then the short-range plans for facilities place their major emphasis on maintenance. The responsibility of the administrator for short-range plans includes periodic inspection of the facility to be certain that the repairs needed are noted and scheduled. The age of the facility in use affects this inspection schedule; older structures will need more frequent inspection. At least twice a year, inspection to determine painting, lighting, or general repair needs must be made and scheduled for vacation intervals unless the educational institution has a maintenance department schedule of similar type. Program needs and increased enrollments often necessitate minor renovations of existing facilities. Minor renovations such as the use of odd corners in old buildings for more offices or for storage areas are usually planned and constructed within a short time span. Estimates are made, bids taken, and contracts signed. Therefore, budget askings either within the department or within the maintenance division of the institution must be foreseen. Outdoor facilities require short-range rotation of play fields for seeding and rest for turf surfaces. Constant friction on turf results in abrasive or muddy field surfaces. Short-range plans may include additional courts for play or lighting for night activity if these items have not been economically feasible in the long-range plans. With constantly increasing enrollments, there is a point where long- and short-range plans overlap. The building of an excessive number of indoor play areas may be questioned by a community. It is good economy, however, to plan the basic construction in such a way that additional facilities may be added, from time to time, without danger to existing foundations and without the expense of foundation construction. One example will suffice. In this day of high-rise construction, perhaps we need to consider a gym-upon-a-gym. Construction of heating tunnels, electrical cables, water lines and other utility factors could be planned less expensively on a long range to accommodate additional short-range additions. By and large, short-range plans are either emergency measures to take care of unexpected needs or they are primarily maintenance measures for existing facilities.

Long-range planning for facilities generally involves capital improvements either in complete renovation of existing facilities or in the construction of new facilities. At this point in our discussion, we will consider the basic thinking with regard to long-range planning.

HOW MUCH WILL IT COST?

A basic consideration is the source of funds for building facilities. The economic structure of the community supporting the educational institution must be carefully analyzed. Physical education facilities cannot be excessively luxuriant, especially when the economic and tax structures are low. Very careful planning is needed to secure the best possible facility under such circumstances. The use of newer building materials and types of structure is recommended as an aid in reducing costs. In public school systems and in colleges, physical education facilities are usually coordinated

PRESENT LEVY AND PROPOSED TAX LEVY

	19XX-19XX	Proposed
Bond Sinking Fund	4.39 mills	5.37 mills
Bond Interest Fund	.98 mills	2.92 mills
Capital Outlay Fund	3.72 mills	1.47 mills
	9.09 mills	9.76 mills

Increase .67 mill

AVERAGE LINCOLN PROPERTY

$5,000	$10,000	$20,000
Actual Valuation	Actual Valuation	Actual Valuation

$1,750 Assessed Valuation	$3,500 Assessed Valuation	$7,000 Assessed Valuation
10¢ per Month	20¢ per Month	40¢ per Month

Fig. 7–3. Sample school bond issue. (Used by permission of the Lincoln Public Schools, Lincoln, Nebraska.)

with total institutional planning. The needs of physical education are specialized and should be specified by the experts in this field. Coordination, however, demands that the voices of all fields be heard and that "give and take" occur in all areas. For example, the author knows of two public school facilities cooperatively planned by a public school system and a university. Due consideration of the economic structure in both instances and consideration of specific needs for teacher education were needed. In the end, the public pays for these facilities. Administratively, charts that speak in terms understood by the public will help to secure public support. Although in this affluent society we glibly speak in terms of millions and billions, we are aghast if such expenditures threaten our personal spending habits. Bond issues and capital improvement funds need public acceptance rather than public resistance. A breakdown into understandable terms, such as relative costs per day to the taxpayer, is a fine administrative procedure.

Figure 7–3 shows a sample school bond issue in terms of the individual taxpayer. The proposed $12 million bond issue based on the school district's present valuation, and sold at an average rate of 3¼ per cent, will cost approximately 67¢ per $1,000 assessed property over the amount now being paid for school building purposes. The retirement of school bonds calls for a fixed amount of dollars over a period of years. The 67¢ additional cost for each $1,000 of assessed property will decrease as the assessed valuation of the district increases.

PLANNING

Public support assumes that the public understands how this planning for physical education facilities fits into the total community plan. To this end, housing and zoning officials should be consulted to ascertain the patterns that both county and urban areas are following. Erection of campus-type schools in an area zoned commercially is a waste of funds since population numbers are gradually reduced. Population trends based on birth and school entrance statistics indicate future needs and should be carefully studied. A campus-type school complete with physical education facilities built at the edge of an urban community may have a few transportation problems during its initial use, but if well planned, it will have adequate outdoor play areas plus enough land for additions to the buildings as needed. Economically, locating new facilities in highly developed industrial or business areas may raise problems in that the acquisition of additional land may be either impossible or prohibitive in price. If the public is carefully apprised of these problems, better rapport is established.

Climate and geographic conditions affect long-range planning. In colder climate, there are rather long stretches of time (early spring and late fall) when outdoor play surfaces become soft and muddy. Two solutions are feasible—more hard surfaces or provision of play porches, Fig. 7–4 (also useful in extreme heat).

The above general factors bring us to consideration of the long-range planning responsibilities of the physical education administrator and his staff. As experts in physical education, the staff should state in writing the specific needs for the various activity areas such as sports, dance, and swimming. Included should be recommended room sizes in relation to official dimensions for courts and swimming pools, and locker formulas. Total planning should certainly take into cognizance formulas for the number of teaching stations needed: [3]

$$\begin{array}{l}\text{Minimum}\\\text{number of}\\\text{teaching stations}\end{array} = \frac{\text{Number of students}}{\begin{array}{c}\text{Average number of}\\\text{students per instructor}\end{array}} \times \frac{\begin{array}{c}\text{Number of periods}\\\text{class meets each week}\end{array}}{\begin{array}{c}\text{Total number of class}\\\text{periods in school week}\end{array}}$$

The formula for computing the number of teaching stations needed for physical education in an elementary school is as follows: [4]

$$\begin{array}{l}\text{Minimum}\\\text{number of}\\\text{teaching stations}\end{array} = \begin{array}{c}\text{Number of classrooms}\\\text{of students}\end{array} \times \frac{\begin{array}{c}\text{Number of physical}\\\text{education periods per}\\\text{week per class}\end{array}}{\begin{array}{c}\text{Total periods in school}\\\text{week}\end{array}}$$

Planning the number of teaching stations also involves the informal program. If a school has two interscholastic squads, an intramural program, an "open gym" program, and a community recreation program, five stations are involved. Comparison of the results of the formula needs of the teaching program with the informal program needs determines the number of teaching stations needed. The larger number of stations is used in stating the total need. [5]

Unfortunately, the number of teaching stations frequently does

[3] *Planning Facilities for Health, Physical Education and Recreation* (rev. ed.; Chicago: The Athletic Institute, 1965), p. 83.
[4] *Ibid.*
[5] *Ibid.*

Fig. 7-4. Play porches. (Courtesy of Lincoln Public Schools, Lincoln, Nebraska.)

161

not reflect the needs in physical education if too small an area or an irregular area is planned. Therefore, descriptive analysis of working areas is needed. Snowberger suggests that no one spectator sport should usurp space at the expense of other activities.[6] Planning for women's facilities places spectator space at a minimum since little if any emphasis is placed on its desirability. When areas must be shared, investigation of the space uses under geodesic domes[7] may be of interest. However, women's departments with separate facilities may question this type of construction because of the lack of privacy for teaching and the acoustical problems with women's voices. Dual uses of the requested activity areas should be indicated both for guidance in the planning and as documentation of the need for each area. With the need for the financial resources of the institution to be allocated to various interests, planning often must be done on the basis of unit-by-unit construction. Such planning limits program offerings but is better than using obsolete or inadequate facilities. Under such circumstances, priorities must be established by the staff in consultation with top administrative officers. Need for a specific facility combined with its anticipated use may form the base for setting these priorities. In like manner, planning may provide for additional units as monies become available.[8] All of this planning occurs within a staff and at first may be nothing more than a "dream." The moment of reality comes when an architect using his knowledge of building and sanitary codes and construction codes and his ability for creative design takes over the dream and translates it into feasible working plans.

Long-range planning for facilities, therefore, is a matter of analysis of community economics, teaching needs, professional dreams, and architectural and engineering know-how. Objective and cooperative action is the goal of the physical education administrator in projecting long-range facility needs.

INDOOR AREAS

There are details of indoor area planning that are pertinent to all levels of physical education. It seems best to structure the dis-

[6] Campbell Snowberger, "A Functional Field House," *Journal of Health, Physical Education, and Recreation*, XXXV, No. 1 (January, 1964), 38.

[7] *Conventional Gymnasiums vs. Geodesic Field House*, Case Studies of Educational Facilities, No. 1 (New York: Educational Facilities Laboratories, Inc.).

[8] Symposium, Bemidji State College, Minnesota, "Focus on Facilities, Long Range Planning," *Journal of Health, Physical Education, and Recreation*, XXXIII, No. 4 (April, 1962), 41.

cussion of these details as a part of the description of secondary school areas for physical education (i.e., floor details, standards for window areas, etc.).

ELEMENTARY SCHOOL INDOOR PLAY AREAS

Physical education activities for grades kindergarten to two do not demand the same indoor play area as for grades three to six. In the lower grades, more informal activities are the practice, while the use of lead-up and modified team games for the upper grades necessitate standard-size courts and higher ceiling areas. The enrollment in a specific elementary school helps to determine the indoor play space that may be provided. A small elementary school needing only one play area should try to provide at least a minimal-size gymnasium. An elementary school carrying dual grade units will probably need two or more teaching stations. Thus, at least two classes from the units (kindergarten to two and three to six) may be scheduled simultaneously. Provision for a gymnasium, a playroom, and/or a multiple-purpose room would then fill this need.

The location of the gymnasium in any school is important. Its location in a small elementary school is vital to fine functioning of the total school. Short concentration and interest spans are characteristic of elementary school children. Distractions may easily occur. Movement and the accompanying noise of movement should be located away from the classroom complex. If possible, the gymnasium or playroom should be located in a separate wing. If this is not feasible, one end of the building should house this facility.

The size of either the elementary school gymnasium or playroom is frequently a matter of expediency or the square footage possible after other needs have been met. Standards for this facility seem to be variable: from 40' × 30' with a height of 18', to 86' × 54' with a height of 20'. However, the standard of 86' × 54' meets the criterion that the length of a gymnasium should be one and a half times the width. Moreover, with the use of a soundproof divider, an area of this size may become two teaching stations of 43' × 54'. Areas of this size will accommodate basketball, volleyball, badminton, paddle tennis, and other court games, with space for climbing ropes, stall bars, horizontal ladders, and similar apparatus. Scott and Westkaemper note that smaller areas, 36' × 50' with 18' ceiling, may suffice for auxiliary playrooms to be used by children in the lower elementary grades.[9]

[9] Harry A. Scott and Richard B. Westkaemper, *From Program to Facilities in Physical Education* (New York: Harper & Row, Inc., 1958), p. 69.

There are desirable features that are too frequently omitted in planning a gymnasium for the elementary school. When a specialist in physical education is employed, he needs an office for planning and for privacy in conferences. Maple floors are as necessary here as in higher educational levels. The resiliency of the wooden floor is needed because of the developing arch in the child's foot. Recessed drinking fountains for informal use solve a time problem. Toilet facilities either adjoining the gymnasium or adjacent to it contribute to better health practices. Storage rooms and cabinets for small equipment add to safety and the appearance of the gymnasium. When classes are scheduled continuously, a door for entrance and a door for exit will aid the traffic flow. Children at play are not silent. Therefore, acoustical treatment of ceilings and walls will help in noise control and reduce the irritations of sound transmission outside the gymnasium.

SECONDARY SCHOOL GYMNASIUMS

Secondary schools (junior high and senior high) have at least one gymnasium and frequently have auxiliary rooms. In the planning of campus schools, gymnasiums are usually located in separate buildings (Fig. 7–5). Some outstanding examples of school facilities are using a wing arrangement similar to the fingers of the hand for location of area teaching. Schematically, this would be as shown in Fig. 7–6(b). In either case, gymnasiums are located so that the noise factor is kept to a minimum. Also, these facilities may be locked off (usually by firedoors) from the rest of the building when the public is admitted as spectators or for recreation. It is obvious that, in either plan, expansion may take place without jeopardizing the original construction. Since facilities are assumed to be usable from forty to seventy years, flexibility is a grave consideration.

In practice, the sizes of gymnasiums run the gamut from the exact size of a basketball court (or less) to multiple teaching areas. The authorities agree that the height of a gymnasium designed to accommodate basketball, volleyball, badminton, and other court games should be at least 22 feet. The recommended size for a junior high school floor ranged from 65' × 86' to 65' × 102', with 72' × 96' recommended if the area is planned for community use. An area 72' × 90' received sanction since it would provide a full basketball court 42' × 74' with bleacher seats for spectators. By using a folding door, this area would provide teaching stations with two cross-courts. Senior high schools require a standard basketball

Fig. 7-5. Architect's model: Holland Senior High School, Holland, Michigan. (From *Profiles of Significant Schools*, 1962. Courtesy of Educational Facilities Laboratories, New York.)

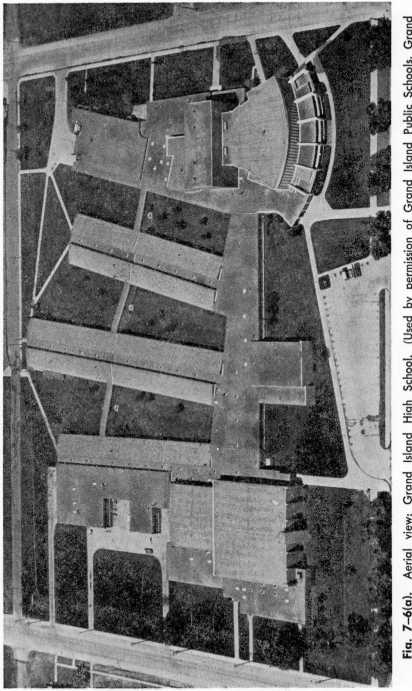

Fig. 7-6(a). Aerial view: Grand Island High School. (Used by permission of Grand Island Public Schools, Grand Island, Nebraska.)

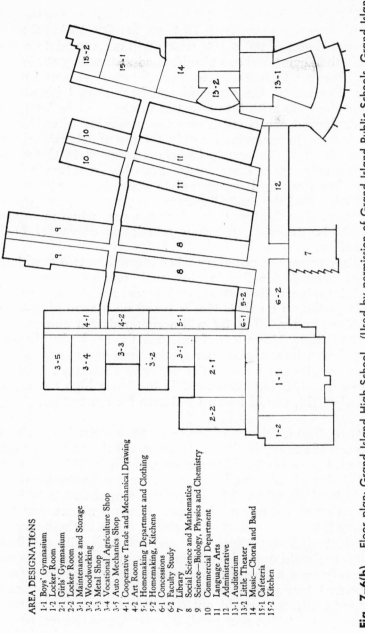

167

AREA DESIGNATIONS

1-1 Boys' Gymnasium
1-2 Locker Room
2-1 Girls' Gymnasium
2-2 Locker Room
3-1 Maintenance and Storage
3-2 Woodworking
3-3 Metal Shop
3-4 Vocational Agriculture Shop
3-5 Auto Mechanics Shop
4-1 Cooperative Trade and Mechanical Drawing
4-2 Art Room
5-1 Homemaking Department and Clothing
5-2 Homemaking, Kitchens
6-1 Concessions
6-2 Faculty Study
7 Library
8 Social Science and Mathematics
9 Science—Biology, Physics and Chemistry
10 Commercial Department
11 Language Arts
12 Administrative
13-1 Auditorium
13-2 Little Theater
14 Music—Choral and Band
15-1 Cafeteria
15-2 Kitchen

Fig. 7–6(b). Floor plan: Grand Island High School. (Used by permission of Grand Island Public Schools, Grand Island, Nebraska.)

court 50′ × 84′ with a resultant increase in the size of area. Again, the areas' dimensions vary from 76′ × 96′ to 94′ × 100′ to the highly recommended size of 90′ × 108′ which will accommodate a regulation basketball court and can also be used as teaching stations—two courts. Planning facilities as to exact court sizes sets up safety hazards. For safety, the side and end lines should be placed 10 feet from the walls with 6 to 8 feet as minimums. At least 10 feet between adjacent courts cuts down the possibility of collisions between players. In programs for girls, the use of extensive space for spectators is poor. Telescopic bleachers recessed in the wall will adequately take care of these needs. Probably from two to five sections of five rows will accommodate spectators for intramurals, sports clinics, and the limited extramural program currently under organization. For the few times during a year when more spectators might be desirable, judicious scheduling of varsity facilities should suffice.

Auxiliary rooms are necessary when more than two teaching stations are needed. Smaller in size, such rooms or areas can be planned into space that would not accommodate a gymnasium. The rule of thumb on their size is based on a ratio of 5 to 3; so, 30′ × 50′ or, better, 40′ × 60′ will accommodate a number of different activities. Movement fundamentals or body mechanics, fencing, dance, recreational sports, adaptives, stunts and tumbling, and free exercise are some of the activities that may be taught in such an area. If it has been feasible to plan a high ceiling, 22 to 24 feet, then this would be an ideal area for apparatus.

Storage. The efficiency of many exercise areas is cut down by the absence of storage facilities. Estimates of the amount of storage area needed for each teaching station vary from 100 to 500 square feet. This is probably true because storage areas were fitted in odd spaces in total planning. The happy medium of 250 to 300 square feet probably would prove adequate. Because pianos, mat trucks, and heavy floor apparatus must be stored, doors to these areas need to be 7 feet high and 6 feet wide and set flush with the flooring. These areas should open directly into the gymnasium. The author has recently seen a blueprint on which the storage area (as outlined above) was placed around a corner from the gymnasium. Since long equipment could not turn this corner, its use was negated. Adjacent to the area used, the piano, and the record player, cabinets and racks to store percussion instruments and cabinets for recordings and music are needed. Locked steel cabinets to house balls, hockey sticks, golf clubs, bats, softball gloves plus protective equipment, and badminton and tennis racquets in frames should be provided. By judicious selection of these cabinets with their component divisions, and with either edged or tilted shelves, a very efficient storage facility fitted to specific needs may be arranged. Use of large-holed pegboards fitted with commercial hooks (single or double) is suggested if cabinets are too expensive. Provision for out-of-season storage will facilitate the use of storage areas adjacent to the exercise areas.

Office. An office for the teacher of secondary school physical education should be provided. This is usually about 10′ × 12′ with viewing windows placed for supervision of both the gymnasium and the locker and shower rooms. Privacy for dressing and showering should always be provided for the teacher. A single shower unit is 4′ × 4′ with the dressing area slightly larger to accommodate toilet and lavatory facilities. The same construction should be used as in the students' area: namely, ceramic tiling, provision for drainage, and partitions and utilities suspended from the ceiling for ease in cleaning. Office furniture needed is discussed in Chapter 8.

Heating and Ventilation. Heating and ventilation are partners. Humidity with no movement of air is a deadening experience. In gymnasiums and locker and shower rooms, it is necessary that heat be controlled. In both areas, radiators should be recessed, and they operate best if placed 10 to 12 feet above the floor. Usually, heat standards are measured 48 to 60 inches above the floor. Authorities agree that with humidity at 60 per cent or less of saturation point, activity areas should be heated at 55° to 60° F. Teacher judgments in specific activities will determine the best temperature under local conditions. The temperature in the locker and shower rooms is usually regulated between 70° and 78° F. Zoned heating for the physical education unit is an economy when the total school facilities are not in use.

Unless ventilation is available, air becomes heavy and oppressive. Moreover, in physical education facilities wherever moisture is present, there is a condensation problem. Under current conditions with classes in session winter and summer, air conditioning is widely used. The advantage of air conditioning lies in its control of heat, humidity, and dust, as well as the circulation of air. If air conditioning is not available, forced air circulation is necessary, especially in locker rooms. During interim seasons, it is well to have outside windows in locker rooms that can be opened for fresh-air circulation.

Locker and Shower Rooms. The location of locker and shower rooms either increases the efficient operation of the program or prevents it. If teachers and students must climb stairs or move across corridors twice each class period, quite a lot of time is lost from the total program. Location of shower rooms in basements often defeats the purpose of providing clean, airy, sanitary, and attractive facilities. Students should be able to enter the dressing rooms from the corridors and enter the gymnasiums from the dressing rooms. In addition, access to the fields saves time and avoids unnecessary disturbance of other classes.

The size of dressing rooms is directly related to the enrollment of the school. Using the peak load, an allowance of 14 square feet per student, in addition to the space occupied by the lockers, will provide adequate facilities. This area is again determined by the size and type of storage used for gymnasium clothes. Self-service tote baskets may be used, or combination units of storage and dress lockers. Using the number of periods per day as the basis, a combination unit of (5-6-7-8) storage lockers plus one dress locker provides a convenient locker system. The size of locker chosen varies, but smaller box lockers (9" × 12" × 24") suffice for younger students, while 12" × 12" × 36" are more suitable for secondary and college girls. Dress lockers are usually 12" × 15" × 60" or 12" × 12" × 72". Placing lockers on concrete bases makes cleaning the area easier, and ventilation of the lockers is easier if space is left between them when they are placed back to back. Benches placed on concrete bases between the rows of lockers are comfortable assets needed by students.

The floors and walls of the locker room are important to the standards of sanitation to be maintained. It is the author's belief that all phases of physical education facilities, especially locker and shower rooms, should be as clean as possible. Probably the least expensive floor would be sealed concrete, but ceramic tile gives a lighter appearance and is easy to clean. Using coved corners and edges, the tile should be used for the lower wall with moisture-treated plaster above and in an acoustically treated ceiling. Drains, large enough to prevent overflow, and well located so that floors may be quickly flushed, scrubbed, and dried, are necessary. Location of hose bibs in relation to drainage facilitates this process.

Shower rooms should adjoin the dressing rooms. Today, open-type showers are becoming more and more acceptable for girls and women. However, provision should be made for those girls who desire privacy. The proportion usually used is 90 per cent open showers and 10 per cent private showers. The size of the single shower is usually 4′ × 4′ with an adjoining dressing area of the same size. In the open showers, ten shower heads for the first thirty girls plus additional shower heads for every four persons thereafter placed at 4-foot intervals is standard. To avoid wet hair for girls, shower heads should be placed at shoulder height and angled toward the floor. Liquid soap dispensers at each shower head are advised for safety and sanitary reasons. With an entrance from the shower room and approximately the same size, a drying or toweling room should be provided. Non-corrosive towel bars and a foot ledge are needed in this room. The same tiling treatment for floors and walls as used in the locker room is needed here. It is especially important that enough floor drains be provided and that the floors slope slightly toward their drains.

Sanitary codes establish the standards for the number of toilets and lavatories needed during periods of peak enrollment. Plumbing arrangements should be planned in the interests of economy. If a group of individual showers are used, these may be placed back to back with an open shower. Toilets and lavatories should not be located in conjunction with shower rooms, but they should be grouped to avoid unnecessary expense. With expanding enrollments, it is wise to leave room in the walls for additional plumbing. In the interest of efficiency in cleaning floors, partitions should be hung from the ceiling, and all items of plumbing equipment should be suspended from the walls.

Locker and dressing rooms for girls and women have numerous accessories that contribute both to comfort and to fine grooming. Several of these have healthful environment implications. The first of these is the placement of gravity-flow liquid soap dispensers above each lavatory. The second is the placement of facial tissue dispensers near lavatories so that lipstick, cold cream, and other greasy substances are not thoughtlessly wiped off with expensive towels. Waste disposal units conveniently placed also contribute to good housekeeping and a healthful environment in dressing areas. In the area of grooming, a few hair dryers for girls whose hair has become damp in the showers adds to the efficiency of the dressing room. Full-length mirrors, strategically placed near the dressing room exits, contribute to a good-grooming appearance both in the playing areas and upon return to the classroom. The author knows of two attractive dressing rooms for girls that are furnished with a bank of small dressing tables and benches rather than the traditional wall mirror with a narrow purse shelf below it. Another item adding to comfort is the location of a refrigerated drinking fountain near the exit. Finally, bulletin boards with attractive, neat displays and announcements are a great convenience for both staff and students. The entire unit of locker and dressing rooms and of shower and drying rooms makes an important impact on the morale of the students. The use of color, attention to nicety of detail, and a spotless environment make the difference between pleasure in coming to the building or dread of the use of these areas.

A word about traffic flow in the dressing area will close this discussion. Students usually enter the dressing area from a corridor, change clothes, and leave for class. They return to the locker area, proceed to pick up a towel, go on to the showers, enter the drying room, and return to the locker area. Location of a small area for the matron near the shower area, for towel service, will facilitate this pattern and will help control the spread of water into the dressing area. (See Fig. 7–7.)

Floors, Walls, and Ceilings. The floor of the gymnasium is one key to its effective use. Experience has proved that a hard maple floor correctly installed gives a resilient, hard-wearing surface. Preparation for the floor should include moisture-proofing and ventilation to prevent dry rot and termites. Long, narrow strips of maple correctly laid on a subflooring attached to sleepers based on the concrete slab give a durable floor. The use of metal angles at the edges of the floor allows for expansion. In construction of new floors, apparatus fastenings may be attached to the concrete base before the floor is finished. If floor creeping is a problem, it has been suggested that floor plates be attached to a heavy wooden beam inserted between the sleepers so that this beam may creep with the floor. After sanding the floor, court markings are placed on before the finish sealer coats. Although tile or vinyl floors are sometimes used for reasons of economy, there is question of safety in activity units where rapid movement and abrupt changes of direction occur. Currently, synthetic surface materials are being developed that may be substituted for wooden floors in certain areas.

The walls of the gymnasium may either enhance or retard the program. Thin, poorly constructed walls result in cold gymnasiums in winter and extremely hot areas in summer. An air space between the inner and outer walls provides insulation that helps with such a problem. Because physical education has many activities that need a rebounding surface, smooth walls 7 to 12 feet high are required. This smooth area may be glazed brick, cement, or hollow glazed tile. If only brick is used for the entire wall, the acoustics are affected. With the noise of activity, echoes develop and sounds are magnified. The use of acoustical plaster for the upper walls and

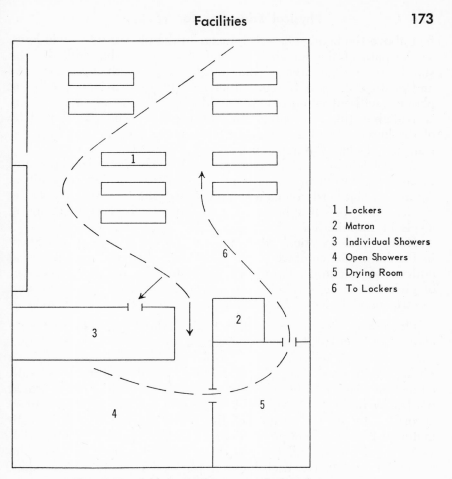

Fig. 7–7. Sample traffic pattern: locker-shower area.

ceiling and beam soffits (acoustical drop panels) make for a more relaxed teaching environment with less strain on both the students and the teacher. In the construction of new facilities, fixtures for suspended apparatus should be installed before walls and ceiling are finished. The use of two sleeves 6 inches apart and placed every 3 or 4 feet in concrete beams provides flexibility for apparatus installations. The stark grim gymnasium of the past is being replaced with the smart modern gymnasium, using color and newer types of wall materials to increase its beauty without an undue increase in cost.

Windows and Lighting. Because wall space is needed in gymnasiums for rebound activities, windows should be placed 10 to 14 feet above the floor. Glare is a factor in the placement of windows, so the path of the sun in a specific place should be studied. The standard window area is one-fourth to one-fifth the floor area and *cross-placement* is used. Increasingly, gymnasiums are being planned without windows. If forced ventilation or air-conditioning is available, this is feasible. In locker rooms, windows should be of the louvre type for ventilation in rainy and colder weather, and translucent glass should be used.

Artificial lighting should be planned to eliminate shadows and to conserve vision in all parts of the physical education facilities. Approved standards of candle power or light intensity should be used. Table 7–3 has been adapted from a chart recommending levels of illumination.

Items in all physical education facilities that add to efficiency in teaching and comfort in their use include numerous electrical outlets for teaching aids, a planned system for quick replacement of globes or tubes, "breaker" panels to avoid replacing fuses, and electric panels placed for efficient and safe control of all areas.

Classrooms. To accommodate health education, activity theory classes, and safety education and school organizations, physical education facilities today usually include a classroom. Located in a physical education wing, this classroom may also be used for adult education classes at hours when opening the entire school would not be desirable. Using movable desks or arm chairs to be arranged according to the varied uses of the room, the size usually is estimated at 20 square feet per student. Chalkboards, outlets for audio-visual equipment, bulletin boards, and shades arranged for film projection add to the usefulness of physical education classrooms.

Swimming Pools. With the increasing emphasis on water sports in leisure time, schools and colleges are giving more heed to the possible safety results in the teaching of swimming. Large public school systems are including swimming pools in the total planning of school facilities, and smaller communities are attempting to provide outdoor pools for summer use. The details of construction and operation of natatoriums would require a volume in itself. The general bases of thinking and the overall standards, therefore, are the subject of this discussion.

LOCATION, SIZE, AND SHAPE. In public schools, swimming pools are located in the physical education building or wing and are placed in such a way that they may serve both boys and girls. The same principle of economy and use may operate on the college

Table 7–3

Levels of Illumination Currently Recommended for Specific School Areas

Area	Minimum Foot-Candles on Tasks	Area	Minimum Foot-Candles on Tasks
Classrooms, lecture rooms, audience area	70	Offices	
Corridors and stairways	20	Accounting, auditing, tabulating, bookkeeping, business-machine operation, reading poor reproductions	150
First-aid rooms, general	50	Regular office work, reading good reproductions, reading or transcribing handwriting in hard pencil or on poor paper, active filing, index references, mail sorting	100
Gymnasiums			
Exhibitions, matches	30		
General exercise and recreation	20		
Dances	5		
Locker and shower rooms	20		
Badminton		Reading or transcribing handwriting in ink or medium pencil on good quality paper, intermittent filing	70
Tournament	30		
Club	20		
Recreational	10	Reading high-contrast or well-printed material, tasks and areas not involving critical or prolonged seeing, such as conferring, interviewing, and inactive filing	30
Basketball			
College and professional	50		
College intramural and high school, with spectators	30		
College intramural and high school, without spectators	20		
		Storerooms	
Volleyball		Inactive	5
Tournament	20	Active	
Recreational	10	Rough bulky	10
Library, reading room, study and notes	70	Medium	20
		Fine	50
Lounges		Swimming pools	
General	10	General and overhead	10
Reading books, magazines, newspapers	30	Underwater	*
		Toilets and washrooms	30

* 100 lamp lumens per square foot of pool surface.

Source: Adapted from *Planning Areas and Facilities for Health, Physical Education and Recreation* (rev. ed.; Chicago: The Athletic Institute, 1965), p. 145.

campus. However, if the college has several pools because of large enrollments, the pools may be assigned specifically to men or women with coeducational hours for recreational swimming established. The day is past, fortunately, when a pool is placed in a basement location. Objections to this plan include difficulties in water line and sewage disposal plus the fact that the use of space above the pool is poor due to condensation problems. A ground floor location preferably on the south side of the building is recommended.

Size and shape of swimming pools are related. When an exten-

sive competitive program is operative, as in some colleges, an L-
or T-shaped pool is recommended. This, however, is an expensive
facility in terms of square-foot construction, space required, and
upkeep. Two principles need to be considered in deciding the size
and shape of the pool: (1) How much can a particular community
afford? (2) Will the additional costs be justified in terms of the
maximum use of the facility? Although small pools may be adequate for classes, especially if the shallow water area is extended,
a rectangular pool 35′ or 42′ × 75′1″ meets both class and competitive swimming needs. To accommodate diving, the height of the
room should be at least 22 feet above the deck.

Pool decks are planned to accommodate teaching and to contribute to safety, particularly behind the deep-water diving area.
Side decks are usually 6 to 8 feet wide, and 10 feet is better, with
end decks 10 to 20 feet wide. Depending upon the needs of the
situation, deck areas may be planned to be narrower on one side
and wider on the other. Outdoor pools require additional deck
area to accommodate sun bathing. Decks should slope slightly
away from the pool and be provided with adequate drainage to
carry away water. Unglazed tile is recommended as a non-slip
surface for pool decks.

CONSTRUCTION FACTORS. The construction and placement of a
shell or basin for a swimming pool is exceedingly important. Before a final decision on the site of a pool is made, an earth core
should be secured to be sure that the soil will sustain the weight
of the shell plus the additional construction features without settling. A number of materials are suggested by experts for this shell.
The expense of the material selected combined with the earth core
result will probably determine this factor. Quality concrete for
indoor pools is to be desired. Location of inlets for water and
drain outlets plus the necessary plumbing must be decided at this
point. It is absolutely necessary to investigate water supply in
relation to pool use and sewer outlets for correct location (no reverse flow) and size so that the pool may be emptied without undue
loss of time. Provision for a repair tunnel, electrically lighted, is
an economy. Plumbing repairs and small leaks may then be controlled without interruption of classes and without the unnecessary
expense of destruction of the pool decks. Overflow gutters around
the entire floor are usually required by the sanitation codes. These
are placed at intervals 10 feet apart and must be deep enough to
remove the water adequately. Most pools use a curved coping
around the edge of the pool to prevent splashing of water onto the

deck and for use in diving. Lanes 7 feet wide are usually marked
with dark tile in contrast to light-colored tile used for the pool lin-
ing. Water depths are carefully marked. The percentage of shallow versus deep water depends upon the use of a specific pool. If
both 1- and 3-meter diving boards are used, the pool must be a
minimum of 12 feet at the deep end with an additional 2 feet advised for safety in teaching diving. Ladders, recessed into the side
walls at each end of the pool, are considered the safest type of entry
and exit from the pool. All pool edges should be rounded to facilitate cleaning. Hose bibs and outlets for vacuum cleaners should
be located so that the pool and the pool room may be kept in spotless condition. If underwater lighting and underwater sound are
used, the installations and types must comply with the electrical
codes. Condensation and acoustical problems are always encoun-
tered in the pool room. Consultation with expert architects is
advised on this and all phases of pool problems.

AUXILIARY AREAS. 1. *Dressing rooms and showers.* The same
standards apply to this area as those planned for the general dressing room area. Banks of hair dryers are needed, and the shower
area is planned so that swimmers must use it before entering the
pool. Entrance to the pool area must be electrically controlled in
this room as well as in the pool office.

2. *Laundry.* Many schools and colleges operate small laundries
in conjunction with the swimming pool. In some instances, towel
laundry is handled as well as tank suits, leotards, fencing jackets,
and other items for use in the department. Institution-size wash-
ing machines and dryers are an economy over domestic-size machines as they take a larger load. Installation of heavy-duty
conduits and outlets for electricity and gas plus water lines and
drains must be planned, and a space that is well ventilated and
treated for humidity should be provided. Storage cabinets for
soaps, detergents, and bleaches plus counter space for folding garments are needed. Tile or concrete is suggested for the floor so
that it may be easily cleaned.

3. *Mechanical room.* In the mechanical room, water heating
and circulation, filtration, and water purification equipment operate.
Here we find the surge tank, hair strainers, coagulation pots, chlorine or other purification agent, sand or diatomaceous earth filters,
heaters, and pumps for recirculation of water. The size of this
room is determined by the size of the type of filter used. It should
be large enough to house all the equipment comfortably and permit easy access for repairs.

4. *Storage room.* It is a mistake to use the edges of the mechanical room for pool storage. Space for an indoor canoe rack and paddles, float lines, kick boards, buoys, poles, and game equipment is necessary.

5. *Pool office.* A pool office should be located at the shallow end of the pool. The equipment for all offices is discussed in Chapter 8. The special features of this office include shower and dressing areas for the swimming staff, controls and equipment for underwater sound systems, and electrical control of the pool entrance for reasons of safety. A large window overlooking the pool enables the swimming instructor to supervise the pool.

6. *Spectator space.* A small gallery at one side of the pool should be provided for spectators. Entrances and exits for this gallery should be separated from the pool area. As in the pool area, the materials used must be easily cleaned, and provision should be made for condensation and acoustical treatment. The size of the area depends upon the needs in a specific situation.

Indoor Traffic Flow. Since no two areas are identical in size, layout, or needs, plots for traffic flow cannot be established. There are, however, principles to be observed. Ample corridor space to accommodate large numbers should be provided to the dressing areas and from dressing areas to the playing fields. In separate buildings, the entrance foyer should give access to corridors leading to spectator space and dressing areas but should not be used for access to wet areas such as the pool or pool dressing areas. Public restrooms and telephone booths should be located off the foyer.

Stairways, if needed, should be wide enough to accommodate traffic in two directions and should be protected from fire hazards. For safety reasons, all equipment such as heating units, display cases, drinking fountains, bulletin boards, and fire extinguishers should be recessed.

All exits should be provided with panic bars and should open outward.

Special provisions for deliveries should be made. These include a delivery entrance and dollies and carts for carrying heavy materials from place to place.

COLLEGE FACILITIES

Except for increased size and number of teaching stations with resultant increases in all types of service areas, college physical education facilities follow the same standards as secondary schools.

There are, however, certain differences in the program that result in different facilities. These will be discussed at this point.

Activities receiving increasing emphasis at the college level, especially for young women, are the individual and dual sports, dance, gymnastics, movement fundamentals, and aquatics. It is therefore important that teaching areas be set up to accommodate fencing, rifling, indoor golf, and tennis, as well as badminton and bowling. Dance in the secondary school is conducted in the usual gymnasium or auxiliary room. A well-designed and well-equipped studio in the college accommodates all forms of dance, with emphasis upon creative dance. The studio often has two floor levels so that one end may be used as a stage. Mirrors, drapes, and lighting for staging increase the possibilities for this use. Storage areas for the piano, recording cabinets and record player, costumes, and percussion instruments should be provided. If well designed, these areas may serve as dressing rooms for dance performances. Indoor golf and tennis may be set up in large gymnasiums. The long narrow room needed for fencing may double as an archery range.

Since physical education in colleges is generally housed in a separate building, a reception office is needed. Such an office should be located near the main entrance of the building and adjoined to the office of the chairman of the department. Offices for all staff members are provided. In the case of staff whose duties include theory classes, advising major students, and graduate teaching assignments, these offices should be private. Staff dressing rooms that provide attractive, convenient, and uncrowded space are needed. In departments serving major students, separate dressing room areas as well as study or seminar rooms help to weld the department into a cohesive unit. Several classrooms are needed to serve the program for major students. With a large staff (fifteen or more), a conference room for staff and committee meetings serves a real need. Students wishing to visit with other students or to wait between classes enjoy a small lounge. The Women's Athletic Association and other professional organizations need a small kitchen to prepare refreshments. It is now customary to provide such facilities in a physical education building for women. All areas of a physical education building should be serviced by telephones and an intercom system.

Research is a responsibility of college departments of physical education. Reuben B. Frost of Springfield College, in an address delivered in 1964, pointed out the responsibility of administrators to see to it that facilities for research are provided. This may be the scheduling of gymnasiums, playing fields, or the swimming pool, and it may also be the provision for a research laboratory. It is impossible to state the type of facility needed; this will vary with the type of research interest. Whether small or large, simple or complex equipment—the college administrator of physical education needs to provide facilities for research if this field is to advance.

NEWER-TYPE FACILITIES

Several indications of changes in program with resulting changes in facilities have been mentioned in this and previous chapters. Team teaching and flexible scheduling that is personalized to student needs and interests may demand a break from the traditional scheduling of facilities. We have mentioned the use of the geodesic dome (a field house type of facility with partial partitions). It may well be that improvements upon this general plan will make this type of facility more comfortable for the use of girls and women, especially if the acoustical treatment can be perfected. Dependent upon more widespread total acceptance of flexible scheduling, facilities could be planned that will contain large instructional units plus smaller practice units. It will take experimentation to determine the relative costs of such planning as compared to more traditional areas. Certainly, no new facility today should ignore the constantly increasing enrollments. Therefore, the structural planning of a new facility should consider footings to hold increased weight. With foundation space at a premium, a gymnasium upon a gymnasium may become one of the answers. Carpeting is currently under experimentation in classrooms for two reasons: (1) its acoustical properties and (2) economy in maintenance. Educational Facilities Laboratory reports experimentation with a "turf-like" surface for sports areas.[10] New developments of any type in construction or maintenance using experimentation should be carefully watched and the possibility for local use judged on the basis of economic feasibility and durability as well as its functioning in a physical education program.

In college planning, we find two trends that need consideration in physical education. The first of these is the construction of intramural or recreational buildings for use by the college community. The thinking behind this plan is that gymnasiums and other play facilities must be available at all times for informal use by college students. Administratively, this is a costly facility, and

[10] Newsletter No. 5. (New York: Educational Facilities Laboratories, Inc.).

there may be times, especially during morning hours, when classes could be held. A second idea that is receiving considerable support is the inclusion of hard-surface play areas, small-size recreational swimming pools, and recreation rooms within a dormitory complex. The thinking here is that, if recreational facilities are conveniently located, participation in such activity will be encouraged. Administrators of physical education should be alert to their role as consultants in such planning and in the operation of such areas.

PLANNING NEW FACILITIES

Many hints on the details of planning new facilities have been included in this chapter. It seems expedient, however, to summarize this process. At any time that there is any indication that new facilities may be considered, the staff and administrator of a department of physical education must be able to produce a statement of needs on very short notice. Such a statement may well be labeled a "dream sequence," as it states the ideals and the desires of the department. However, it seems wiser to plan ideally and cut realistically rather than to patch inadequate askings later. In fact, this latter course is often impossible.

Preliminary planning includes a statement of the program needs as based upon the philosophy of the department. Using either current enrollment figures or, more frequently, predicted enrollment figures, time schedules, and class size, the formulas will produce the number of teaching stations needed. This arithmetical result, however, does not always give the best space planning in terms of program needs and in terms of the uses of the various stations. Therefore, this statement, prepared by the staff for the architect, spells out specialized problems such as heights of activity areas, the amount and kind of wall space, apparatus and sports installations, safety specifications, audio-visual needs, and size and type of storage areas. In a women's building, a great deal of care and attention should be given to attractive, spacious, and well-designed locker and shower rooms. The use of color and acoustical considerations will enhance the value of a building for women. A small lounge, with kitchenette for group meetings, is now a standard practice in construction planning. Statements of multiple-use possibilities for each area will strengthen the cause in preliminary planning. Thus, the staff dreams but comes face to face with reality in fitting dreams to the allocated funds for such a building.

Although the staff should be consulted with regard to needs and with regard to final approval of building plans, the architect has the know-how for the design of the building. A functional building may thus evolve based on two types of expertise. The architect has his knowledge of stress factors, building codes, construction costs, and use of new materials. The staff, on the other hand, know the needs and the place of physical education in the total educational picture. There may be a need for expert consultants, however, such as a swimming pool specialist; yet the use of consultants is limited both by fees and the possible duplication of such services with that of a fine architect.

Planning for a building, especially in a college program, is a coordinated activity. Most colleges employ a construction engineer, either on a full- or a part-time basis, to supervise the building program. With his background and his knowledge in regard to the capacity of utility lines, heating or air-cooling plants, and access tunnels, plus his knowledge of building and sanitary codes, valuable time and energy is saved by his reading of the blueprints and checking of the tables of specifications and of the various contracts and subcontracts. By coordinating the efforts of such a person with those of the purchasing agent, the business manager of the college is able to obtain the best possible result from the monies available.

As this process evolves, the staff is asked to review the layout drawings. Every detail of these should be carefully analyzed and suggestions made for needed changes. When the architect has prepared the first drawings and when specifications are reviewed by the governing body of the institution, the contracts are let. Bidding is the usual procedure. Once the contracts have been signed, changes are extremely expensive or may even be prohibited. The staff, therefore, must be aware of common errors found in physical education construction [11] and be alert to any indication of these in the blueprints. The staff must also use every possible source of information regarding standards and best practices in constructing physical education facilities if discerning judgments are to be made.

Another staff responsibility, as indicated in Chapter 8, is the preparation of equipment lists (Fig. 7–8) and installation requirements for the activity program. Complete information with regard to detailed specifications and probable costs must be prepared by the staff early in the planning for a building. This involves detailed, careful, comparative price shopping to avoid undue expense.

[11] A Guide for Planning Facilities for Health, Physical Education and Recreation (rev. ed.; Chicago: The Athletic Institute, 1962), pp. 64 and 70.

						Cost		In	

UNIVERSITY OF_____

EQUIPMENT PLANNING LIST   PROPOSED_____BUILDING____

DEPARTMENT OR SERVICE_____IN CHARGE_____DATE_____

						FOR EQUIPMENT DIVISION			
Item	Utility Require-ments*	No. Req.	O. H.	To Pur-chase	Cost Unit	Cost Total	In Arch. Contract	Comment	

*Utility Requirements - Elect. amp. & voltage; st =steam; H. W.= Hot Water; C. W.= Cold Water; W=Waste; G=Gas

ROOM NO._____

Fig. 7–8. Sample equipment planning list.

After a building has been constructed, there is usually a short time lapse before it is accepted by the authorities. Within this time, any unexpected problems relative to the construction should be resolved. Planning new facilities and seeing the project through to its materialization as a functional unit for a physical education program is a heavy but rewarding responsibility.

RESPONSIBILITIES OF THE ADMINISTRATOR

In the development and maintenance of facilities, the administrator has definite responsibilities as follows:

1. Knowledge of the standards that have been established for both indoor and outdoor facilities will enable the administrator to plan functional units for all levels of education.
2. Contingency planning on a long-range basis as well as short-range improvements is needed for growth of the program.
3. An understanding of the economic base and community mores is needed by the administrator in order to gain public support for construction of physical education facilities.
4. Land acquisition and its development for play areas are major re-

sponsibilities of the physical education administrator. Knowledge of differing space needs, as well as activity needs, of the various educational levels will contribute to intelligent planning.

5. The details of construction for gymnasiums and other play areas must be readily available. A physical education administrator is expected to advise school personnel and the public on the optimum size of areas, types of floors to be used, traffic considerations, service units, and storage problems.

6. Maintenance costs should cover adequate upkeep of the facilities and thus should protect the original investment. This is a serious problem for administrators. Budgets for this purpose are either cut or eliminated when funds are scant.

7. Scheduling the best use of facilities and establishing policies for their use by community groups are other administrative duties.

8. Finally, supervision of facilities in the interest of cleanliness, safety, and respect for public property is a major administrative responsibility.

SUMMARY

The administrator has constant responsibilities in the area of facilities. Not only must standards be met in developing new or renovating old facilities, but also there is the problem of daily and weekly upkeep. The health education of the student is a factor to be faced. Safety precautions, safety inspections, and traffic flow must be constantly included in the considerations of the administrator. In brief, facilities demand planning, supervising, scheduling, and the establishment of policies for both use and maintenance on the part of the administrator.

PROBLEMS

1. Formulate a policy for the use of the gymnasium area by outside groups. Write the regulations necessary to control this use.

2. Plan a swimming facility for a community of 1,000 in your state. Investigate health and sanitation codes, water supply, and sewage levels. Plan the pool complete with bathhouse; state its size, mechanical controls, and design of the traffic flow.

3. Outline the span of planning for a new physical education building for a college or university.

4. Design a dressing-shower room for a secondary school with an enrollment of 900 girls (600 in required physical education plus electives) with a schedule of six class periods per day.

5. Write a set of policies for community use of a small high school gymnasium in a town of approximately 5,000 people.

6. Plan an indoor wing of an elementary school with separate facilities for lunchroom and kitchen, auditorium, and gymnasium. Consider economy in entrances, use of plumbing, and use of space. Make this a functional unit.

7. Diagram the various surfaces used for play areas, and list the activity uses possible by elementary, secondary, and college classes on each type of surfacing.

8. Outline the facilities available in a public school known to you. Point out the advantages of these and also the errors in the original planning. Could any of these errors be corrected without undue expense? If so, how?

9. Plan a play area layout for each of the following:

a) An elementary school of 500 in an urban community

b) A consolidated secondary school serving a rural county with sparse population

c) A small college with an enrollment of 800 girls

8

Administration of Equipment

"Equipment" is a term that is used with varied meanings in physical education. To some persons, the term denotes the articles commonly used in the sports program; to others, it refers to gymnastic apparatus. In this discussion, permanent equipment is identified as those large items that are purchased or replaced on a long-term basis, for example, parallel bars, climbing ropes, pianos, and steel files. Seasonal or activity equipment is identified as those items that must be replaced annually or, perhaps, within a shorter time span. Supplies, in this discussion, refer to office materials, health or first-aid needs, and other small items necessary to the program but not specifically used in activities.

ELEMENTARY SCHOOLS

Although there are numerous general types of equipment used throughout the education span, such as balls and ropes, there are differences in type, size, and kind in use at the various age levels. At the elementary school level, if a gymnasium, playroom or multipurpose room is available, permanent equipment such as climbing ropes, balance beams, volleyball standards, low basketball backboards, and mats add to the enrichment of the program. On the playground, permanent equipment is changing from the traditional slide, seesaws, and swings to equipment that challenges the child to find activity. Short tunnels made from culvert commercial piping, roughened concrete ramps and steps, and varied-height concrete or brick walls are often provided for the smaller children; tether ball standards, basketball backboards, horizontal bars at varying heights, rings, and ladders are available for all ages. The following suggestions are pertinent to this discussion of playground equipment.

Installation

Proper installation of horizontal bars, climbing apparatus, slides adjacent to fences or buildings is important.

Action should be planned parallel to the line of the fence or building.

Apparatus should be placed a safe distance away for complete freedom of action without touching any obstacle.

There should be adequate play space provided exclusively for younger children with apparatus reduced in height to meet their age needs.[1]

Precautions

Broken chains, loosened sections, or broken parts of apparatus should be removed from apparatus, repaired, and replaced promptly.

Upright posts should be buried deep enough for safety or embedded in concrete blocks. Iron posts are more desirable than wooden ones. The latter, unless they are redwood, will rot.

Horizontal bars should be so fastened that they do not turn in the hands and cannot work out of their frames.

The ground beneath apparatus should be free from stumps and rocks and hard surfacing; the landing area should be softened regularly by spading up the earth. Sand and shavings may also be used to soften landing areas.

Safety teachings:

Children should be taught to use each piece of apparatus safely.

They should be taught to follow directions when group participation is necessary.

They should be taught to have a concern for the safety of others.[2]

From time to time, a Parent-Teacher Association becomes interested in adding to the permanent equipment of an elementary school. Several standards must be borne in mind in advising a committee from this organization. First, some piece of equipment that is currently popular may have caught the attention of the group. Second, the suggestions made by the committee may be based upon the experiences of these parents in physical education several years prior to this need. Third, the parents are often unaware of developments in physical education and thereby omit possible items from consideration. Advice to a Parent-Teacher Association on what to consider should include information on the physiological activity advantages of various types of equipment, comparative prices of several suggested items, as well as the cost

---

[1] *Physical Education for Nebraska Elementary Schools.* Prepared under the supervision of Dudley Ashton, University of Nebraska. Edited by George E. Rotter, Curriculum Coordinator. Issued by Division of Supervision and Curriculum, Floyd A. Miller, Assistant Commissioner, State Capitol, Lincoln, Nebraska. January, 1957, p. 34.

[2] *Ibid.*, pp. 34 and 35.

of upkeep of any contribution that automatically becomes the property of the school.[3]

Seasonal activity equipment for many elementary schools in rural areas is difficult to obtain because of limited budgets, but a suggested list, based upon experience, follows: [4]

1 volleyball (rubber, leather)
1 basketball (junior size) (rubber, leather)
1 soccer ball (rubber, leather)
3 rubber balls (6 inch, 8 inch, 10 inch)
2 12-inch outseam softballs
2 or 3 bats (light to heavy, junior size to regular)
3 or 4 eyeguards

In urban schools, a full supply of seasonal equipment for every classroom is again almost prohibitive because of the expense. Basic lists, however, have been prepared and basic standards established. A rule of thumb used is that of one ball of a type for each six to eight children. The practice of purchasing one volleyball, one soccer ball, one softball, and one general-use rubber ball for a class of thirty to thirty-two children is a mistake. The use of these balls would be in error since a volleyball should not be kicked, the soccer ball would be too heavy for volleying, and the softball has a limited season. More advantageous is the practice of purchasing a supply (four or more of various types) to be used cooperatively by the classrooms of a school. A "ball box," which is light in construction so that two children may carry it, is kept in a central place and checked out and returned by classrooms taking turns in the use of this equipment. Rubber or rubberized balls have longer life than leather ones when used outdoors on rough surfaces or in damp weather. Newer manufacturing processes are improving such balls and standardizing their weight. It would be wise to investigate these balls before deciding on the type to purchase. Both footballs and basketballs now come in junior size. The weight and graduated size of these balls lend themselves to better skill teaching at the elementary level.

Movement exploration is enhanced by the use of small hand equipment. A supply of individual jumping ropes (No. 9 sash cord with the ends dipped in paint to prevent fraying; standard, one rope for every four children), several long ropes, beanbags, colored cloth bands, and hoops are useful in this program. Home-

---

[3] Suggestions credited to Eunice Johnson, Coordinator of Elementary and Secondary Girls Physical Education, Public Schools, Lincoln, Nebraska.
[4] *Physical Education for Nebraska Elementary Schools, op. cit.,* p. 35.

made equipment is not to be discounted. When expense is a major factor, homemade articles such as paddles for paddle tennis, low bars for jumping, and target games for indoor use can be made from scrap material. A maze for running and jumping activities can be easily set up using large tin cans. Discarded containers from detergents with a few beans inside each make excellent rhythmic instruments for creative gymnastic sequences. Beanbags are useful for the same purpose as well as for games. The elementary school probably can use homemade equipment to the best advantage, but table tennis equipment and other items that vary the program are useful at higher levels.

Rhythm band equipment may serve two purposes: use in the music lesson and use for creative movement in physical education. Many schools now have record players available for use in various classes. Recordings for free creative dance, folk dance, play party games, and square dance should certainly be standard items of equipment for elementary schools. Often, a lending library of recordings is established so that each school may have opportunity for a wider selection of materials than would be possible in a single school supply.

Care of large equipment for elementary schools should include:

1. Use of bright paints and seasonal cleaning of apparatus.
2. Protection of ropes, nets, and wood to prevent weathering.
3. Setting upright equipment in concrete with sand below the apparatus.
4. Removing damaged equipment and apparatus promptly for repair.
5. Keeping soft ground under apparatus dug up and raked to prevent packing.
6. Keeping small equipment in orderly and clean style in equipment boxes.
7. Protecting mats by scheduled cleaning and by never dragging them.[5]

Care of balls is discussed later in this chapter.

A final word on equipment for the elementary schools—if the elementary school is the golden age for the learning of motor skills, then adequate equipment should be furnished without question. In the past, the elementary school has often been treated shabbily, with its equipment consisting of discards from other programs or of substandard materials.

[5] Adapted from Elizabeth Halsey and Lorena Porter, *Physical Education for Children, A Developmental Program* (rev. ed.; New York: Holt, Rinehart & Winston, Inc., 1963), p. 123.

SECONDARY SCHOOLS AND COLLEGES

Both permanent and seasonal equipment in secondary schools and colleges are similar. They may vary in quality, in quantity, and in point of emphasis. It takes time to perfect skills; therefore, repetition in the type of activity with progression in skill bases occurs. This fact is sometimes questioned in physical education by those who do not realize how long it takes to establish fine skills. The same instrument, such as the piano, could be used by a music student from early childhood to the launching of a professional career and no one would question the need for this equipment. It is a commentary on physical education personnel that we have not educated our publics to the need for adequate equipment for developing the skills of physical education. The differing emphases at these levels have been discussed in Chapter 2. As far as smaller schools and colleges are concerned, budget limitations may make it necessary to concentrate on fewer types of activities or to spread budget planning over a span of several years, whereas the larger institutions may be able to offer a more varied program. This discussion will concern itself with the types of equipment needed in these programs.

PERMANENT EQUIPMENT

The majority of the permanent equipment for physical education is purchased and installed at the time when the building is erected. Replacements and additional items for new activities are purchased when needed. It seems relevant, therefore, to discuss general policies and practices in the selection of such equipment. The first premise should be the use of the equipment. Will its use be worth the money spent? Permanent equipment is quite expensive, and departments of physical education should be able to justify such expenditures. Second, will this be stationary equipment, or is storage space available for it? Many large pieces of apparatus have been purchased and left at the edge of a gymnasium to become either safety hazards or sources of irritation when facilities are shared. Finally, was every resource exhausted in comparative paper shopping plus consultation with previous users to be sure that the best equipment at the best price was the final decision?

Items such as basketball backboards and goals, installation for net games, diving boards with fulcrum, climbing ropes, stall bars, and telescopic bleachers are usually installed in a building. The exact specifications for the activity situation must be met. Although the woman's program usually does not demand full spectator space, bleachers are needed for demonstrations and clinics. As competition for women increases, there is a need to look ahead and to be sure that any permanent installations that are made will meet the standards for competitive events.

Gymnastic equipment for women is rapidly coming into widespread use. Parallel bars, uneven parallel bars, the buck, the Swedish box, low and high balance beams, several types of mats, and trampolines, plus the accessories needed for these, are being added to the permanent equipment lists for women. Grave consideration must be given to the safety factors. To purchase parallel bars without the special mats needed or a trampoline without safety pads is to jeopardize the usefulness of the equipment.

The reader is advised to consult the excellent lists and installation suggestions available from the Athletic Institute for complete coverage of the above types of permanent equipment.[6, 7] Office furniture will be discussed as a separate category later in this chapter.

SEASONAL EQUIPMENT

Team Sports. It would be ideal if classes could be scheduled for team numbers plus numerous substitutes, but this seldom happens. The solution is enough equipment in both team and individual sports for skill practice to occur at the sides of the courts. Games such as hockey and lacrosse are expensive since each individual must have several articles of equipment, plus the protective equipment needed for the goalies. Soccer, speedball, speed-a-way, volleyball, basketball, and softball are played with one ball, but practice is impossible without at least one ball for every four players. Bats in various weights are needed for softball. Safety equipment is also needed, such as shin guards, goal guards, catchers' masks, mitts, gloves, and chest protectors. Field games require installation of goals (either permanent or marked by flags). Young women appreciate a game in which a football is used and a few of the rules and strategies of the game explained. Because of the size of the girls' hands, a junior size football is advised.

Individual Sports. Because of the nature of the activity, it is difficult to teach individual sports in large classes. Therefore, this

---

6 *Planning Facilities for Health, Physical Education and Recreation* (rev. ed.; Chicago: The Athletic Institute, 1965).

7 *Equipment and Supplies for Athletics* (Chicago: The Athletic Institute, 1960).

program is found in secondary schools when classes can be small, for example, elective activities. At the college level, an effort is made to emphasize individual sports. Probably the most widely used individual sports for women and girls are badminton, archery, golf, and tennis. Each of these sports demands equipment for every player. By ascertaining the average size class in a situation and by judicious purchase over a period of time, classes in these sports can be equipped. Players are frequently asked to furnish their own golf or tennis balls, badminton birds, and, in some instances, arrows. Racquets for tennis and badminton, matching sets of golf clubs, and bows, arrows, arm guards, finger tabs, and targets for archery are usually furnished. There are additional items needed to teach these activities. Arrow quivers for archery, and putting cups, composition mats, and, if possible, a golf cage are used.

Fencing is taught when the department can afford the equipment and has personnel able to teach this sport. A special rack to hold the foils is necessary to prevent breakage. Each student must have a foil, a mask, and a fencing jacket (quilted cotton or padded canvas). Rubber tips for foils, extra blades, and extra bibs for the masks are additional items needed.

Very few departments of physical education for women have their own bowling alleys. Usually, facilities in the community or the college are used. Girls should be taught the correct weight of bowling ball (10–14 lbs.) to use, good taste in clothing to secure freedom of movement, and the use of bowling shoes on the alleys.

Track and Field. Track and field, after years of retirement from the program, is coming to the front again. Most classes use the running events without benefit of starting blocks. If an indoor or an outdoor track can be shared with the men, more sophisticated events can be scheduled. The same balls used in the sports program may be utilized again for distance throws. If safety can be controlled, the javelin and the discus are well liked by girls. A practice rubber discus is less dangerous than the official discus and should be utilized in early practices. These are inexpensive. Metal measuring tapes and stop watches are absolutely necessary.

Dance. A good piano or a good record player is the basic equipment needed for all types of dance. Over a period of years, a library of dance recordings can be built up so that a department has at hand materials for modern, folk, square, and social dance. Percussion instruments add to the interest and the variety of dance experiences. Starting with a dance drum and adding gradually, a fine collection of percussion instruments is possible. Included in such a collection should be gongs, cymbals, wood blocks, scrapers, xylophones, triangles, tone sticks, clappers, bells, castanets, tambourines, and maracas. Excellent storage must be provided so that recordings do not become cracked, broken, or warped. A cabinet with slits and shelves for each recording is suggested. Percussion instruments react to changes in temperature and are affected by humidity. A percussion closet should be ventilated and provided with both temperature and humidity controls.

Aquatics. The aquatic program is no longer limited to swimming and diving. Scuba diving, synchronized water ballet, lifesaving classes, and various forms of small craft instruction have expanded the program. Equipment to teach all these forms, along with necessary safety devices, has now been added. Lifesaving equipment (jackets), as well as buoys, ropes, poles, and pool-testing kits, is as necessary as flutter boards, water game balls and goals, and diving boards. The opportunity to learn to handle small craft (canoes, rowboats, and sailboats) adds to the equipment needs in this area.

Self-testing Areas. The same mats used for gymnastics may be used for stunts and tumbling. Small items such as beat and reuther boards are sometimes used. There is an overlap here in the use of some game equipment and in the use of permanently installed devices.

Adaptives. A specifically equipped area for persons who have physical limitations is usually provided for adaptive exercise. Certain permanent installations found in this area are stall bars, suspension apparatus, wall mirrors, and pulleys with weights. Plinths, trucks with small, light-weight mats for individual exercise, scales, bicycle ergometers, a rowing machine, weights on dollies, and various kinds of recreational sports equipment are also used. A silhouettograph, screens, a camera, floodlights, a conformateur, and picture developing equipment add to the value of the posture program. This area and its equipment should be restricted to the use of the adaptive program and should be carefully supervised.

First-Aid and Rest Rooms. All schools and colleges provide first-aid and rest rooms. A white sanitary cabinet should be provided for storage plus constant availability of first-aid supplies. Standards for first-aid supplies change as knowledge in this field advances; therefore, the listing below needs to be supplemented annually. The basic first-aid supplies are:

Soap (tincture of green preferred)
Triangular bandages and splints (new plastic splints are available)

Scissors
Antiseptic applicators
Rubbing alcohol
Merthiolate
Sterilized bandages—1- and 2-inch widths
Sterilized gauze in glass jar
Sterilized absorbent cotton in glass jar
Adhesive tape
Band-aids in several sizes and types
Unguentine or other preparation for burns
Wooden tongue depressors
Clinical thermometer
Chemical cold packs (a second supply should be kept with field
    equipment)

The usual office equipment of desk, chair, and filing cabinet is
needed. Such an office should be equipped with running hot and
cold water and a telephone. Scales with a stadiometer, eye charts,
and a full-length mirror add to the usefulness of the first-aid room.
For students who are ill or who need rest, cots should be available.
Sheets, pillow slips, and washable blankets are needed. Laundry
is often a problem, so the use of paper pillow shams is suggested.

Lockers and Baskets. Lockers and storage baskets come in a
number of sizes and combinations of types and are generally purchased as a part of the permanent equipment at the time that a
building is erected. When enrollments increase or when this equipment reaches the point where repairs are too expensive for the
projected usefulness of the equipment, replacements become a
budget item. Consideration of the standards to use and of types
of such equipment available has been discussed in Chapter 7. If
lockers with built-in locks are used, one problem is solved. Padlocks, however, are usually provided for baskets that are individually used, and padlocks are often used to secure lockers. Selection
of padlocks is a matter of evaluation of samples and the feasibility
of the use of combinations with a master key for emergency use by
a staff member. Although the initial expense is large, the administration of padlocks is comparatively simple. Code sheets are prepared for the locker record, and a double locker card is used in assigning students to lockers. If lockers have been arranged in groups
of six for use in a six-period day, one locker from each group is
assigned to one student in each period (code sheets so arranged)
in order to facilitate speed in dressing for class. At the same time,
the double card is filled out; one half is placed on file, and the other
half is given to the student. Each student is held financially responsible for the padlock issued and must check in the padlock

at the end of the activity season. Samples of a code sheet and a locker or basket assignment card are given in Fig. 8–1.

OFFICE EQUIPMENT AND SUPPLIES

Every teacher of physical education at any level needs a minimum of a desk and chair, a file, and a bookcase. In elementary

```
┌─────────────────────────────────────────────────────────────┐
│  ┌──────────┐        LOCKER RECORD         ┌──────────┐       │
│  │          │        Womens' Gym           │          │       │
│  └──────────┘                              └──────────┘       │
│  Locker No.                                 Padlock No.        │
│                                                               │
│  Name_____        │
│  Receipt No._____ Fr.____ Soph.____ Jr.____ Sr.____   │
│  Date_____        │
│  - - - - - - - - - - - - - - - - - - - - - - - - - - -        │
│                                                               │
│                      Student Copy                             │
│                                                               │
│  Grant East_____        Coliseum_____          │
│  Grant West_____        Ag College_____        │
│                                                               │
│                 HOW TO OPEN THIS LOCK                         │
│              Depress shackle before operating                 │
│                                                               │
│  Turn right two whole turns and stop at        No._____    │
│  Turn left one whole turn past above                          │
│  number and stop at                            No._____    │
│  Turn to right and stop at                     No._____    │
│  TO CLOSE—Snap shackle in lock.                               │
└─────────────────────────────────────────────────────────────┘
```

Fig. 8–1(a). Sample locker record card.

Locker No.	Name	Padlock No.	Combination
101		54582	14-26-39
102		54128	10-18-28
103		54379	12-24-0
104		54267	8-32-15

Fig. 8–1(b). Sample locker record sheet.

schools and in small secondary schools, it is often futile to expect more, and this equipment may be placed in an equipment room or at the edge of a gymnasium. If the staff is to do the best possible work, privacy for preparation and conferences and equipment with which to work are needed. A flat-top metal desk, double pedestal style, is probably the best buy. Desk chairs that can be adjusted for correct height are conducive to better sitting posture. Open metal bookcases, a metal two-drawer letter file with small card spaces above, and a small extra chair should complete this minimum office equipment.

Staff members in large schools and colleges need storage space for records and books, a typewriter with table, and, often, tables or counters for work space.

The main office of a department of physical education needs counter space with locked file drawers in various sizes underneath it (Fig. 8–2). A bank of locked letter files, desks and chairs for

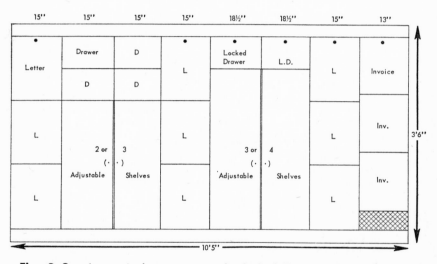

Fig. 8–2. A practical arrangement for locked-file space beneath counters (standard-size units used).

secretaries, typewriters, an adding machine, a duplicating machine (mimeograph, copying machine, ditto), work tables, and desk lamps are necessary. If dictating machines are in use, the transcriber must be placed beside the typewriter. The reception section of the office needs a small magazine table, a lamp, and several comfortable chairs.

Office equipment is generally furnished to the teacher or the administrator without consultation. When new facilities are planned, there is an opportunity to improve the efficiency of the office by judicious selection of office equipment.

Office supplies depend upon budget allocations. In public school systems, the format of roll books, grading sheets, and departmental forms are decisions made by central administrative officers. Letterheads and general office supplies are made available by the central office of each school. In college departments, there is usually a budget allocation for office supplies. The necessary printing is included with supplies drawn by requisition from general stores at cost price.

EQUIPMENT PRIORITIES

Several principles hold fast in equipment priorities: (1) the greatest good for the greatest number, (2) maximum use of the equipment, (3) use of equipment under local conditions. Equipment is too expensive to allow the money expended to go to waste. Therefore, it is only common sense to set priorities and to hold to these. The purchase of a trampoline that can accommodate only one or two persons at a time and at an expense that would supply numerous types of game equipment for large numbers is an example under priority one. The purchase of hockey equipment is a fine expenditure but not if only one class in the entire school is to be scheduled to play hockey. It then becomes a violation of priority two. Skiing is an excellent sport and can be handled satisfactorily in classes. Skiing equipment that is provided for classes at an institution on the edges of the snow belt may be used infrequently. Local conditions demand the purchase of another type of equipment. Perhaps compasses to be used in a pioneering project would be a better investment. Definite priorities to fit all conditions cannot be stated. The fact remains that each administrator needs to look at his program, his facilities, his students, and his environment and set his priorities accordingly.

CRITERIA FOR PURCHASING EQUIPMENT

The first criterion in the purchase of equipment is implied in the priorities listed above. The equipment recommended for purchase must fit the program. Extraneous purchasing is inexcusable. Recommendations for equipment must not exceed budget allocations;

so, it is wise to investigate prices (comparative shopping) in order to stay within one's ability to pay. The use of standardized equipment that meets sports specifications enables one to buy from open stock, and, in the case of large departments, quantity buying represents a saving for the department. Administrators are advised to be sure of specifications, however, as the word "official" stamped on equipment is no longer a guarantee of quality or of the latest specifications. Quality buying saves money in the long run. Testing equipment within a department to ascertain the best use and the lasting qualities, in relation to a local program, is highly recommended. Cut-rate cheap balls, racquets, clothing items, or even gymnasium mats often prove to be expensive. It is unnecessary, however, to pay for extra styling. Usually, purchase of quality equipment in the medium price range from reputable firms will be sufficient. The practice of marking equipment with the departmental name and date of purchase enables one not only to identify and thus prevent certain losses in equipment but also to judge the wearing qualities of these purchases.

DETAILS OF ADMINISTRATION OF EQUIPMENT

A listing of these details seems more expedient than a full discussion:

1. Inventories with subsequent ordering at the end of an activity season expedites the program.
2. Marking equipment enables one to study wearing qualities and also informs the student that the department values the equipment. Use of different paint colors enables the teacher to identify such items as length of hockey sticks. Marking pens, stencils, and marking irons are standard items of equipment.
3. Students must be taught to respect their equipment. Such malpractices as sitting on balls, banging the heads of racquets against hard surfaces, using hockey sticks or lacrosse equipment as crutches, dragging mats across floors, using apparatus while wearing street shoes, and removing stains with expensive towels are open opportunities for "teachable moments."
4. The staff may become lax in notifying ancillary personnel of their need for items of either permanent or seasonal equipment that is kept in dead storage. A weekly request sheet to be given to the custodian or matron on Friday may solve this difficulty.
5. Both students and staff must be reminded that equipment cannot be carelessly handled or left behind in activity areas. It is good physical education to teach students to distribute, to collect, and to

report equipment at each class period, and each teacher should record the exact equipment in use by individual students. This constant check enables repairs to be made at once and forecasts needs for replacements. A check-out system enables the department to keep these factors under control (see Fig. 8–3). An equipment counter for check-out purposes speeds this process.

6. All equipment must be kept in good condition for immediate use. Rainy seasons, inadequate storage, and lack of small-repair know-how of equipment cause these problems to multiply. A small reserve supply of seasonal equipment, if financially feasible, is advised.

7. Storage of equipment in well-planned storage areas (shelves, bins, hangers) prolongs the life of equipment and contributes to the efficiency of the department. Humidity and temperature controls plus excellent ventilation are needed for such areas.

8. Safety equipment such as shin guards, chest protectors, gloves and mitts, arm guards, and, above all else, guards for glasses must be provided, and the students must be educated to their use. A new problem is the increasing use of contact lenses, particularly on the part of young women. Teachers should find out who wears contacts and watch this situation closely.

CLOTHING

Students usually furnish their own costumes for classes in physical education. In a few places where local laws permit the prac-

DEPARTMENT OF PHYSICAL EDUCATION FOR WOMEN					
CLASS EQUIPMENT CHECK-OUT SHEET					
Items	Number	Day and Class Hour	Out – Teacher's Initials	In – Teacher's Initials	Remarks

Fig. 8–3. Sample equipment check-out sheet.

tice, clean costumes are furnished each time the class meets, with the students furnishing their own socks and tennis shoes. Using marking pencils to identify each student's personal equipment at the beginning of the school year is time well spent. Under either circumstance, the department of physical education should extend effort to judge the quality of the materials in use. Costumes for girls and women should be easily washable, pretested for shrinkage, and colorfast. Many fabrics are difficult to judge; therefore, one must depend upon reliable manufacturers to maintain these standards. If textile laboratories are available in the institution or in a nearby institution, the cooperation of the department of home economics can often be secured, and fabrics tested for tensile strength, a thread count made, and advice secured on the general attributes of the material in question. In like manner, a joint project on the care of costumes for physical education may be undertaken by these two departments covering the best laundry practices, repair of garments, and personal grooming for activities.

Girls and women use lightweight tank suits for the swimming program. Although in many instances, students would be quite willing to bring their own suits, there are sanitary reasons prohibiting such a practice. Every suit must be thoroughly washed and dried after every use in water temperatures established by sanitary needs. Modern bathing suits are constructed from a variety of materials that react differently to laundering routines. It would be impossible to administer the institutional laundry without destruction of some fabrics in personally owned bathing suits. A conservative style suit is also advised for school and college use. Knit tank suits of cotton fibers, mixtures of cotton and wool, cotton and nylon, or other synthetic fibers now may be procured in attractive colors. A *double*-knit suit keeps its shape and stands up well under daily use. All-nylon suits are attractive but quite expensive. All suits must be carefully checked out and in with a small reserve supply kept under lock and key. Too large a reserve supply is a waste, as knit materials deteriorate as they lie unused on shelves.

Leotards for the modern dance program are used in high school dance clubs and in the total college program. Currently, many students own their own leotards. In other instances, they are rented for a small fee or furnished by the department. Leotard materials are usually the same fabrics as tank suits, with some experimentation with other stretch fabrics. In selecting leotards, a material heavy enough to maintain its contours yet easy to launder should be chosen. Leotards come in many colors, but basic black is probably the best choice.

Towels are a major problem in physical education. The best practice is to furnish one towel per student for use at the end of each class. An administrator may figure his towel needs based upon peak load times the number of classes per day times the number of completed laundry services per week. A reserve supply of 10 per cent will usually cover the total need. Towels are made of heavy cotton terry cloth weave. Usually 18″ × 36″ or 20″ × 40″ towels are used. When commercial laundry resources must be used, towel laundering is a major budget item.

MISCELLANEOUS ITEMS

Depending upon the program offered in the department of physical education, there are numerous miscellaneous items of equipment needed. Some of these are sanitary needs such as liquid soap; others are instructional needs such as a good skeleton and several muscle charts for anatomy and kinesiology classes. A sewing machine (used) is a good investment; with its use, the need for sewing supplies arises. Many of these items defy classification, but the need is apparent. A small contingency fund on the budget will help to cover such needs as they arise.

CARE, REPAIR, AND MAINTENANCE

The details of care, repair, and maintenance of equipment need a volume all their own. The presentation in Table 8–1 is an outline of certain major factors to be observed in the use of various equipment *materials* in physical education. See also Table 8–2.

Table 8–1

Materials Used in Physical Education *

Items	Descriptive Properties	Care
Natural Fibers		
1. Cotton	Advantages:	
	Absorbent, cool, comfortable	Wash carefully after each use
	Inexpensive upkeep	May be laundered at high water temperature
	Launders well	Vacuum and brush cotton canvas mats; air periodically
	Stronger when wet	

* Information on fibers courtesy of June Ericson, Associate Professor, Department of Home Economics, Arizona State University, Tempe, Arizona.

Items	Descriptive Properties	Care
	Disadvantages: 　Subject to mold, silver- 　　fish, crickets 　Lacks elasticity; 　　wrinkles 　Excessive chlorine 　　bleaches—bleeding 　Subject to ultraviolet 　　light—weather de- 　　teriorates it	Cotton tank suits should 　be carefully stored Outdoor cotton nets 　should be tarred and 　taken down when not 　in use
Wash and wear finish	Advantages: 　Wrinkle resistant Disadvantages: 　Reduced tear strength 　May retain chlorine 　Picks up oily soils more 　　easily	Better to air dry and 　hang up wet Machine dry at cool cycle 　and remove at once Avoid unreasonable soil- 　ing and pretreat soiled 　spots No bleaches unless tag on 　garment indicates their 　use
Types: 　Gabardines: may be 　wool, cotton, rayon, 　or combinations; nylon 　blend for strength	Firmly woven, warp- 　faced cloth, closely 　set, raised diagonal 　ribs or cords	Launder or dry clean 　carefully dependent 　upon fiber content
Poplin	Horizontal ribs run across 　from selvage to selvage Coarser rib than broad- 　cloth Heavier weights may be 　preshrunk, and wind 　and water repellent 　treatment possible	Outdoor garments of 　heavier weight—if 　water repellent 　treated, washable 　with care
Cotton duck	Can be finished to resist 　mold and mildew and 　to be water repellent; 　can be treated with fire 　retardant	Launder cotton duck 　shower curtains 　regularly
Terry cloth—pile weave	Absorbent finish	Towels should be laun- 　dered in hot water 　and fluff dried
Stretch cottons	Slack-mercerized Minimal stretch Comfortable	Avoid excessive heat in 　laundering Avoid wringing
2. Wool	Advantages: 　Absorbs moisture with- 　　out feeling wet (30%)	

Items	Descriptive Properties	Care
	Has elasticity—does not wrinkle	
	Resists abrasion	Substitute other materials
	Takes color easily	if individuals are
	Has warmth	allergic to wool
	Soft—easy to wear	
	Disadvantages:	
	Absorbs and holds odors	A sanitized finish helps prevent this
	Felting problem—shrinks and becomes stiff	
	Friction accumulates some static electricity	Humidifiers will help
	Low tensile strength	Dry cleaning recommended unless labeled washable (follow directions)
	Weaker wet than dry	Launder carefully with mild soap in low water temperature
	Subject to loss of strength in sunlight	"Block" before drying
	Subject to moths and carpet beetles	Keep garments clean—use moth preventives and store in sealed boxes

Note: Labeling laws demand that wool be tagged (1) Virgin; (2) Reworked—as reprocessed from scraps or reused from worn clothing.

Types:		
Worsted	Long fibers lie parallel in the yarn; will give good wear	
Woolens	Short fibers—a loosely spun yarn	

Man-Made Fibers

Non-thermoplastic (not softened or melted by heat but will scorch)

1. Rayon	Advantages: Inexpensive (viscose)	
Trade-names:	Absorbent—easy to dye	
Avisco Rayon	Comfortable, soft, easy to wear	
Enka Rayon	Does not accumulate static electricity	
Celanese Rayon	Not subject to moths	
	Does not pill	

Items	Descriptive Properties	Care
	Disadvantages:	
	Does not launder as satisfactorily as cotton; loss of strength when wet	Press carefully to avoid scorching or burning
	Lacks elasticity and resilience; wrinkles	May be treated with resin
	Lacks staple dimensional stability (when cut in short lengths)	
	Loses body gradually when laundered or dry cleaned	
	Loses strength on exposure to sunlight	
Dope-dyed Rayon	Advantages:	
	Can be solution dyed	
Trade-names:	Does not fade	
Avicolor		
Coloray		
Colorspun Rayon		
Jetspun		
Dy-lok		
2. Newer forms		
a. Avron	Advantages:	
	Stronger than regular rayon; approved fabrics carry label	Less care required in laundering than regular rayons
	Good abrasion resistance; resists scuffing wear	
	Can be resin treated for wrinkle resistance	
	Disadvantages:	
	Not as shrinkage resistant as high-wet modulus	
	Higher priced than regular rayon	
b. Fortisan	Advantages:	
	Great strength yet lightweight	May be laundered at high temperatures
	Little loss of strength when wet	
	Good light and weather resistance	
	Dimensionally stable	
	Disadvantages:	
	Poor wrinkle resistance	
	Expensive	

Items	Descriptive Properties	Care
c. Corval	Advantages: Dimensional stability— no progressive shrinkage With resin finish, less fraying, less loss of tear strength than regular rayon Can be slack- mercerized for stretch fabrics	
d. High-wet modulus Trade-names: Avril Zantrel Lirelle Moyver	Advantages: Can be resin treated for crease resistance Absorbent, comfortable Blends well with ther- moplastic fibers such as nylon, dacron, acrilan, orlon; re- stricts movement of these fibers in yarns Stability equal to cotton Higher wet and dry strengths Can be mercerized and sanforized Does not accumulate static electricity	

Thermoplastic (will soften with heat, become pliable, and may melt under high temperature)

Items	Descriptive Properties	Care
1. Acetate Trade-names: Celanese Acetate Acele Acetate Estron Acetate Avisco Acetate	Advantages: Resists sunlight and creasing better than cellulose Soft, pleasant feel Resists staining and soiling Inexpensive Moth and mildew resistant Dries more quickly than cellulose fibers	Sharkskin—used for ten- nis costumes Washes easily—must be carefully ironed at low temperatures Boiling water may damage the fabric
Dope-dyed acetate Trade-names: Chromspun Celaperm Color Sealed Color Spun	Disadvantages: Weaker when wet Subject to gas fading unless solution dyed Heat softness at low temperature	

Items	Descriptive Properties	Care
2. Arnel Jersey Sharkskin	Advantages: More wrinkle resistant than acetate Somewhat higher resistance to gas fading than acetate Can be heat set and permanently pleated Disadvantages: Lower absorbency than cellulose Some accumulation of static electricity	Dance costumes—completely washable, dries quickly Hot water does not damage the fabric May be ironed at higher temperatures than acetate
3. Nylons	Advantages: Elasticity Strength Resists abrasion; long wear Dimensionally stable Light in weight but has the warmth of wool Disadvantages: Non-absorbent; in heat, it is uncomfortable Develops static electricity Expensive Transparent, translucent—untextured yarns lack cover Heavy or oily soil is difficult to remove	Washable; dries quickly Woven nylon—use of temperature hot enough to remove soil may develop permanent wrinkles Press only at low temperatures Will pick up other colors in laundering so whites must be washed alone Avoid white or pastels for costumes
Newer forms: Antron Cantrece Textured nylons a. Stretch b. Bulked Trade-names: Ban-Lon Texturalized Spunized Tycora Taslan Skyloft	Better cover Excellent shape retention Bulk developed for better cover	Used for leotards, tank suits Launder after each use

Items	Descriptive Properties	Care
4. Polyesters	**Advantages:**	
	Resists wrinkling best, wet or dry	Wash carefully by hand or use the wash and
Dacron		wear cycle on machine
Kodel	Less translucent than nylon	
Kodel IV	Dimensionally stable	
Fortrel	High strength, elongation, abrasion resistance	
	Built-in whiteness	
Vycron	Resists pill (used in knitted fabrics)	
	Blends with other fibers	
	Disadvantages:	
	Pills (balls of fibers pull to surface)	
	Wicks resistance—moisture travels along the fiber out or in	
	Oily soil difficult to remove	Pretreat heavy and oily soil
	Static electricity develops	
5. Acrylics	**Advantages:**	
	Lightweight but warm	
Orlon	Good covering power	
	Good breaking strength	
	Crease and abrasion resistant	
	Resists weather and ultraviolet light	Ideal for outdoor use
	Disadvantages:	
	Alkali yellows white (soap or detergent content)	Better to wash than dry clean
	Develops static electricity	Knitted garments tend to shrink and discolor
	Staple pills	
Acrilan	Melts at lower temperature than orlon	
	Crisp, springy fibers	
Creslan	Dyes better than orlon	Used for knits, sweaters
	Manufacturer permits label only on approved article that meets the standards	Pile fabrics—fake fur, pile liners for warm coats

Items	Descriptive Properties	Care
Zefran	Dyes more easily than other acrylics Lower pill Blends well with other fibers	Use in play clothes expected to increase

6. Modacrylics	Advantages:
	  Good insulation
	  Resilient
	  Fire resistant
	  Mold resistant
	  Dyes easily and is colorfast
		Used as pile liner in ski boots, parkas
		Must be laundered at low temperatures
		Air drying best

	Disadvantages:
	  Heat sensitive; stiffens, delusters
	  In sunlight, deteriorates at same rate as cotton
		Do not iron pile liners

Verel	Resists weathering Low pill Wrinkle resistant Strong, high tensile strength	
7. Olefins	Advantages: Lightweight, will float on water; does not deteriorate in salt water	Used for marine lines Ski boot liners
Vectra Reevon	Chemically inert Not absorbent	

Herculon	Disadvantages:
	  Brittle in low temperatures
	  Sensitive to ultraviolet light—degradation
	  Will melt under low heat
	  Takes dye poorly
	  Under stretch—will not recover	

Elastic Fibers		

1. Rubber	Advantages:
	  Highly elastic
	  Absorbent, comfortable
	  Completely washable
		Hand wash and air dry
		Do not use bleaches

Lastex Lactron	Disadvantages: Deteriorates at high temperatures, from body and other oils, and under dry cleaning solvents	

Items	Descriptive Properties	Care
2. Yarns (thermoplastic fibers) Helanca Superloft Fluflon Agilon		
3. Spandex Lycra Blue C Duraspan Spandelle Vyrene	Advantages: Spandex core with fiber sheath Quite elastic Equal resistance to elongation as rubber but lighter weight Resists perspiration and body oils Good abrasion resistance Tightens under tension Disadvantages: Low strength but compensated by elongation Yellows under heat and light Sticks at 34° F	Used in woven and knit sportswear Machine wash and dry carefully at low temperature Used in swimming suits, support bandages, foundation garments
Metals (iron, wire, steel)	Advantages: Durability Low upkeep Disadvantages: Must be protected against rusting Scratches	Store in dry place Heavy—store on floor to avoid accidents Outdoor equipment— paint to protect Lacquer metal parts of equipment Racquets—oil carefully to prevent rusting Fencing foils—hang separately on a rack Fencing masks—store in separate compartments
Feathers	Advantages: Lightweight Can control flight action Disadvantages: Very fragile	Store in cool place—use humidifier Feathers (arrows) can be replaced with care
Leathers	Advantages: Strength—kangaroo hide Durability—cowhide, kangaroo hide Softness and pliability —sheepskin, kan-	Use deterrents for mice If wet, dry gradually at room temperature Store in cool, dry place in separate compartments

Items	Descriptive Properties	Care
	garoo hide	Use saddle soap to clean
	Water resistance—	balls
	kangaroo hide	Keep balls inflated to
	Scuff resistance—horse-	stated pressures in
	hide, kangaroo hide	season—partially de-
		flated for storage
	Disadvantages:	Repair rips or tears
	Brittle under heat	
	Subject to deteriora-	
	tion from grease or	
	oil	
Wood	Advantages:	
	Hard woods—strength,	Keep sticks, bats, and
	resiliency, light-	playground equipment
	weight	smooth and free from
	Plywood—a good ply	splinters
	used for certain	Never store on damp
	equipment; easy to	floors
	clean and less likely	Rack items horizontally
	to warp and split	to prevent warping
	with grain than solid	Use varnish to lengthen
		life of item
		Rub hockey sticks with
		linseed oil
	Disadvantages:	
	May warp	Racquets—clean with
	May break if brittle	damp cloth; place in
		presses to prevent
		warping
		Archery bows—hang
		unstrung
Fiberglas (laminated)	Advantages:	
	Flexible	May be washed in light
	Heat resistant	soap and water; rinsed
	Very strong	and air dried
	Lightweight	
Rubber		
Vulcanized	Advantages:	
	Elasticity	Clean with mild soap
	Waterproof	and water
	High shock absorption	Clean and paint field
	High frictional re-	hockey balls
	sistance on dry sur-	Replace broken valves
	faces	in balls
	Disadvantages:	
	Slick when wet	Do not expose to oils and
	Brittle under extreme	grease
	temperature	Do not expose to extreme
		heat or cold
Foam	Advantages:	
	Shock absorption	Clean mat covers with
		mild soap and water

Items	Descriptive Properties	Care
	Disadvantages: Explosive Becomes moisture soaked and loses its life Unless covered, deteriorates from industrial or heating fumes	Avoid rolling Store in dry place
Plastics (usually protective equipment)	Advantages: Molds easily Supported with knit on woven backing—more resistant to tearing	Easily cleaned with soap and water
	Disadvantages: Sensitive to extreme heat and cold Brittle—will snap; ages and becomes stiff because of loss of plasticizer Sensitive to chemical reactions	Avoid extreme temperature Avoid strain, such as rolling mats Do not place in contact with lacquers or paint

Table 8–2

Normal Stretch Qualities of Fabrics

	Stretch Levels Needed (as represented by two leading manufacturers)		
	Company A		Company B
Elbow flex	Vertical:	35–40%	19%
	Horizontal:	15–22	
Shoulder flex		13–16	15
Knee flex	Vertical:	35–45	40
	Horizontal:	12–14	13
Seat flex		4–6	5
Spectator sportswear		20–35	45–60
Active sportswear		35–50	65–70

TERMS USED:

Power stretch (action stretch). Stretch fabrics with more extensibility and quicker recovery (30–50%). Particularly adapted to sportswear.

Comfort stretch. Garments for everyday use. Stretch factor (30%).

Core spinning. A spinning process enclosing an elastic fiber under stretch in a sheath of staple fibers. The yarn is elastic to the point of original elongation (stretch).

SUMMARY

This chapter has been concerned with the equipment needs of physical education at various age levels and under various conditions. Permanent equipment conducive to the development of children and youth and seasonal activity equipment have been suggested. The supplies needed to support the physical education program have been stated. Priorities, criteria, and details of the administration have been discussed. The care and maintenance of the materials used in physical education have received attention. It is the hope of the author that realization of the tools needed to conduct physical education together with responsibility for their care and maintenance will produce finer and finer products for use in the physical education program.

PROBLEMS

1. Select an area of physical education (for example, golf). List the essential equipment required to conduct a class of thirty, and state how to care for and repair this equipment.

2. Plan ideal playground equipment for a class of twenty-four younger children (kindergarten to grade two).

3. Plan developmental playground equipment for the intermediate grades, and state the developmental properties of the equipment chosen.

4. Discuss the need for adequate protection of all types of physical education seasonal equipment. Set up a plan for staff responsibility for equipment on a daily, seasonal, and an annual basis.

5. Select one of the new synthetic materials. Trace its use in *all* types of physical education equipment, and indicate the type of care it requires.

6. Discuss the advantages and the limitations in the use of a custodian for equipment issue and collection.

7. List and justify your priorities in activity equipment for an elementary school of 75 children. For a secondary school with 500 girls enrolled in physical education. For a small college with coeducational classes (250 men and women in physical education).

9

Business Techniques

Widening sources of leisure time, together with an awakening awareness of the necessity for physical fitness, have more firmly established interest in sports and other leisure-time pursuits in our culture. Concurrently, the amount of money spent on sports equipment and sports facilities of various types is extending the economic contribution of such pursuits. With cultural pressure of this kind, demands for the introduction of new activities, the building of more and better facilities, and upgrading in the preparation of personnel are resulting. Each of these factors has economic import. No one has ever denied that physical education is relatively expensive as compared with the use of classroom areas for certain academic pursuits. This being the case, business techniques are of major importance to the administration of physical education if the best possible program is to result.

FINANCING THE PROGRAM

Ideally, an administrator would like to develop a program in physical education and assume that it would be supported by the college or local community. In reality, financial support for the physical education program may determine its extent. The management of funds assigned to the program of physical education is one of the major responsibilities of the administrator. Whether funds are generous or scanty, the administrator has an obligation to handle his resources carefully and in the best interest of both his students and the public(s) supplying his support.

SOURCES OF FINANCE

The public schools and state-supported colleges of this country are supported primarily by taxation. This support may occur in a variety of ways: by local and/or state property tax levies, by

213

state aid in an attempt to equate opportunities between low and high economic-level communities, and by federal aid for special projects (supported by federal taxes). Although physical education has advanced to the point where minimal programs are generally supported by tax funds, the administrator often finds himself in the role of supplicator, either when needs increase or when enriched programs are under consideration. Moreover, we are not sophisticated in the matter of securing federal aid for research. Such items as format for presentation of research proposals, formulas for ascertaining costs of overhead, and reimbursement to cover additional staff when the professional staff is released for research are matters to which administrators in physical education must give grave attention in the near future.

Private schools and colleges rely, to a large degree, upon tuition fees and private endowments for their support. Public colleges also include tuition fees in their sources of income and are increasingly seeking endowments for educational purposes from foundations and alumni.

In both public and private secondary schools and colleges, student fees may be set up to cover the costs of physical education and athletics. Depending upon local or state laws, instruction in physical education may be supported by funds, but athletics, where gate receipts are charged, are considered an amusement and must rely upon their own resources. The battle to secure adequate support for instructional programs for girls and women has been grim and is still not completely resolved. If athletics have educational values, then it follows that they deserve support. This point is made in the interest of maintaining the educational values in competition for women lest we find ourselves with tax support withdrawn and facing the financial pressures and problems long known in athletics for men.

There are schools and colleges that rely upon money-raising devices to support physical education and athletics. Concession rights operated by the school itself or by a subsidiary group within the school may become the source of extensive revenues. Dances, bake sales, circus events, joy nights (skits), or even a box supper may be the vehicle if financial support is not available from regular sources. Needless to say, budgets based upon such events are on a precarious footing.

CAPITAL IMPROVEMENT

In planning long-term capital improvements, special appropriations from legislatures and building fund endowments from private sources are the usual financial sources tapped in colleges. In public schools, physical education facilities are included in the askings when school bond issues (a form of deferred taxation) are placed before the public for vote. In both cases, the administrator has a responsible assignment in preplanning and seeing to the end the facilities under consideration. Details of such planning are discussed in Chapter 7.

BUDGETS

Having determined where the financial support for the physical education program can be secured, it is then necessary to plan carefully how this money may be spent. This process is called "budgeting." There are numerous reasons for developing a budget. The careful planning necessary controls expenditures in terms of the amount of money available and in terms of the relative values of the various phases of the program. Thus, the instructional phases of the program would be allocated more funds than the recreational phases. The budget calls attention to activities needing more or better equipment, to omissions in the program, to activities on the decline, and to the development of enrichment activities. Budgets, with the resultant accounting of funds allocated, protect the staff and the administrator from claims of fraudulent practices in relation to expenditure of public funds. Very seldom is money actually handled by a physical education administrator, but the public is definitely entitled to know how its money is to be expended. Budgets plus the planned expenditures are usually paper transactions, with the actual payments made either by a comptroller, purchasing agent, superintendent of schools, or the treasurer of the board of education.

There are two principal types of budgets: capital budgets and operating budgets (biennial and annual). Capital improvement funds covering acquisition of land, new facilities, and repairs and renovations are usually formulated and allocations assigned by the top administrative officials. It is the obligation of the administrator of physical education to work within such an allocation in planning new facilities or the renovation of old facilities. Under tight controls, suggestions for the wisest expenditure of funds in forwarding a fine program of physical education are made (see Chapter 7). Operating budgets may be prepared over a long projection of years. Salary scales of a school system planned to cover ten to twenty years influence the projection of the budget. Projections of enrollment will also influence the personnel section of an operating budget in terms of additional instructors needed or restrictions operative when birth rates have changed. In the public schools, personnel budgets are prepared by the principal, who recommends to the supervisory staff and to the superintendent regular salary scale increments or merit raises as the case may be. These are reviewed and with attached recommendations are forwarded to the board of education for action. A number of practices are used in college personnel budgets. In small colleges, the personnel budget may be the direct responsibility of the president or the dean of instruction. In larger colleges and universities, a comptroller or vice-president in charge of finance sets up bases for judgment as well as financial limits to be observed by the deans of the various colleges. The deans then consult with departmental chairmen, and personnel budgets including increments are drawn up. These personnel budgets are then reviewed in reverse order and finally are submitted to the governing board for approval. Personnel budgets frequently include funds for professional improvement in advisory or special consultant services. It is obvious that these budgets cover both academic and non-academic personnel.

Maintenance operations (equipment, supplies, etc.) may be projected, if desired, over a period of years, but usually these are planned on an annual or biennial basis. Maintenance budgets in physical education generally cover supplies, equipment, office needs, laundry, medical services, transportation, and similar needs. In public schools, these may be prepared in the central administrative offices, or the principal of either the elementary or the secondary school may have this duty delegated to him. Either the central administration or the principal may require the physical education teacher to submit budget sheets stating his needs and his projected planning. In most colleges and universities, the chairman of the department submits maintenance budgets at the same time and via the same channels as the personnel budget. Separate maintenance budgets may be in order in both secondary schools and colleges for interscholastic sports if these sports are not supported by tax funds. Women should become increasingly aware of these practices as the competitive program develops.

The basic construction of budgets follows two patterns: a blanket budget or a line budget. In the blanket budget, X number of dollars is allocated to a department for its expenses with distribution of the monies assigned by the chairman. It is relatively simple to shift funds when unexpected circumstances occur. In a line budget, a code line number is used; for example, personnel may be designated A-1, A-2, and so on. General expense factors are broken down to fit a numerical code in use throughout the school system or the college. Once a slot or line is assigned to a service or need, its designation does not change, and the administrator is expected to hold to his askings for this line. Line by line, the administrator works out his educated guesses on his biennial or annual needs. Slight shifts are tolerated by the top administration, but shifts in large sums require special permission.

Construction of either blanket or line budgets requires the same information. Data to justify requests must be gathered with regard to equipment needs, activity by activity. After an activity has been established, this is usually replacement, but in initiation of an activity, it may be necessary to spread the expense over a period of years to avoid retrenchment in other activities. For example, to initiate lacrosse, crosses and balls to supply one class might be purchased the first year and use made temporarily of hockey cages and goalie pads. In the second year, a few crosses, lacrosse goalie pads, and more balls could be added. Official lacrosse goals plus the usual replacement and enough crosses to supply a second class could be added the third year. With constant changes in prices of athletic equipment, every department needs current sports catalogs. In visiting exhibitors at professional conferences, it is well to pursue paper comparative buying and to inquire into price trends. Data should be compiled over at least five years, showing cost trends in laundry services, job pool charges (minor repairs), telephone services, office supplies, printing, medical services, insurance, mailing, transportation, and other current expenses. In locales where it is legal, a small cash fund ($25–$50) eases the payment of minor expenses of $1 or so. A contingency item on the budget is an excellent practice. However, this may not be possible on a line budget. In public school systems and in colleges, the spending of monies is accomplished by paper work. Requisitions are written, bids on large items are submitted, orders are placed, and vouchers are received after services or equipment delivery has been completed. A part of the administrator's responsibility is the checking of services, equipment, and supplies before a voucher for payment is signed. See Fig. 9–1.

NON-RECURRING FUNDS

From time to time, school systems or colleges will make available to all departments the opportunity to request equipment on a non-recurring basis. This is generally a special budget, and expendable equipment and supplies are not recognized in this category. Large equipment or apparatus, musical instruments, and

Items	Cost Table					Biennial Asking	Current Year	Summary of Expenditures
	19XX	19XX	19XX	19XX	19XX	19XX-19XX	19XX	19XX
810 Postage	X$	+X$	+X$	-X$	+X$			
811 Telephone	X$	+X$	+X$	+X$	+X$			
812 Printing	X$	+X$	+X$	-X$	-X$			
815 Laundry								
820 Office Supplies								
821 Office Equipment								
822 Office Equipment Repair								
830 Instruction Supplies								
831 Instruction Equipment								
832 Instruction Equipment Repair								
840 Household								
850 Building								

+ = increase in askings.
− = decrease in askings.

Fig. 9—1. Sample budget form.

large or expensive office equipment could be requested under such a category. The source of such a fund varies, but usually it is an institutional contingency fund that has not been exhausted.

ROTATING FUNDS

Elementary schools, secondary schools, and colleges frequently maintain rotating funds. The source of these funds are student activities, including interscholastic athletics. All monies charged for admission to musical events and dramatic presentations, game tickets, student activity tickets, or other fund-raising events are deposited in a rotating fund. These monies are then handled in one of two ways. Funds deposited by a specific activity may be earmarked for use by that activity. In this case, a budget (for example, in athletics) would be prepared similar to the departmental budget with the exception of differing items. Proposals from year to year would take into account expected receipts with proposed expenditures held within these bounds. The second manner in which rotating funds could be handled would be the deposit of income into a general rotating budget. In this case, an activity wishing to make expenditures would be required to present its needs to a committee for action. Rotating funds are not tax derived. A bonded treasurer is needed with a small charge against each activity to cover the cost of administering these funds.

SPENDING THE BUDGET

There are items in the budget for which lump-sum payments are made, such as a yearly station telephone bill. Other items are paid monthly, such as laundry charges, toll telephone calls, and job pool charges. Based upon inventories, budgets for the various activities are established. An administrator must constantly analyze his budget expenditures. A running account is kept, and monthly accounting statements are carefully checked to be sure that departmental funds are conscientiously expended. One suggestion that has proved its worth is the division of the budget into quarters, with adherence to this amount insofar as possible. This practice also avoids accumulation of funds to the end of the year. Sudden spending just at the end of the fiscal year is subject to question of its need.

PURCHASING

The process of purchasing is the same for a one-teacher department in a small public school or a large college department. There are minor differences in the channels used, but briefly this process is as follows:

1. Inventory of equipment in use
2. Requisitions
3. Bids, if necessary
4. Purchase orders
5. Invoices and checking
6. Payment of bills

In a one-teacher situation or a small department, the above process may be carried out in full by the person in charge of the program. For the protection of all persons serving the public, it is recommended that payment be channeled to either the comptroller or the treasurer of the board of education. Every step of the process needs to be geared to the use of carbons for reference filing, and standard forms of a standard size should be developed. Time is a factor in small departments. Therefore, short cuts are a temptation. Time, worry, and energy are saved, in the long run, by objective and accurate purchasing records.

In small schools and in public schools, channels for the forwarding of requisitions are usually routed via the principal's office for clearance. In some colleges, a control similar to that of the principal is operative in that requisitions above a stated amount need the signature of the dean of the college. Occasionally, requisitions are routed directly to the superintendent's office for approval. In larger school systems and in colleges, a central purchasing agent is employed. He assists in the gathering of cost-quality information, places items on bid, places orders, and finally, after clearing with the department on acceptance of materials, releases the vouchers for payment by the authority designated.

Pressures to buy locally are frequently found. An administrator of physical education needs to be aware of these pressures and to be on guard professionally. It is considered unethical to accept personal discounts or gifts for personal sports use, or to allow friendships to color the transactions in the purchase of supplies and equipment. If quality merchandise from reputable sources can be secured locally and the price range is comparable to other sources, the placement of orders with a local firm is on an objective basis. If more than one firm is available and prices are comparable, it is considered good practice to rotate the orders.

INVENTORIES

The first item in the purchasing process is an inventory of the materials in use. Overbuying or underbuying is avoided by this process. A full discussion of inventories is included later in this chapter.

REQUISITIONS

Requisitions are written to cover the departmental needs. These are usually placed on standard forms, $8\frac{1}{2}'' \times 5\frac{1}{2}''$ or $8\frac{1}{2}'' \times 11''$ sheets (Fig. 9–2) with a code used for the items on a line budget. Each requisition should carry the departmental budget number and should carry a purchase order number (to appear on all subsequent forms). In the case of sports equipment, apparatus, dance recordings, and costume items, an exact description plus the catalog number of the items should be supplied. The standard required for the program should be stated (for standards, see Chapter 8). Office supplies, soaps, and antiseptic solutions are usually purchased by large school systems and colleges in bulk and distributed by requisition from general stores or scientific stores. Departments may save for other budget uses by using such sources. Every requisition should be in writing and should carry at least one carbon for departmental records. An oral order has questionable legality and can lead to difficulties in executing the contract. Not only are requisitions written for materials but also for various services such

SEND THIS COPY TO DIVISION OF PURCHASES
511 Administration Bldg.

THE UNIVERSITY OF ____________

REQUISITION

DATE ____________ 19____

PURCHASE ORDER NO.

Account Number | Department Name

DELIVER TO: ____________ Location

PLEASE FURNISH THE FOLLOWING

DATE NEEDED

QUANTITY	UNIT	GIVE COMPLETE SPECIFICATIONS—CATALOG NAME AND NUMBER WHERE APPLICABLE	EST. COST	OBJECT CLASS.

TO BE USED FOR: B

SUGGESTED VENDOR

NAME ____________ REQUESTED BY ____________ Department Chairman — Del.

ADDRESS ____________ RECOMMENDED BY ____________ Dean, Director, Manager, Etc. — I

T

CHECK ONE OF THE FOLLOWING IF ITEM OR SERVICE IS TO BE FURNISHED BY A UNIVERSITY DEPARTMENT

☐ GENERAL STORES ☐ PRINTING DEPARTMENT ☐ AUTO REPAIR SHOP ☐ OTHER UNIVERSITY DEPARTMENTS — F.O.B.

☐ SCIENTIFIC STORES ☐ FOOD STORES ☐ AUTO RENTAL POOL

☐ PHOTOGRAPHIC LAB. ☐ JOB POOL ☐ KEY DEPARTMENT — FA

1. Articles to be ordered from different vendors should appear on separate requisitions.
2. In specifying date of need, please allow ample time for advantageous purchase and delivery.
3. Suggestion as to additional vendors are invited. (Use other side for listing).

Fig. 9–2. Sample requisition form.

as telephones, job pool repair of equipment, or moving of large equipment items.

BIDS

To insure equities and to protect the public monies, many institutions require that bids be let on purchases over a specified amount ($25–$100). This practice is time-consuming, but the saving is often worth the time. The administrator simply schedules requests earlier so that bids may be taken. The type, quality, and quantity of materials needed are specified in the bid letting. Therefore, a low bid with inferior merchandise could be rejected.

PURCHASE ORDERS

Upon completion of requisitions and bids, if necessary, purchase orders are written. These orders carry the requisition number and are prepared in duplicate or triplicate. Standard forms (8½″ × 11″) are used, and voucher sheets (in duplicate or triplicate) for use by the supplier accompany the purchase order. At this point, the commitment is firm and can only be voided by the inability of the supplier to furnish the materials under order.

INVOICES

An invoice (Fig. 9–3), or statement of the shipment, accompanies every order. These should be checked against the written order to be sure the shipment carries the same materials. If not,

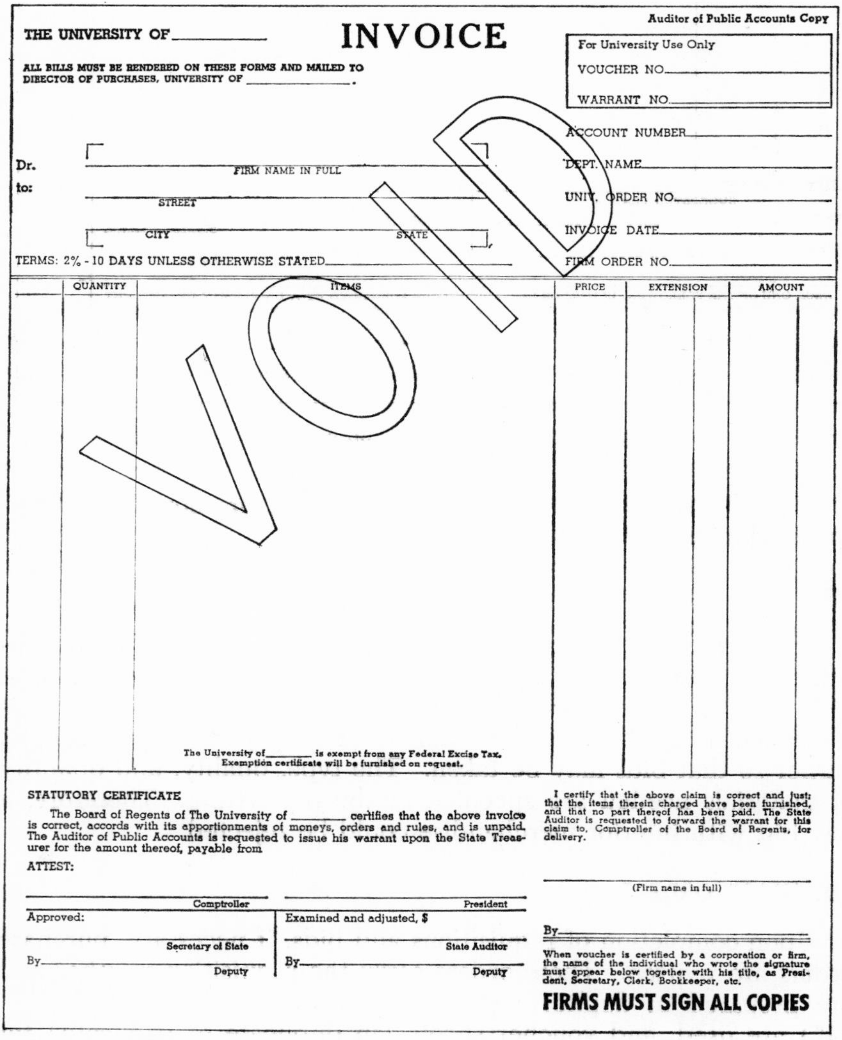

Auditor of Public Accounts Copy

THE UNIVERSITY OF__________

INVOICE

ALL BILLS MUST BE RENDERED ON THESE FORMS AND MAILED TO DIRECTOR OF PURCHASES, UNIVERSITY OF __________.

For University Use Only
VOUCHER NO.__________
WARRANT NO.__________

Dr. to:
FIRM NAME IN FULL
STREET
CITY STATE

ACCOUNT NUMBER__________
DEPT. NAME__________
UNIV. ORDER NO.__________
INVOICE DATE__________
FIRM ORDER NO.__________

TERMS: 2% - 10 DAYS UNLESS OTHERWISE STATED__________

QUANTITY	ITEMS	PRICE	EXTENSION	AMOUNT

VOID

The University of________ is exempt from any Federal Excise Tax. Exemption certificate will be furnished on request.

STATUTORY CERTIFICATE

The Board of Regents of The University of ________ certifies that the above invoice is correct, accords with its apportionments of moneys, orders and rules, and is unpaid. The Auditor of Public Accounts is requested to issue his warrant upon the State Treasurer for the amount thereof, payable from

ATTEST:

__________ Comptroller
__________ President

Approved:
__________ Secretary of State
By__________ Deputy

Examined and adjusted, $
__________ State Auditor
By__________ Deputy

I certify that the above claim is correct and just; that the items therein charged have been furnished, and that no part thereof has been paid. The State Auditor is requested to forward the warrant for this claim to, Comptroller of the Board of Regents, for delivery.

__________ (Firm name in full)

By__________

When voucher is certified by a corporation or firm, the name of the individual who wrote the signature must appear below together with his title, as President, Secretary, Clerk, Bookkeeper, etc.

FIRMS MUST SIGN ALL COPIES

Fig. 9–3. Sample invoice.

the package should be rejected. If the shipment is correct and in order, the invoices are signed. There is no redress after the invoice has been signed. An invoice often carries a notation, "Rush for discount." This is a legitimate discount, usually 2 per cent if the bill is paid within ten days, and is one means of stretching the budget a bit.

PAYMENT OF BILLS

All bills should be paid by check or by warrant—never in cash. Most institutions meet their obligations on a monthly basis with due accounting to the department concerned. Thus, the cycle of purchasing is concluded, and the department is kept aware of its ability to cover purchases.

The timing of purchases is important. Three months before the material is needed is a sound rule, as this interval allows time for delivery and checking of equipment before it is used. In the case of costumes or uniforms, ordering off season gives the manufacturer work during a slow period. Better workmanship and more accurate regard for specifications are possible during this time than is true with rush orders. Good workmanship is found in quality merchandise. In physical education, we often buy in large quantities. By comparing prices, specifications, and guarantees, quality and quantity can be combined for the benefit of the department. Reputable, well-established firms are willing to stand behind their products. As new firms enter the field, it is well to try out one or two of their items before entering into contracts for large amounts of merchandise.

INVENTORIES

Many physical education instructors think that a sports equipment inventory is all that is used in administering a physical education department. All inventories serve the same purpose: namely, to enumerate items of value, to state the condition of these, and to indicate needed purchases. If a perpetual inventory is used, seasonal inventory procedures are simple. The running record of materials on hand and items to be repaired or discarded clearly indicates the items needed. With due attention to budget allotments, purchases are then made. This is possible in departments where the budget may be used as a departmental responsibility. In school systems and in some colleges, purchasing of equipment and supplies occurs as an annual activity. In this case, a yearly inventory is made and requisitions for the year's needs are written, countersigned by the principal or the dean, reviewed by the purchasing agent, and forwarded to the governing board for approval before orders are placed. All items in use in a department of physical education are inventoried—sports equipment, costumes, towels, apparatus, and office supplies. In addition to departmental inventories, institutional inventories are used to check filing cabinets, furniture, office equipment, and similar items in general use (Fig. 9–4).

	DEPARTMENT OF PHYSICAL EDUCATION FOR WOMEN Classification _____									Inventoried by _____
Items	Description	On Hand	Purchase	Discard	Lost	On Hand	Purchase	Discard	Lost	On Hand

Fig. 9–4. Sample institutional inventory.

BOOKKEEPING AND AUDITING

Although most institutions and public school systems have an auditor's office for clearance and auditing of purchases and subsequent payment, simple line bookkeeping is necessary in a department. A cross-check of sums expended for any specific area of the program should be available at all times. The monthly expenditures plus encumbered expenses (ordered but not yet paid) appear on the statement from the auditor's office. Attention to the balance each month will enable an administrator to remain within the budget and to keep his spending well distributed throughout the fiscal year. Simple bookkeeping is a great assistance to the administrator in line budgets. A page may be devoted to each activity, with equipment items listed in detail. A composite page will show the year's expenditures. Comparison of the yearly columns enables the administrator to forecast his budget needs more accurately.

FILING

Filing serves two purposes: to systematize the records of the department, and, simultaneously, to serve as a source of information in conducting departmental business. In a one-teacher situation, it will be necessary to take care of one's own files. Any system that serves the purposes best will meet the needs. In large departments, public school or college, filing must be carefully planned or its purposes will be defeated. Numerous items must be filed, such as all correspondence, copies of requisitions, course outlines, student records, catalogs, roll books, and departmental reports of various kinds. Files are usually arranged alphabetically or numerically. Within the alphabetical filing, subject-matter filing occurs. Business files such as requisitions, purchase orders, and invoices are usually filed numerically.

Two types of files are maintained: active files and dead files. Current records over an established period of years (the educational span of the institution plus one year is suggested) make up the active files. Availability of information is mandatory for the administrator of the program. Therefore, when files are checked out for a brief period of time, a record should be made and files returned promptly to the main office. It is especially important that files concerned with students be kept under lock and key. At established intervals, correspondence files should be reviewed, and only items of major importance retained. Departmental records, as they become inactive, should be moved to the dead file for storage. Free access to all files destroys efficiency in a department. What is "everybody's business is nobody's business" is an axiom in this instance. All staff should have free access to certain files, but confidential files should be maintained for use by the administrator only.

A final word on filing seems pertinent. Microfilming is becoming more accessible, and IBM programming is being introduced into more educational institutions. As these practices spread, physical education administrators need to study the possibilities and thereby reduce the space needed for dead files.

LETTERS

One-teacher situations and school system teachers do not receive as many letters as do supervisory staffs and college departments of physical education. In either case, letters relative to professional organization work are answered by the recipient. If policies or procedures are involved, it may be necessary for the teacher or the staff member to consult a higher administrative authority. Invitations to participate in professional conferences or letters of inquiry regarding pupil reactions or student attainments may need administrative clearance. Under any circumstances, it is wise to inform the administrator of the situation. Lack of such communication can lead to confusion, misunderstandings, and a negative reaction on the part of the administrator. The staff member also protects himself by such consultation when the parents or other publics are involved. Some school systems have policies that route letters to parents from the principal's office or that require that such letters be countersigned by an administrative officer.

There are many routine letters in a department of physical education: letters of invitation to departmental events, letters of congratulation to colleagues, letters of condolence, letters announcing a staff opening, letters to prospective students, and routine letters covering equipment orders and similar items. For some of these, a form letter can be constructed (Fig. 9–5). For others, a form letter plus a personalized paragraph is the answer (Fig. 9–6). An efficient secretary can find numerous places where a form letter or a modification of it may be useful.

Professional letters concerned with staff morale or departmental progress or welfare should be carefully written. Certain letters require thought and judgment and should never be rushed off on the spur of the moment. "Sleeping over the problem" is a good idea. Letters concerned with staff promotions, supporting reasons for budget increases, interdepartmental scheduling, and definite offers for a staff position are typical problem areas that should be treated with care.

All letters coming to the department should be answered. It is absurd to expect busy people to answer on the same day as the receipt of the letter; within a week is a more realistic practice. All letters should be prepared with carbon copies, set up correctly, typed neatly, and proofread before signing. The reputation of the department for accuracy and efficiency is there for all to see in the letters forwarded to its clients, its supporters, and its various publics.

OFFICE MANAGEMENT

In one-teacher situations at any level, you are your own office manager, and usually you must cover your own secretarial work. This situation has changed slightly, however, in schools where team

THE UNIVERSITY OF_____
PHYSICAL EDUCATION FOR WOMEN
October 22, 19___

We are now planning our thirteenth annual coffee hour
for parents of major and minor students in physical education
for women. These occasions have been well attended by a
fine representation of parents. The staff feels that this is a
valuable experience to meet the parents of our students and
to give all of you an opportunity to know us. Of course, your
daughter will also be invited.

Therefore, we are planning a coffee hour from 9:30 to
11:30 a.m. on Saturday, November 6, 19___ (Parents Day).
Your daughter and the members of this staff will be eager to
greet you at_____ Hall 203, University of
_____. It is our hope that you will be able
to accept this invitation.

Sincerely yours,

Chairman

- -

You are cordially invited to a coffee hour, Saturday,
November 6, 19___, at 9:30 a.m., _____Hall 203.

Please reply by mailing the lower half of this sheet.

_____ (We) (I) plan to attend the coffee hour,
November 6, 19___.

_____ (We) (I) do not plan to attend.

Signed_____

Fig. 9–5. Sample departmental form letter.

THE UNIVERSITY OF_____
PHYSICAL EDUCATION FOR WOMEN

Your physical education teacher has told us that you
are thinking about teaching physical education. We are
happy to hear that you are interested in this course. This
is a promising field in which to work and there are many
opportunities for service in this activity area and many good
positions open at the present time. In this letter, I am
enclosing copies of our brochure on physical education as
a profession. I shall also enclose a copy of the major curriculum as found in the Teachers College catalogue.

I think that you will find that all majors in physical
education are friendly people and that this is a department
with a homey atmosphere. We are pleased to know that you
are interested in the University of_____and we
hope that you will become a major in this department. We
shall be most happy to make you welcome. If you happen to
be in the vicinity, we shall be happy to have you visit us.
Please do not hesitate to write if you have other questions.

Sincerely yours,

Chairman

Enclosures

Fig. 9–6. Sample personalized form letter.

teaching is in operation. A team usually includes at least a part-
time secretary or a student secretarial assistant. In large secondary
schools, colleges, and universities, it is the practice to employ one
or more full-time secretaries. In colleges with limited funds, student secretarial assistance is frequently used. Regardless of the
situation, it is necessary to consider the secretarial and office duties
needed in the department and to plan these carefully. The work

of the department is coordinated and expedited by efficient functioning in the office.

OFFICE FUNCTIONS

The office of the department serves as the reception center for visitors. It should, therefore, be located close to the main entrance of the building or of the department if the building is shared. As the coordinating center for the department, the work of the office must be scheduled and must meet deadlines. The various types of files needed in the conduct of physical education should be housed in this office. Suitable office machines should be made available, and space should be so allocated that their use is expedited. Centralization of office functions is increasing. If a pool of secretaries, part-time, full-time, or student assistants, is operative, an adjoining working area is needed to avoid the noise of several machines at work and to maintain the confidential status of both student and staff counseling. The central office of the department sets the tone of the department. It should be kept clean of clutter; suitable drapes, rugs, pictures, and, when feasible, flowers add to its attractiveness. Business in this office should be conducted calmly and in a well-bred manner.

The work of the central office is the key to the work of the department. In small schools and colleges, the teacher often has to conduct her office work between classes or use a free period for it. About the only difference in slightly larger schools is the use of additional time for clerical work. Necessarily, in these instances, the work must take short cuts and, frequently, the records of the department are fragmentary. When full-scale secretarial assistance is available, the office routines are quite similar to those of business firms. The departmental secretary is the office manager. She allocates duties to her assistant. Either formally or informally, she sets job descriptions, follows the progress of the work, and checks on its accuracy. Physical education has many detailed office routines that must function daily as well as those of seasonal or annual occurrence. Daily, there is correspondence, filing, receiving callers, answering student inquiries, telephone messages, making appointments, preparing minutes of staff meetings, clipping departmental news items, receiving and sorting mail, keeping staff bulletin boards orderly and up to date, and opening and closing the office. Seasonal duties, on the other hand, may be duties that occur from time to time but are repeated within the space of the year's work. Locker assignments, monthly payrolls for student assistants, preparation of course outlines, rosters, checking staff roll books, student grade cards, departmental reports, course examinations, dummies for fliers, bulletins, pamphlets or programs for departmental events, departmental announcements and invitations, departmental schedules, and assisting the administrator in gathering information and materials fall in this category. Annually, there are budgets to be prepared. Tables giving information on comparative costs need to be maintained as a basis for judgments on budget allocations. It requires careful work and thought on the part of the secretary to have such information ready for use and to note unexpected needs as the year progresses. In many institutions, an annual report is submitted by the department of physical education. Such a report varies from a brief description of the year's problems and accomplishments to detailed analysis of program progress and plans, staff loads, financial forecasting of personnel and maintenance needs, digests of budget spending, and total plans for the coming year. Another annual duty in some departments, and suggested as important for all, is the maintenance of historical records. An annual newsletter serves two purposes: the gathering of information from alumni and a statement of staff and departmental accomplishments for the year. A file of such newsletters provides an invaluable source of historical materials. A departmental scrapbook compiled annually is another historical record as well as maintenance of a card file for each graduating class of majors, listing of staff year by year, and notes on placement of major students. It takes an excellent sense of first-things-first and painstaking organization to keep an office for physical education functioning at top efficiency.

STUDENT ASSISTANCE

Secretarial assistance for teachers in public schools has been at a premium over the years. This situation is gradually coming into review, and it may be that the future holds some promise for professional help for these teachers. Meanwhile, in public schools and in colleges, student assistance at hourly rates is often available. When remuneration is not possible, departments of business education may be interested in assigning laboratory experiences to students. The teacher of physical education who gains assistance by such an assignment has the responsibility of making sure that the student has the type of experience she needs and that the standards of business education are adhered to. Careful orientation of the student assistants will set the stage for conscientious work on their part and understanding of the confidential nature of certain phases of work to which they may be assigned, for example, the recording of grades.

WORK SCHEDULES—ANCILLARY PERSONNEL

Departments of physical education for women at both the secondary and the college level employ matrons to supervise the shower and dressing rooms. In certain instances, these matrons manage the equipment cage and check equipment out and in. They clean the shower and locker rooms and the teachers' offices, and assist students when needed in the locker rooms. A matron for the swimming pool area generally has her work restricted to the pool dressing room. She usually operates an electric washer and dryer to service clean suits for every class. Towel laundry is usually done commercially because of the size and volume of this operation. The pool matron is charged with keeping her dressing and shower areas spotlessly clean. A sewing machine adds to the department's efficiency and is an economy since the matron can repair tank suits and also take care of small sewing needs within the department. A custodian in a department of physical education for women needs an interest in the equipment and should have special skills. He keeps the gymnasium, corridors, and walks clean. Because of time elements and also because of the weight of

THE UNIVERSITY OF _____ Department of Physical Education for Women EQUIPMENT NEEDED FOR COMING WEEK (to be turned in not later than Friday beforehand)		
Items	Date Out	Date In

Fig. 9–7. Sample equipment request.

some apparatus, the custodian services the department by setting up nets when needed, moving apparatus, helping to store equipment at the end of one season, and preparing other equipment at the beginning of another season. He should know how to repair small equipment such as archery arrows; he inflates balls, oils hockey sticks, and takes care of fencing and lacrosse needs. Weekly requests for equipment facilitate the preparation of these materials and reduce friction between the staff and the custodian (Fig. 9–7).

If feasible, the custodian is the ideal person to clean and service the swimming area, including the daily water-testing program. Other duties that are too numerous to mention are performed by ancillary personnel. If all these duties are to be remembered so that the department may be well serviced, it is necessary to write work schedules for each member of the ancillary staff. Figure 9–8 is a sample of such a schedule, giving daily, weekly, and annual duties.

CUSTODIAN'S DUTIES
October, 19XX

Hours: MTWTF   6:30– 2:30   Lunch: 11:00 A.M.–12 Noon
       Sat.   6:30–10:30

Hall   6:30 A.M.–12 Noon.

Daily: Sweep all area floors before 8:15 A.M.
          Sweep all corridors and wet mop entrance from boneroom as needed (not the wooden floor—the concrete).
          Assist staff as needed in setting up equipment in various areas and taking field equipment down on the elevator.
          Pick up and straighten equipment, benches, etc., in various areas.
          Empty trash containers.
          Clean the floor and dust both the equipment rooms.
          Straighten up both equipment rooms.

Saturday: Lock staff areas, turn off all lights, and lock equipment rooms at 10 A.M. (The only exception will be a few Saturday events, and these dates will be given to you in advance.)

Hall   12 Noon–2:30 P.M.

Daily: Clean men's restroom off the northwest entrance.
          Empty wastebaskets.
          Clean two staff offices and/or classrooms thoroughly each day as follows:
          Sweep, dust, wipe ledges.
          Day I   Room 201 and Room 200,
          Day II   Room 202 and cloakroom and Room 203 and cloakroom,
          Day III   Room 206 and Room 208,
          and repeat.

Fig. 9–8. Sample schedule of custodian's duties.

Monthly: Clean inside windows and hall windows, using above schedule.

Yearly: Houseclean these areas, during Christmas vacation and late August.

Hall

Weekly: Change mops. Check and replenish cleaning supplies.

Dust all equipment and window ledges in all areas.

Get out equipment (Saturday A.M.) as requested by staff for following week. Put away equipment no longer in use.

In Season

Hockey:
1. Rub linseed oil into hockey sticks—for three successive days before storing.
2. Sandpaper rough places on hockey sticks.
3. Paint hockey balls before storing.
4. Brush shin guards before storing.

Balls (leather):
1. Inflate balls as needed.
2. Clean all leather equipment with "ball cleaner."
3. Repaint letters on all balls marked by department, as needed.
4. Deflate balls to be put in storage, leaving a little air in each.

Nets:
1. Repair tears.
2. Repair ropes.

Equipment Cabinets:
Clean inside and outside in January and July.

Golf:
1. Clean metal parts of golf clubs at end of season, with scouring powder if necessary to keep them shining.
2. Set up and store large golf equipment as needed.

Archery:
1. Keep equipment repaired.
2. Put out arrows for classes.
3. Assist with storage.

Movement Fundamentals:
Move heavy equipment to teaching area.

Paddles and Bats:
Oil, sandpaper, and varnish as needed.

Set up chairs as needed for testing session four times yearly.

Fig. 9–8. (*Continued.*)

THE SECRETARY

It takes an efficient as well as a personable secretary to carry out the duties as outlined in this chapter. The personal qualities of this secretary are just as important, if not more so, as her secretarial skills. She must present a well-groomed appearance and must be able to receive the public in a courteous, calm, and attentive manner. Visitors to the office as well as callers on the telephone must recognize her interest in their problems and her desire to serve the department well. Her public-relations function sets the pace for her assistants. If she confers quietly, carefully, and sincerely with students, parents, staff, and institutional personnel, her assistants will tend to follow her example. It takes patience and tact to meet the varying demands and myriad details of the office in a large department of physical education. As supervisor of student assistants, she watches carefully their relationships to the staff and stresses the need for objectivity and a reserved manner in the conduct of office business. Fortunate, indeed, is the department with a secretary who understands the profession of physical education or whose interest in the field can be fostered. Across the secretary's desk and by consultation with the administrator, she learns many confidential departmental matters. The administrator needs a secretary who can keep confidences and upon whom he can rely for loyalty and integrity in departmental affairs. Since the administrator and the departmental secretary spend a great deal of time together, it is imperative that their personalities be compatible.

The secretary needs many office skills. Probably the greatest of these is office management. Her decisions on what to allocate and how to allocate work to her assistants will determine, to a large extent, the efficiency of the office. Within the role of office manager, she must teach student assistants how to answer the telephone and how to take messages. She must teach them how to operate office machines such as the mimeograph, the ditto machine, and the Thermofax or the Xerox copiers. Employment as a student assistant usually demands typing skill, but the secretary must review stencils and letters to be sure that the reputation of the department does not suffer by carelessness.

Shorthand is a fine skill for an office secretary, but a dictaphone is often a timesaver for the administrator who can then work alone while the secretary is busy at other tasks. Filing and simple bookkeeping, as indicated in previous sections, are necessary skills for the secretary.

After some experience in working together, the administrator can delegate the use of form letters and the answering of routine matters to the secretary. Mass mailings are often needed in a department of physical education. The secretary organizes her assistants and handles all these details. Finally, the secretary keeps track of the administrator's appointments and smoothly protects his time by judicious warnings when a visitor remains overtime. Since the secretary is expected to be able to reach the administrator at any time, the administrator should keep her informed of his plans when he leaves the office. The administrator of physical education and the secretary work as a team. Mutual appreciation of each other's problems, mutual effort, and mutual respect add to the team's efficiency.

CALENDARS

Calendars that are carefully checked add to the efficiency of business techniques in physical education. The procedure is the same for one teacher or complex departments. Daily calendars are maintained on the desks of all staff members. It is imperative that both the secretary and the chairman of a department keep identical calendars of appointments. An alert secretary, by a reminder, may avoid departmental embarrassment when emergencies arise. At the end of each calendar year, the regular monthly or seasonal deadlines and regular monthly activities are recorded for the following year. It takes experience in each situation to learn the approximate dates on yearly deadlines. Sometimes, institutional handbooks carry this information, but again it may only be made available by mimeographed instructions or notices when reports are needed. It is imperative that the administrator meet every institutional deadline. Careful analysis of the approximate dates for summer session planning and appointments, departmental class reports, rosters of grades, budget askings, recommendations for promotions, work-load reports, and similar items enables the administrator to plan a yearly calendar and thus add to the efficiency of the office. A running calendar of the major professional meetings in which the staff may be involved should be available at least one year in advance.

PLANNING THE YEAR'S WORK

Paralleling the use of calendars is the business function of planning the year's work. Many public school systems require their teachers to return to duty before the students report for classes. Workshops for in-service education are held at this time with a few days for preplanning sessions. Colleges and universities require their teaching personnel to return during Freshman week and before classes are scheduled to begin. During this time, departmental personnel have an opportunity to pace the year's work. Units of the program may be roughly blocked out in time spans, arrangements for dual use of facilities discussed and scheduled, and special events, not previously dated, may be set up and their dates cleared. An administrator of physical education looks ahead in September and sets tentative dates for all staff meetings. Taking cognizance of professional commitments on the part of the staff, he sets the dates and assigns responsibilities for departmental events for the year. As each month comes up from September to June, he plans ahead to meet all administrative deadlines in spite of various professional responsibilities he may also be carrying. He plans, when feasible, staff seminars to alternate with staff meetings and sets the problems for discussions. He must be alert for changes in institutional policies or procedures that may influence his planning, and he must keep some time open to meet unexpected problems or emergencies. During the summer months, he plans ahead for the following year. At this time, he revises form letters, plans and has printed new record forms, schedules needed repairs, and, in general, devotes a great deal of thought to the overall effectiveness of the department and how it may be improved. The year's cycle then repeats but always with differing administrative problems. Every situation has its own schedule of administrative details; therefore, it is difficult to set a pattern. One device that has been used to assist in planning the year's work is the preparation of a handbook for the secretary. A monthly outline of duties for the secretary also helps the administrator to think ahead. A sample month's outline is included here for guidance in the preparation of such materials.

EXCERPT FROM SECRETARY'S HANDBOOK

June

1. Request Head of the course in Physical Education for the Elementary School to indicate mimeographing necessary for the first two weeks in September, before she leaves for the summer.
2. Prepare outlines, courses of study, bibliographies, library reserve lists, etc., for summer session classes, as requested.
3. Prepare lockers and combination cards sufficient for expected numbers for the summer session.
4. Prepare class grade cards for summer session classes after first class meetings.
5. Collect roll books of past semester and check through that essential details (name of activity, time, calendar number, name of instructor, year, semester, etc.) are included.
6. Check inventory sheets turned in by staff members. Make a list of equipment lost and broken and list of equipment needed. Secretary inventories all that is not sports equipment—as locker rooms and offices.
7. Recommendation Slips from Health Service begin coming in, in June (through early September). These must be filed in alphabetical order.
8. Supervise student assistants in removing locker padlocks, replacing locker padlocks, listing locker numbers and padlock numbers, looking up com-

binations and listing these in the locker book, and then preparing locker cards to be assigned to students at first class meeting in September.

DEPARTMENTAL RECORDS

Departments of physical education differ from institution to institution; therefore, no set forms for departmental records can be recommended. The types of records in use, however, are fairly constant. At appropriate points in this book, examples of records in use may be found. In keeping a record of attendance and the achievement of each student, roll books are used. The importance of careful recording in these books is emphasized when departments are asked to verify a student's record years after his attendance. Most departments have one or more student record cards for filing final grades. Forms for health examination and for participation recommendations are usually in use. Schedule forms for the department and for the individual, inventory sheets, intramural records, game reports, publicity forms, accident reports, employee records, and special permission forms are examples of some of the needs of the department. It is wise to have a trial run when a form is revised before a quantity is printed. It is also advisable to limit the supply to use for one or two years, as the needs of the department may change. Samples of forms in use are given in Figs. 9–9 and 9–10.

DEPARTMENT OF PHYSICAL EDUCATION FOR WOMEN
UNIVERSITY OF _____

NAME ....

P.E. 51 First Sem.............................   P.E. 52 Second Sem.......................

Fall...   Winter...

Hour & Days ....   Hour & Days ....

       Grade ....   Grade............................

Winter.......................................   Spring..

Hour & Days..................................   Hour & Days................................

       Grade............................   Grade............................

To complete work................................   To complete work ....

FINAL GRADE..................................   FINAL GRADE............................

Fig. 9–9. Sample student record card.

PUBLIC RELATIONS REPORT

Name_____

Position _____

Convention Material:

    Attendance or contemplated attendance

    Program appearances

    Officer responsibilities

    Committee responsibilities

Other Professional Contributions or Commitments:

Community Contributions or Involvements:

Other:

Fig. 9–10. Sample public relations report.

SUMMARY

Physical education is complex in its organization and expensive in its functioning. It is, therefore, imperative that sound business techniques be employed in the conduct of physical education. This chapter has reviewed the possible channels for financing the physical education program and the controls exercised by and with sound budget practices in disbursing these funds via the budget. The paper regime in the form of requisitions, invoices, inventories, and other forms necessary for purchasing equipment and supplies has been noted. The conduct of office work by dated planning schedules, filing, bookkeeping, correspondence demands, and office management has been discussed. Finally, the contributions of all forms of clerical and ancillary assistance, with special emphasis on the role of the secretary, have been presented. Physical education needs to employ the techniques used in business in order to increase its efficient operation.

PROBLEMS

1. Make a list of the many types of records needed in physical education. Develop "forms" for three of these.

2. You have a young and attractive chief secretary. You notice that the office is becoming a popular place for several staff members and students to spend ten to fifteen minutes in social conversation. How would you solve this problem?

3. What is the function of the inventory in relation to purchasing procedures? Explain the uses of several types of inventories. Set up an inventory sheet for a specific sport of your choice.

4. Prepare a portfolio of sample form letters for use by an administrator of physical education.

5. Prepare a portfolio of sample letters relative to staff institutional problems for use by an administrator of physical education.

6. Set up job analysis sheets for the following persons:
    a) Custodian
    b) Matron
    c) Student secretary (secondary school)

7. Prepare a five-year budget spread for introducing a new activity into the curriculum. Assume that you have $100 for the first year and $50 for each of the remaining four years.

8. Write the directions for a complete filing system for a large department of physical education at the college level.

9. Construct an interview sheet for use in hiring a new departmental secretary.

10

Appraisal Techniques

The title of this chapter is frequently interpreted to mean testing and measuring devices with the resultant grading techniques. The author will include this concept in the discussion that follows, but appraisal will be treated as a total concept of the entire physical education program and personnel with due regard to the locale, administrative setup in the school system or college, and the level of instruction. Since appraisal carries the connotation of general estimation of value, there are judgments involved as well as the application of known measuring devices or even established criteria. It is difficult to decide upon a method of attack for this problem. No one decision will ever be satisfactory to all concerned. The matter of appraisal in its various forms is a perennial problem that is brought to the attention of both staff and administrators.

TANGIBLES

Appraisal of concrete things is probably the simplest form, but it sometimes is a frustrating experience. The administrator must constantly assess facilities and equipment. Is the available space adequate, not only for the current program, but also for future enrollments and future plans? Many school systems and colleges secure the services of industrial consultants to advise on such needs based upon ratios of enrollment forecasts. The administrator of physical education must be prepared to submit tables showing current needs and changing needs over a period of time. The extent of use of both indoor and outdoor facilities for every phase of a given program must be analyzed.

Safety factors must be constantly judged. In this instance, protective devices, scheduling, traffic flow, and, above all else, daily housekeeping are prime factors. Quality and quantity of equipment must be appraised for optimum use and, also, for best program functioning. A number of appraisal devices as well as subjective judgments may be employed. Inspections of facilities and equipment may be scheduled yearly (for major needs, on a longer time basis); seasonally, for changes in arrangement or equipment use; weekly or daily, for safety and housekeeping needs. Standards of safety should be constantly under surveillance. For example, in programming, enough mats for optimum use are needed, and consideration of traffic flow is indicated in sequence of classes. Personnel, both professional and ancillary, need reminders related to appraisal of their own actions relative to the safety of students.

HEALTH EXAMINATIONS

Every administrator confronts liaison problems in the setup for health examinations. Knowledge of the status of the individual for participation in the varied activities of physical education affords protection for both student and staff. It is currently standard practice to secure the results of health examinations from a physician of the family's choice. The philosophy underlying this procedure is that this physician knows the entire situation and thus, by following the development of the student, may base his judgments upon family history, the personal health history of the student, and etiological factors that may occur. The mobility operative in this country sometimes defeats this purpose, but the intent of the practice is sound. Definitive policies as to the spacing of these examinations are usually established. A common pattern is the preschool examination followed by examinations at grades three, six, junior high school entrance, senior high school entrance, and in senior high school graduation year. Many colleges require pre-entrance examinations with follow-up appraisal and decision by the Student Health Services (with due consultation if desirable) on the student's status for participation in activities. To enable the physician to advise on participation status, forms have been developed by both public school systems and college health services (see Figs. 10–1(a)–(f).

Physical education may contribute to social factors as well as to mental hygiene; therefore, students with limitations should be provided with scheduling specific to their needs. Adaptive exercise programs or rest may be indicated for some; others may need programs limited to low-level activity. The staff (teachers, nurses, physicians, dentists, guidance counselors), together with parents,

LINCOLN PUBLIC SCHOOLS
Department of Health, Physical Education, and Safety

PARENTS' NOTICE REGARDING PHYSICAL EXAMINATION

Dear Parent or Guardian:

The Board of Education, at its September 14, 1954 meeting, has recommended that "each child enrolled in K, 3, 6, and 9 grades will be expected to present a physical examination report from his family physician. This is not a requirement for admission to these grades but is to be encouraged." It is extremely important that any physical defects might be discovered at these age levels to prevent more serious difficulties in your child.

The form below should be filled out by the doctor when the examination is given, then returned to the school nurse. If you have seen your physician recently, please send the blank below to him to be filled out, or if you intend to go within the next few months, take it to him then. This report will be recorded on the pupil's permanent school health record.

APPROVED: , Superintendent

- -

REPORT OF PHYSICAL EXAMINATION

Name_____ School_____

Address_____ Age_____ Date_____

I have examined_____
            (first name)   (last name)

and found him or her to be in_____condition.

Significant findings and remarks: _____
_____
_____

Recent immunizations: DPT: Date_____ Smallpox: Date_____

    Polio: SALK____ ____ ____ ____ SABIN ORAL____ ____ ____
                 (Dates)   (Dates)

    TB Test: Reaction_____ Date_____

    Other:_____ Date_____

              Examining Physician_____

              Phone_____

Classification:_____

Code:

Regular: Any student who may participate in the regular program of physical education, recreation, intramurals, or athletics, without undue risk or injury.

Adapted: Any student who has a condition which might risk sustaining injury from participation in the regular program on needs a special adapted program as indicated by the consulting physician. Re-examine each year.

Exempt: Any student who has a severe handicap which might risk sustaining injury from participation in the regular or adapted programs. These students should be re-examined for possible re-classification at the end of the exemption period.

Fig. 10—1(a). (Used by permission of the Lincoln Public Schools, Lincoln, Nebraska.)

LINCOLN PUBLIC SCHOOLS

Department of

Health, Physical Education, and Safety

HEALTH INVENTORY

Date..

Name.. Birth Date...

Parent or
Guardian .... Address ....

Phone...

Please check the illnesses the child has had:

Approximate Date		Approximate Date
Chicken pox	Asthma	
Measles	Hay Fever	
Mumps	Eczema	
Whooping cough	Heart disorder	
Poliomyelitis	Ear infections	
Pneumonia	What operations	
Scarlet fever		
Rheumatic fever	What accidents	
Tuberculosis		
Self	Other serious illnesses	
Family		

Has the child had the following?

Headaches................................... Nose bleeds ....
Tires easily .... Growing pains ....
Fainting or convulsions .... Bed wetting ....

Has the child been immunized against the following?

	Yes	No	Date of Initial	Date of Booster
Diphtheria				
Tetanus				
Whooping cough				
Small pox				
Others				
Poliomyelitis.......			1...... 2...... 3...... 4......	

Family history:

List who lives in the home: Health condition of:

Father   Father ....
Mother   Mother ....
Brothers (older) .... (younger) ....   Brothers ....
Sisters (older) .... (younger) ....   Sisters ....
Others ....   Others ....

Date of last physical
examination..................................... By Dr. ....

Date of last dental
examination..................................... By Dr. ....

Give any other health information you feel we should have..........

Signature of Parent

Fig. 10–1(b). (Used by permission of the Lincoln Public Schools, Lincoln, Nebraska.)

LINCOLN PUBLIC SCHOOLS
Department of Health, Physical Education, and Safety

PARENTS' CONSENT RECORD FOR PARTICIPATION
IN ADAPTED PHYSICAL EDUCATION

Date _____

Dear _____

Your child _____ has been suggested by _____ for the adapted program of physical education now being conducted in the Lincoln Public Schools. Your permission is desired so that he may participate in this program.

Will you please indicate your wish in this matter on the form provided below. Sign the form and return it to the principal of your child's school.

Thank you for your cooperation.

- -

I would like to have my child participate in the adapted program of physical education.

Comments: _____

_____

Signed _____
(Parent or Guardian)

Fig. 10—1(c).   (Used by permission of the Lincoln Public Schools, Lincoln, Nebraska.)

LINCOLN PUBLIC SCHOOLS
Department of Health, Physical Education, and Safety

PROGRAM OF ADAPTED PHYSICAL EDUCATION

The Lincoln Public Schools seek to provide optimum opportunities for the physical development of each child.

1. Objective:

    To provide a regular, supervised program of modified activities and exercises for pupils who have difficulty in performing the usual game skills and fundamental skills.

2. Procedure for Selection of Pupils:

    a. Referral by nurse and principal.

    b. Review of health records and discussions with nurse and principal.

    c. Consultation with pupil.

    d. Consultation with parent.

    e. Consultation with physician following parent approval.

3. Program:

    a. Fundamental skills, game skills, activities, and exercises.

    b. Evaluation:
       1) Observation
       2) Tests and measurements
       3) Consultations

    c. Nature of instruction — small group activities and exercises.

Director
Health, Physical Education,
and Safety

Approved:
Superintendent of Schools

Fig. 10—1(d). (Used by permission of the Lincoln Public Schools, Lincoln, Nebraska.)

LINCOLN PUBLIC SCHOOLS
Department of Health, Physical Education, and Safety

The parents of _____ have requested
participation in the school program of adapted physical education.

In order for us to provide the best possible program that will meet his
needs, it is requested that you use the form below to report his diagnosis
and recommend a program of modified games and adapted exercises for us
to follow. Your cooperation in this matter is sincerely appreciated.

Respectfully yours,

Director
Health, Physical Education, and Safety

- -

School_____ Grade_____ Date_____

Address_____ Birth Date_____ Ht._____ Wt._____

Name of Parent or Guardian _____ Tel._____

Diagnosis:

Program:

Remarks:

Fig. 10—1(e). (Used by permission of the Lincoln Public Schools, Lincoln,
Nebraska.)

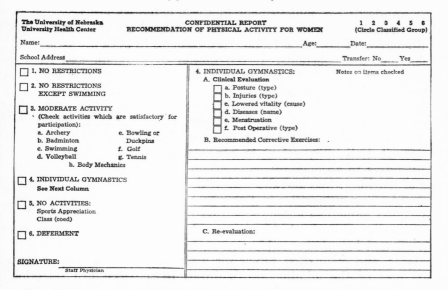

Fig. 10–1(f). (Used by permission of the University of Nebraska, Lincoln, Nebraska.)

enters into cooperative decisions in the best interest of the student. It follows that school or college personnel should be trained to pick up cues by observation and to request medical cooperation as needed. It also follows that when a student's health status improves, machinery should be available for reappraisal with subsequent return to the regular program.

With the increased interest of the medical profession in the role of exercise in the maintenance of stamina and efficiency, physical educators may look forward to more cooperative efforts for the benefit of students and the general public. As physical education steps up its physiological demands in physical fitness programs, in conditioning programs, and in gymnastics, sports, and dance, definitive reports from the medical profession will be necessary. It is the administrator's role to coordinate these efforts and to facilitate safeguarding the health of the student.

PROGRAM EVALUATIONS

Appraisal of the program in physical education takes numerous forms. The types of appraisal, accurate measurement plus qualitative evaluation, indicate to the student, the parents, and the various publics the objectives of the program. The activities selected plus standards for achievement in these activities are revealed in the evaluation results obtained. As indicated by the consistency of discussion of appraisal techniques, changes in both programs and techniques are constants. If the matter of program and its appraisal were settled, we would be balanced at status quo with no progress or advancement possible.

The standards for selection of tests (both objective and subjective) are a matter of record. Validity refers to the objectivity of the measurement—does the technique measure what it aims to measure? Reliability refers to consistency in test results. Objectivity refers to absence of bias. Administrative efficiency refers to use of teaching time and the ease with which a particular test may be used. The authorities in this phase of physical education have developed numerous instruments that meet the above criteria. We have measures of physical capacity, diagnostic measures, measures of skill and knowledge achievement, measures for classification of students, and evaluation tables for attitudes, to name only a few. It is part of the administrator's duties to see that test selection pertinent to the situation and the problem takes place. Correct use of evaluation techniques should help improve instruction. Too many test results become "dust catchers" rather than a source of stimulus for better programs. As Scott and French phrase this: "Every test should serve the student in some way." [1] When the teacher feels threatened by the testing situation, it is evident that the pupils' needs have been discarded. If pupil needs are the crux of the problem, then the pupil must be informed of his status and encouraged to improve it.

GRADING

A discussion of grading could logically be included in the chapter on organization. If appraisal includes reporting results to students, then grading belongs in the discussion of appraisal. The preceding remark clearly indicates then a need for specific grading rather than the use of the vague terms "satisfactory" or "unsatisfactory."

If evaluation is to be reported in terms of the outcomes of the objectives of a program, it follows that weighting of the grading components would be based on this principle. The day is past when attendance, costumes, use of showers, and such items may be used with impunity. It is now customary to base grades on a combination of skill and knowledge achievement plus subjective

[1] M. Gladys Scott and Esther French, *Measurement and Evaluation in Physical Education* (Dubuque: W. C. Brown Co., 1959), p. 4.

ratings of classwork and attitude by the instructor. If grading is used to measure progress, then both the student and the parent must understand the basis for grading and the given results. Explanation of the weighting of grades must be repeated. It is obvious that there must be consistency within a specific school or department with regard to the basis for assignment of grades.

Physical education teachers teach large numbers of pupils. Grading systems must necessarily be simple in structure and economical of the teacher's time. In keeping with the thinking that physical education should support the procedures adopted for the total school program, grading in physical education should use the same symbolic system.

Closely allied with grading is the question of credit. Physical education is a laboratory course and in line with accepted procedures should be so credited. As long as the educational structure stresses grades and credits, physical education should expect reciprocal respect by meeting the established standards for grades and credits.

ELEMENTARY SCHOOL

In the discussion of programs for elementary school children, it was stated that a sizable percentage of these students was taught by the regular classroom teacher. In those programs where a specialist is teaching, the scheduling usually occurs two or three times a week, with interim programs left to the classroom teacher. Espenschade has identified the objectives for the elementary school as "physical fitness, skills, attitudes, and knowledge"; citing the fact that, in primary grades, few performance tests can be used, Espenschade suggests the use of observation, checklists, ratings, and anecdotal records.[2] Latchaw and Piatt suggest the use of an evaluation checklist at the close of each lesson.[3, 4] Specific testing materials are available for middle and upper-grade children.[5] The administrator of an elementary school program needs to be constantly aware of the physical status of the child. Therefore, reports

[2] Anna S. Espenschade, *What Research Says to the Teacher, Physical Education in the Elementary Schools No. 27*, American Education Research Association of the National Education Association (Washington, D.C.: Department of Classroom Teachers, 1963), pp. 5 and 22–25.

[3] Marjorie Latchaw, *A Pocket Guide of Games and Rhythms for the Elementary School* (Englewood Cliffs, N.J.: Prentice-Hall, Inc., 1956).

[4] Marjorie Latchaw and Jean Piatt, *A Pocket Guide of Dance Activities* (Englewood Cliffs, N.J.: Prentice-Hall, Inc., 1958).

[5] American Association for Health, Physical Education, and Recreation, Department of the National Education Association, *Your Fitness Test Manual* (Washington, D.C.: AAHPER, 1958).

and follow-up of medical examinations are a must. He needs to know and respect the growth and development patterns of children, particularly in relation to fatigue and the amounts of exercise advised for children of differing growth patterns and motor achievement. If testing is used for motivation, the child's natural desire to excel may create a hazard. Halsey and Porter urge caution in the use of national norms for elementary school children; their use to assess progress rather than to compare status of a selected group of children is suggested.[6] A rewarding experience for the teacher is the keeping of short anecdotal records on the reactions of each child in physical education. Not only may the teacher observe skill but also he may identify social learnings. An adequate background in the emotional patterns and resultant needs of children will assist the administrator in planning to utilize formal and informal studies of individuals and of peer group reactions. Certain simple skill tests are feasible, but the administrator needs to review carefully the written test to be sure that it is not blocked in results by the reading vocabulary demanded. The administrator needs to be sure that elementary school physical education class time is used primarily for instruction and that a testing program does not become "the" program. A simple but effective physical education progress record is given in Fig. 10–2.

SECONDARY SCHOOL

Appraisal techniques for the secondary school can be more formalized than is the case for the elementary school. Several reasons underlie this fact. Secondary school programs are usually taught by specialists in physical education whose undergraduate preparation has introduced them to the philosophy, principles, and procedures of evaluation. Most physical education classes are organized to follow a seasonal offering in activities with units used as the *modus operandi*. Within the activity unit, testing and measuring are planned areas. A greater number of standardized evaluating procedures have been prepared than is true in the elementary school situation. It is quite possible and is a stimulus to analyzation of the needs of students in a specific situation for the teacher to prepare his own testing program. In the interest of time and space, no exhaustive treatment of the "whys and wherefores" of

---

[6] Elizabeth Halsey and Lorena Porter, *Physical Education for Children, A Development Program* (rev. ed.; New York: Holt, Rinehart & Winston, Inc., 1963), p. 160.

LINCOLN PUBLIC SCHOOLS

Department of
Health, Physical Education, and Safety

PHYSICAL EDUCATION PROGRESS RECORD

Room_____ Teacher_____ Grade_____ P.E. Teacher_____

Code:

1. Outstanding.
2. Very Good.
3. Progress Is Satisfactory.
4. Progress Is Slow.
5. Unsatisfactory Performance.
   A Check (√) Shows Need
   for Improvement.

	1st Quarter				2nd Quarter				3rd Quarter				4th Quarter			
	Grade	Observes Rules of Games	Shows Growth in Physical Skills	Practices Good Sportsmanship	Grade	Observes Rules of Games	Shows Growth in Physical Skills	Practices Good Sportsmanship	Grade	Observes Rules of Games	Shows Growth in Physical Skills	Practices Good Sportsmanship	Grade	Observes Rules of Games	Shows Growth in Physical Skills	Practices Good Sportsmanship

Fig. 10–2. Sample progress record. (Used by permission of Lincoln Public Schools, Lincoln, Nebraska.)

possible evaluative devices is presented. Table 10–1 clearly indicates the range of testing possible in a total program of physical education.

Table 10–1

Types of Evaluating Devices in Relation to Their Purposes

Physical Development	Understandings and Attitudes	Skills	Quality of Program
Medical examinations	Teacher observations	Activity, skill tests	Surveys
Health appraisals	Profile records	Observations	Checklists
Body-type appraisals	Student-teacher conferences	Game-skill tests	Observations
Height, weight, and growth measurements	Self-appraisals	Rating scales	Student response
Cardiovascular tests	Anecdotal records	Self-appraisals	Rating scales
Strength tests	Group appraisals	Situation tests	
Relaxation tests	Sociometric and role-playing tests	Athletic-achievement tests	
Tests of coordination	Projective tests	Classification tests	
Observations	The wishing well	Motor-ability tests	
Self-appraisals	Rating scales	Motor-educability tests	
Anthropometric measurements	Interest inventories		
Body typing	Tests of choice		
Fitness tests	Diaries and autobiography		
Tests of nutrition	Grading devices		
	Knowledge tests		
	Character and personality		

SOURCE: Delbert Oberteuffer and Celeste Ulrich, *Physical Education* (3d ed.; New York: Harper & Row, Inc., 1962), pp. 420–21.

We are concerned, at this point, with the administration of the secondary school appraisal program rather than with its specifics. In spite of the fact that tests and measurement courses set out the general rules for the best administration of tests, it is often necessary to assist the teacher with these plans. Preparation of score sheets, assigning testing assistants, arranging space and equipment for testing, and other minor details are boons for busy secondary school teachers with heavy class enrollments. Because the teacher's time is limited, cumulative records are frequently used to record test results. From such records, grades are calculated and progress noted. Cowell and Schwehn suggest seven principles of good cumulative records.[7]

[7] Charles C. Cowell and Hilda M. Schwehn, *Modern Principles and Methods in Secondary School Physical Education* (2d ed.; Boston: Allyn & Bacon, Inc., 1964), p. 306.

PRINCIPLES OF GOOD CUMULATIVE RECORDS

1. They should be based on objective evidence and reliable descriptions of behavior.
2. They should show trends of development of abilities and interests.
3. They should provide a means for recording measures in comparable and meaningful terms.
4. They should provide informational data in such form and order that they show the interrelationships between separate items.
5. They should be of the graphic type, with high "glance value," so that rapid generalizations may be achieved and trends in development easily noted by visualizing the data.
6. They should be organized into annual divisions and present an all-round picture of the student's developmental progress and not merely his academic achievement.
7. They should be administratively convenient and quickly reproduceable [*sic*] by photostatic or similar process.

A cumulative record may cover growth patterns, classification for activity, motor skill abilities, fitness scores, achievement scores, and similar items. Because of the lack of clerical assistance, the secondary school cumulative record form should offer the teacher speed in recording scores, a full record of the physical education experience, and some record of the leadership roles the student has been able to assume. The more detail that is spelled out on the card, the easier it is for the hard-pressed teacher to use it. (See Fig. 10–3.)

The AAHPER has constructed evaluative criteria to be used as guidelines in improving our schools. An interesting adaptation of these criteria has been evolved based upon the need to encourage schools in states where conditions are less than ideal. Using selected basic needs as the criteria and then raising the standards as the schools improved, an award certificate and banner have been incentives toward improved programs. (See Appendix No. 11.)

COLLEGE

General Program. The physical education program for the general college student offers, in depth and in more sophisticated form, some of the same activities as the secondary school. Standardized scores and norms for certain sports and fitness items have been constructed for the college level and are available in the various sources for tests and measurements. Knowledge of the "why" and "how" of activities receives more emphasis at the college level; therefore, the construction of knowledge tests becomes a matter of major concern. All forms of appraisal are important at all levels,

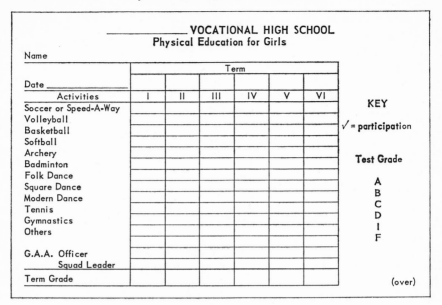

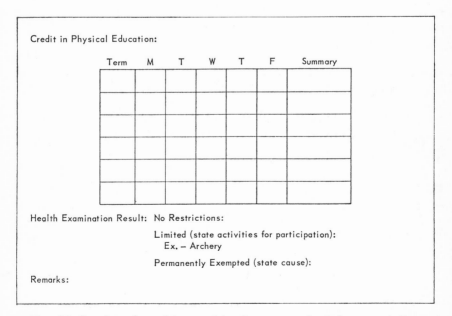

Fig. 10–3. Sample activity participation report: (*top*) front, and (*bottom*) back.

but it is particularly important that the general college student develop insight into the values of activity. It follows that the testing program that is motivational in nature serves a real function at this level. Administratively, staff consensus is needed as to the type of skill and knowledge or attitude tests in use, scheduling intervals to be established, and the weighting assigned objective tests in the final grade for the course. In colleges where large enrollments are found, the mechanics of machine or hand scoring must be established as well as the preparation of the testing materials. Scaling the scores is usually the responsibility of a specialist in tests or measurements or the staff testing committee.

Since all phases of evaluation should be used in the guidance of students, departments are usually interested in the opinions of students relative to the values inherent in courses. Checklists can be used to secure this data. Open-end questionnaires, however, give the student a chance to state his likes and dislikes without prejudice and, at the same time, offer valuable information to the instructors. Careful analysis of the reasons why students like or dislike certain activities and attention to the comments of students may provide incentive for changes in curricular emphasis. Two examples of open-end questionnaires that have been used successfully may be found in Appendix No. 12 and Appendix No. 13. In an effort to assist colleges to evaluate their general physical education instructional programs, a checklist was prepared by the Conference on Physical Education for College Men and Women (see Appendix No. 14). Use of this set of criteria is suggested as a device for the staff in a self-survey situation.

PROFESSIONAL PROGRAMS

Professional programs are necessarily in a constant state of being appraised. They stand or fall based upon the preparation and resultant contributions of their students as they enter the profession. Professional programs use testing devices similar to the general college programs plus additions to assist in the best preparation of teachers. There is growing interest in competency in skills as a qualification for the professional student.[8] Students in professional programs also face retention hurdles. The qualifications for endorsement and certification demand a professional education program. Physical education has set standards in general education, in the background sciences, and in the professional sequence that

---

[8] Ruth Wilson, "Competency Testing," *Journal of Health, Physical Education, and Recreation,* XXXV, No. 2, February, 1964.

are designed to demand fine preparation.[9] Profile charts (Appendix No. 4), analytical records, and similar devices are used in screening and retaining students with superior professional potential.[10] At the crux of the preparation stands the student teaching experience with a galaxy of appraisal devices to improve and prepare the student to enter the profession. Lesson and unit plans are appraised; the appearance, poise, and manner of the student is evaluated; teaching techniques and pupil achievement come under scrutiny. The cycle is completed when the student enters the profession with a follow-up evaluation initiated by the major department (Appendix No. 15).

One cannot leave the discussion of the professional program without mentioning the appraisals of the total program that are based upon accreditation. The various regional accrediting agencies prepare institutional standards upon which institutional evaluation is based. The National Council for Accreditation of Teacher Education standards are the basis for the evaluation of teacher education programs. The preparation of reports for either of these appraisal techniques is often the basis for staff self-surveys. Regardless of the results of the use of these standards, the experience is a valuable one for staff members.

INTANGIBLES

Although we have discussed the grading of physical education as a tangible possibility, the fact remains that the portion assigned to subjective judgment has characteristics that are intangible. This fact is also true when evaluative criteria or opinion polls are used. Prejudice and bias are intangibles, as are enthusiasm and professional interest. Discussions of ratings, bases for promotion, and forms of appraisal contain intangibles that must be faced by both a member of a staff and the administrator. Every administrator carries the onus of objective thinking in these relationships.

PERSONNEL

One of the most sensitive areas in physical education is that of evaluation of personnel. In highly structured educational systems,

[9] American Association for Health, Physical Education, and Recreation, Department of the National Education Association, *Professional Preparation in Health Education, Physical Education, Recreation Education* (Washington, D.C.: AAHPER, 1962). A Report of a National Conference.

[10] Deane Richardson, "A Start in Selective Retention," *Journal of Health, Physical Education, and Recreation*, XXXVI, No. 1, January, 1965.

reports that are varied in type are requested by various sources. These reports may be informal or extremely formal in type. Ancillary personnel may be listed on departmental budgets or on non-academic budgets, but the supervision and reporting are wholly or partially the responsibility of the department being serviced. The administrator is asked to comment and to rate the work of clerical staff. If indicated, either by requests for promotion or by obvious inefficiency, a clerical analyst may visit the department or school to observe and to confer with the administrator. Frequently, raises in classification are based upon these appraisals. The custodial staff is usually supervised officially by a head custodian. Careful liaison between the head custodian and the administrator in physical education will pay dividends in the form of courteous and more effective work.

Appraisal of academic personnel is definitely assigned to administrators. In public school systems, step-interval salary scales may be in operation. Unless definitive negative reports are received, such interval salary increases are automatic. However, two phases of this scale receive careful consideration. The first phase is that of the tenure year (usually the third year of experience). Tenure depends upon careful evaluation of the teacher's ability, cooperative efforts, and professional promise. Tenure reports should be thoughtfully and objectively prepared. The second phase that receives special attention is the step interval upon the completion of an advanced degree by the teacher. The attainment of advanced status would, hopefully, be based upon counseling with its implied appraisal of the professional needs of the individual teacher. Merit raises are in operation both in school systems and in colleges. These can be a blessing or a danger to morale. Reports from several superiors are generally the answer. Such reports must be unbiased and must set forth clearly the effectiveness of the staff member as a teacher and as a member of the profession. Certainly, every teacher should understand the basis for consideration in merit raises and should receive a copy of all appraisals.

Raises in rank in colleges are not automatic. They are recommended to the governing board by the head of a department who is in turn supported by the Dean of the college and the top echelon of administration. Carefully constructed forms are used to present a review of the candidate's professional preparation, professional experience, professional contributions by committee membership or by holding offices in professional organizations, and creative work (literature, choreography, etc.). Promotions to professorial ranks are generally dependent upon the attainment of a doctoral degree and the pursuit of scholarly work in the postdoctoral period. More and more emphasis is being placed on scholarly work in physical education. The instructor who is willing to experiment with the newer technical aids, to read widely, and to bring his thinking into focus by increased competency in teaching and by writing finds his efforts appreciated in the profession.

Research offers an open door to the professionally minded. The administrator is expected to provide scheduling conducive to research needs, to support requests for research equipment, and to encourage and sustain interest in research on the part of the staff. Furthermore, interdisciplinary research is offering wider opportunities. Appraisal of the possibilities among physiological inquiry and fitness programs; cooperative projects with psychology related to concepts, attitudes, and skill learnings; anthropological interest in body types and functions; and sociological interest in group structure are merely samples of these possibilities.

To close this discussion of appraisal, the administrator's work comes under scrutiny. Those higher in the administrative line evaluate the work of the administrator in terms of the attainments of the department, its effectiveness in school and college contacts, its reputation within the profession, and its contributions to the community that it serves.

SUMMARY

We have been concerned with appraisals of the tangible and the intangible factors operative in physical education programs from elementary through college level. Appraisal techniques have been discussed, and the administrative duties entailed have been indicated. Briefly, the administrator's duties may be recorded as assisting in the planning for appraisal techniques in the program and providing time, supplies, and personnel to put these techniques into use. Appraisal of staff effectiveness, together with suitable support of research, has been cited. Appraisal has been focused on reaching the objectives of physical education.

PROBLEMS

1. Discuss the terms "appraisal," "techniques," "measurement," "evaluation."
2. Set up a staff discussion of the cumulative record of a class (Freshman, Sophomore, Junior, or Senior majors).
3. In-service staff training is often needed in the use of skill tests, ratings,

and anecdotal records. Select a circumstance for each of these types, and set up the guidelines for a staff training session.

4. Set up a process for keeping and evaluating anecdotal records for an elementary school physical education class.

5. Write a ten-item checklist of specific phases of sportsmanship that could be used at the junior high school level.

6. State the administrator's possible responsibilities for "action research" in a junior high school sports class.

7. Cite and discuss the bases feasible in the use of merit promotions.

8. What are the advantages in the use of cumulative records in a secondary school?

9. Personnel appraisal is a sensitive area. Cite the wise use of several techniques in a staff situation.

10. What responsibilities does the administrator carry in forwarding research as a phase of appraisal?

11

Special Administrative Problems

Each day brings problems to the administrator in physical education. Fortunately, most of these are minor in nature and require decisions that are also minor in nature. A great many of the major problems of administration have been discussed in the previous chapters. There remain, however, certain problems that occur intermittently and certain trends in the field that will probably cause changes in administrative techniques.

INTERMITTENT PROBLEMS

In both public schools and colleges, self-surveys are conducted from time to time. The administrator is asked to organize his staff in seminar fashion for study of a specific situation. The details of self-surveys differ. Usually, the physical plant receives attention, the preparation and experience of the personnel are reviewed, and the philosophy and objectives of the program are examined in terms of the program and recommendations for progress are invited. Accreditation procedures involve a similar process. In fact, within the scope of the preparation of accreditation reports, staff members in either public school or college situations become aware of both the potentialities and the limitations with which they are working. The administrator of physical education has definite responsibilities in the preparation of such reports. If the staff is accustomed to seminar discussions or committee study techniques, the process of gathering the data and preparing the materials included in the report is almost automatic. However, if such techniques are new to a staff, gradual orientation and the establishment of rapport are needed before the actual work may take place. The administrator as the group leader sets the pace, senses the group reaction, and gradually establishes an atmosphere for cooperative action. The analysis of aims and objectives of the department, professional preparation and professional contributions of the staff, available facilities, and the program presented in the department results in new appreciations on the part of the staff. At any time that an administrator senses the need for the staff to become better informed with regard to the contributions of a department, self-analysis is an excellent technique.

Another intermittent administrative technique that is needed from time to time is the preparation of a "hearing"—although this term is not used in a legal sense. Perhaps it is a presentation before an official committee or an official board. Many times, such presentations are defensive or protective in nature. The author has found that these invitations are often couched in the phrase: "Will you visit with us about this matter?" The atmosphere that the administrator encounters may be hospitable and pleasant, or it may be biased and hostile. Regardless of the sensed reaction, any such presentation must be thoroughly prepared, well thought out, and well presented. A study must be made of the thinking behind such a request, the personnel involved, and the form in which materials may be most adequately presented. Data are gathered pertinent to both local and parallel situations. Short, easily answered surveys accompanied by stamped, self-addressed cards or envelopes for reply are quickly heeded by one's colleagues. Affirmative arguments supported by the research in the field are prepared. All materials are assembled and placed in folders for use by the members of the committee calling the meeting. The fact that many heads are better than one in thinking out such problems and that involvement increases interest points to participation by the staff in these projects. All "hearings" are not defensive. The presentation of a revised curriculum or the application for approval of an advanced degree are examples of the positive approach. Course outlines that have been meticulously constructed to present the current trends and to avoid duplication in content are made available to the committee. Staffing standards and budget coverage are included in such a report. Whether this is a defensive or an affirmative presentation, the administrator of physical education needs to think ahead and identify possible question areas. The ability to think on one's feet and to speak clearly, concisely, and authoritatively in response to committee reactions is a skill that the administrator of physical education needs to develop. An example of a presentation given to preserve a playing field for departmental use follows:

HEARING PRESENTATION

Date _____

To the Building Committee:

The Department of Physical Education for Women presents the following materials relative to the use of the playing fields (bounded by Phillips, Fourteenth Street, Franklin, and Twelfth Street) assigned to its use.

Introduction

The philosophy of the program in this department is based upon these principles: namely, the greatest good for the greatest number, respect for the interests and the needs of the individual student, and the education of the individual as a "whole"—mentally, physically, morally, and spiritually.

The department covers the following programs: a service or activity program for Freshman and Sophomore women, a professional program for majors and minors, an intramural program for university women, recreational clubs for university women, and limited recreational offerings for faculty wives and university personnel.

Administratively, the department is assigned to _____ College. Our professional program is, naturally, a part of the general teacher education function of that college. Our service program cuts across a larger area in that women in all colleges are contacted.

The history of the facilities used by this department points to the fact that for a number of years, the outdoor program has been curtailed for lack of playing fields. The report of the Building Committee, dated _____, page _____, stated a need for these fields. In September, 19___, after years of work and effort on the part of your committee and all persons concerned, these fields were placed in use.

Use of Fields

The fields are in constant use during the fall and spring seasons. Departmental plans call for winter use of the fields as soon as such a program can be efficiently planned and administered. The fall schedule, 19___, for field sports was: Monday, Tuesday, Wednesday, and Thursday: 8:00 A.M. to 12:00 Noon, and 1:00 P.M. to 6:00 P.M.; Friday, 10:00 A.M. to 12:00 Noon. This schedule includes women's intramurals from 5:00 to 6:00 P.M. The schedule planned for spring 19___ increases the use of the field on Friday from 2:00 to 5:00 P.M. It has been possible in this scheduling to care for the needs of Laboratory School girls (an elective class). (See Table I.)

By an agreement made in the spring of 19___ by Mr. _____ _____, Chairman of Physical Education and Intramurals for Men, and Miss _____ _____, former chairman of this department, men's intramurals were permitted the use of the western third of the field, and space not in use by the women was open for men's classes except for the eastern hockey field. The fields were closely scheduled and widely used for men's intramurals in the fall, 19___. A few classes, such as golf, used narrow areas at the west end when the women were not using this space. The arrangement has been entirely satisfactory this year. (Copies of this agreement will be furnished if you so desire.)

On September 15, 19____, the Military units requested use of the fields for laboratory periods—Thursdays, 3:00 to 6:00 P.M. The west portion of the field, usually in use for men's intramurals, was allocated for this purpose when the men's department withdrew their intramural program on Thursdays. (Copies of this agreement will be furnished if you so desire.)

Conclusion

The Department of Physical Education for Women desires to offer a program of which the University and the State may be proud. Such a program means an expanded use of outdoor facilities plus future planning for modern and adequate indoor facilities. Such a program means activities based upon the cultural interests as evidenced in this country and the physical and mental needs of a society geared to sedentary occupations and mechanical gadgets that reduce physical work load but increase nervous tensions (the statisticians tell us that one out of twenty people are destined to be mental cases); and such a program demands that we build our physical stamina, learn to conserve both muscular and nervous energy, and follow well-rounded health and personal living patterns.

Interest in the promotion of a program of physical education has been evidenced in _____ _____'s address at the student convocation, October, 19____. At that time, interest was stressed in intramurals for all students, in enlarged numbers of tennis courts, and in class scheduling that would permit participation in activity. In an informal conference, the administration has stated interest in a sports program for women, the definite need to attract more women to the campus, and the fact that all departmental needs should be considered in the total program of the University.

Dean _____ _____ and Dean _____ _____ are interested in this problem as evidenced by the communications you have received. Dr. _____ _____ is interested in physical education both as a source of physical efficiency in daily living and as a preventive outlet conducive to better mental hygiene. The Women's Athletic Association has a deep interest. This organization has grown in effectiveness in spite of handicaps rather than because of facilities made available to them.

In 19____, the Building Committee of the University of _____ was faced with a similar decision—that of placing a girls' dormitory on the fields. After due consideration, the decision was made to keep the fields and locate the dormitories elsewhere. Since that time, _____ has enlarged its playing areas. (See Table II.)

The Department of Physical Education for Women has no quarrel with the obvious need for a new and adequate High School. The department is, however, interested in protecting its present program and in providing opportunity for educationally sound programs in the future.

The preplanning for the High School includes noon-hour and before-school activities, intramurals for boys and girls, classes in physical education, and a football interscholastic program for boys. The assumption seems to be that unlimited use of the playing fields will be insured by virtue of placing the building on the fields. Dean _____ has stated that "all interests of the departments concerned be taken into consideration." If this is done, such unlimited use is impossible. The Department of Physical Education for Women feels its responsibility with respect to the program for girls in the High School and will provide for these activities. The department needs written assurance that its program for University students in a University situation will be respected and that provision for a High School program involving approximately

200 students will not supersede and impede the progress and function of a University department.

In closing, may we point out that the girls who will benefit or lose from the decision to be made are not on campus—many of them are unborn. However, the decision will stand as a symbol of the University of ＿＿＿＿＿＿＿'s attitude toward coeducation. If the Building Committee wishes to provide tangible assurance that girls are needed and welcomed on this campus, space, facilities, and educational programs to attract girls must be provided. The Building Committee has the support of the Department of Physical Education for Women, and the department understands fully the problems involved in making fair and just decisions with regard to allocation of space. These fields, assigned for the use of women, have resulted in the implementation of a program to meet the interests and needs of our present society. The fields serve large numbers of students. Their use to greater advantage is the plan for the future. This department asks your consideration and assistance in insuring that these facilities once set aside for this use are not encroached upon.

Respectfully submitted,

＿＿＿＿＿＿＿ ＿＿＿＿＿＿＿, Chairman

Table I

Weekly Use of Fields, Fall, 19＿＿＿

Total enrollment in physical education for women	1,880
Freshman and Sophomore classes using fields	525
Professional women students using fields	121
Women's intramurals	*
Men's classes	175
Men's intramurals	2,000
Military (estimate)	1,000

* Varies.

Table II

Comparative Space Allocations for Physical Education for Women at Seven Regional Colleges

Institution	Fields
University of A	74,733 sq. yds. plus two new intramural fields and one golf driving range to double the entire space
A State College	100,889 sq. yds.
University of ＿＿＿＿＿＿＿*	43,173 sq. yds. (includes the slope on ＿＿＿＿＿ Street)
University of B	33,000 sq. yds.
B State College	28,050 sq. yds.
University of C	9,000 sq. yds.
University of D	7,800 sq. yds. plus use of golf course

* Note where reduction of space will move the University of ＿＿＿＿＿＿＿ on this table.

RESEARCH

As research needs increase along with research competency, the administrator finds himself faced with many problems. In public schools, there is increased emphasis upon cooperation with research projects initiated either by local colleges or by national agencies. Heads of departments of physical education in large secondary schools, principals of both elementary and secondary schools, and directors of physical education are asked to initiate action research in classes as well as to supply data for more sophisticated designs. With federal assistance for research under Title I of the Elementary-Secondary Education Act of 1965, there is provision not only for research but also for materials, facilities, and programs for areas with families having low incomes. Title IV of this Act provides for educational research and training, including problems of learning. Title V strengthens state departments of education by funding needed areas. Administrators have responsibilities with regard to the above opportunities. School systems and coordinating agencies within school systems will probably apply for grants under this Act. The administrator of physical education needs to learn the format and lines of communication used in applying for such grants. He needs to gather the local data used in the application and to coordinate the efforts of local personnel in both the application and, if granted, the implementation of programs functioning under federal auspices.

Research by college staffs has enjoyed support and prestige over a period of years. However, some of its prestige has been gained in the past in spite of rather than because of administrative support. Currently, research is a favored child. Staff members with the necessary know-how, interest, and drive to pursue research are encouraged to secure funds from local or regional-national sources. Facilities such as research laboratories and research equipment become more and more feasible. Scheduling is tailored to local research needs, and blocks of time are provided for research-oriented personnel. Unfortunately, it takes persistence, deep and constant application to details, and a talent for interpreting the data secured to produce tangible results. There is far too much research that remains "in process" over a long period of time. The administrator of the college program, therefore, has responsibility in encouraging completion plus publication of research results. A final word is in order on the administrator's duties relative to research. Physical education started its early programs with heavy emphasis on the activity areas. There was, at that time, great interest in fine teaching based upon anthropometric research. There has been continued interest over the years in fine teaching, and the types of research have expanded and have been integrated with associated areas of learning. Without intent and without realization of the trend, staff prestige at the college level has become focused upon research per se. Now, there is emerging a trend to recognize excellent teachers whose interests lie in teaching rather than in research. The administrator of physical education at the college level needs to establish a fine balance in staffing, in scheduling, in time allotments, in budgets, and in promotions both academic and financial. Upon the results of fine instruction as well as upon the results of fine research hangs the future of physical education.

TRENDS IN PHYSICAL EDUCATION

CAMPUS RECREATION

In the past, several isolated agencies have planned and managed recreation for the college student. Comprehensive programs of both men's and women's intramurals have been operated by the respective departments as a subdivision of the department or under the aegis of a departmental organization. Student Unions directed by a student board have offered numerous recreational opportunities. Included in the listing of concerts, forums, discussion groups, and dances has been tournament bowling, lessons in ballroom dancing, skit competitions, and other physical activities. Various living-unit groups have sponsored special events such as a Greek Day or Spring Days (stunt relays, etc.). Within the last five to ten years, concurrent with the population explosion on the campus, the office of student affairs has become deeply concerned with recreational facilities and recreational opportunities on the campus. Administratively, coordination of all campus efforts for recreation seems to be an emerging pattern. On some campuses, this move has resulted in provision for intramural buildings. In other colleges, recreational facilities in dormitory units that combine physical activity and music or quiet games and snack bars have been placed in operation or are in the planning stage. Administratively, these changes impose certain new problems. The usual procedures are followed relative to maintenance and custodial duties. If the recreational room is small and informal, its use is generally restricted to those persons in the living unit. The trend seems, however, to be pointed toward multiple units (gymnasiums, sports courts for handball and badminton), archery and golf ranges, and swimming pools. Sometimes fees are levied at each student registration to finance these facilities. As a coordinated facility, these facilities are usually controlled by a student-staff committee or board. Questions of policy in the use of facilities, regulations for conduct, hours available, and similar items then arise. There may be hours when such a fine facility has few students using it because of academic scheduling. The board of control must then decide whether or not the department of physical education may use the space at designated hours. Such a facility attracts the attention of outside groups who want to schedule activities for its use. The board must decide if this use is feasible and whether or not prime hours will be released for such use. In addition, regulations with regard to supervision, janitorial services, and breakage or damage must be established if outside use is permitted. Prior scheduling, deadlines, and fees are also needed so that student use of the facility is not jeopardized. Priorities in the use of the facility are also needed to avoid conflicts and ill will. Finally, the lines of administrative authority must be carefully spelled out and placed in writing to establish the authority of the governing board.

EXTRAMURAL COMPETITION

There is a steadily growing trend for participation by girls and women in extramural competitive sports. The Division for Girls and Women's Sports of the American Association for Health, Physical Education, and Recreation believes that this activity can be controlled and that valid practices can be established. The statement of policies emphasizes that such a program should "complement the intramural and instructional program." (See Appendix No. 2.) Such programs require excellent leadership, time, and funds. Such programs require a fine program of instruction in physical education and a broad program of intramurals for the majority of the girls and women served.

Over the years, there has been grave concern with regard to the amount and type of interscholastic competition that is advisable for boys at the junior high school level. Since growth and development patterns for both boys and girls are uneven at this stage, The Division for Girls and Women's Sports has been concerned that competition for junior high school girls be carefully planned and rigorously supervised, and that the experience offer opportunity as an extension of the class and intramural level. To this end, in the September, 1966, issue of *Journal of Health, Physical Educa-*

tion, and Recreation, "Guidelines for Junior High School Girls' Participation in Sports" was published for the first time (Appendix No. 16). Since many teachers have had little or no experience with this type of organization, the sample schedules in Figs. 11–1 and 11–2 are provided from a successful program.

Schedules similar to the one below were set up for seventh-grade soccer-baseball and Nebraska ball, eighth-grade volleyball and Nebraska ball, and ninth-grade softball. Each team was scheduled for two games. Track and field activities as well as co-recreational volleyball were held on Saturday mornings. *All* girls who wished to be a part of the extramural program were permitted and urged to participate. No results of the games were kept as a part of any record. The main purpose of the program was to provide a competitive experience in a controlled situation with no direct pressure on winning. The emphasis was placed on participation.

Activity	Dates	Numbers Participating
Soccer-baseball (7th grade)	Oct. 11–14	240
Volleyball (9th grade)	Oct. 21–25	260
Volleyball (8th grade)	Nov. 1–9	350
Nebraska ball (8th grade)	Feb. 24–Mar. 3	340
Nebraska ball (7th grade)	Apr. 4–7	320
Track and field (7th, 8th, 9th grades)	May 14, 21	425
Softball (9th grade)	May 23–26	165

The extramural games were usually played on Mondays and Thursdays after the intramurals were over or at about 4:30 and continued for one hour. The financing for the teachers, officials, buses, and extra custodial help was provided by the board of education as a regular budgetary procedure.

Fig. 11–1. Sample schedule for extramural activities.

Both men and women in physical education have been concerned that extramural competition for girls and women avoid certain problems that have developed in competitive sports for boys and men. The usual recommendations are made for medical clearance and supervision of players, for schedules based upon physiological maturity, for insurance coverage of players, and for safe transportation. In addition, efforts are being made to avoid commercialization of these activities by minimizing personal glorification of both coaches and players, by setting up approved rules for play, and by stating that the salary and retention of instructors should not be based upon the outcomes of the game (Appendix No. 17). It is highly recommended that some type of social event, wherein the participants may learn to know and respect each other, accompany all competitive events for girls and women. The Guidelines for Interscholastic Athletic Programs for High School Girls (Appendix

LINCOLN PUBLIC SCHOOLS
Department of Health, Physical Education, and Safety

October 19, 19xx

To: Teachers and Principals
Re: 9th Grade Volleyball Extramurals

The following schedule has been established for the 9th Grade Volleyball Extramurals. Games will be played in 10 minute halves, no assist on serve, and using the one-hit rule. Host schools will provide scorekeepers. Officials will again be provided.

Thursday, October 21

At Lefler   At Mickle

Whittier I vs. Lefler I   Pound I vs. Mickle I
Irving I vs. Lefler II   Pound II vs. Mickle II
Lefler II vs. Irving II
Whittier II vs. Irving III

Monday, October 25

At Dawes   At Culler

Everett I vs. Dawes I   Lefler I vs. Culler I
Everett II vs. Dawes II   Lefler II vs. Culler II
                                   Lefler III vs. Culler III

Fig. 11–2. Sample extramural volleyball schedule. (Courtesy of Eunice Johnson, Coordinator, Physical Education, Lincoln Public Schools, Lincoln, Nebraska.)

No. 18) also state that students must be successfully carrying full academic loads, that only certified teachers employed by the board of education should be responsible for the welfare of the girls, that limited seasons and limited geographic areas should be operative, and that students should be limited to play on only one interscholastic team during a season. The Guidelines for Intercollegiate

Athletic Programs (Appendix No. 19) have similar standards plus prohibition of participation on or against a men's intercollegiate team. General college eligibility requirements are used as the basis for participation, and athletic scholarships and financial assistance for women athletes per se are taboo.

Over a period of years, golf, archery, and bowling tournaments for women have been sponsored by various colleges. The National Association of Physical Education for College Women and the Division of Girls and Women's Sports, as well as individual college staffs, have been concerned that these competitive events be well-planned functions of which women could be proud. There have been several cumbersome documents setting forth these regulations, stating standards, and outlining procedures. Realizing that student sponsorship is temporary and that on-going programs will need faculty responsibility with student assistance, a Commission on Intercollegiate Sports for Women has been established under DGWS sponsorship. The functions of this commission are stated as (1) to encourage organizations of colleges and universities or organizations of physical educators to govern intercollegiate competition for women by providing a framework and organizational pattern appropriate for the conduct of intercollegiate athletic opportunities for college women, (2) to sanction closed intercollegiate events (in which only college or university students participate) to which more than five colleges are invited, and (3) to sponsor DGWS national tournaments as the need for them becomes apparent. It is hoped that this organization, using streamlined standards and regulatory procedures, will forward developments in intercollegiate athletics for women in a manner that will reflect credit upon the profession and the young women who will be the participants.[1]

This phase of physical education for women has not been entered into lightly. The Division for Girls and Women's Sports has studied the question over a long period of time. There is still doubt in the minds of many persons whether or not women will be able to hold these controls and keep them operative. There are schools in this country that use interschool athletics (meaning primarily team sports) as a substitute for physical education. There are schools that concentrate on a specific sport from September through June. DGWS advises that we "make haste slowly" by the introduction of extramural competition in one sport and then evaluate the situation before enlarging the program. It is the administrator's duty to

[1] Phebe M. Scott and Celeste Ulrich, "Commission on Intercollegiate Sports for Women," *Journal of Health, Physical Education, and Recreation*, XXXVIII, October, 1966.

realize the implications of this entire situation, building a firm base for intramurals and offering extramurals to the extent that these can be afforded as far as finances and the demands on staff time are concerned. Orlo Miller, Coordinator of Health, Physical Education, and Safety, State Department of Public Instruction, writing in the *Wisconsin Journal of Education,* points to the need for the development of girls' sports programs which are "educationally sound, sane and sensible." He spells out this principle in the following statement:

> There should be little similarity to the boys' sports program. The basic emphasis is on sports participation with school identification non-existent or limited. Intensive interscholastic competition, as symbolized by leagues and tournaments, is not desirable for junior or senior high school girls and is not included in the four types of extramural activities outlined in the bulletin. These, too, should have precedence over sports days. . . . Very tight controls have been outlined to guide the organization and conduct of sports days. Needless to say, these are aimed particularly at basketball, which could become a real offender if unchecked.[2]

The question has been raised whether or not there are channels to direct and to control carefully the development of interscholastic school programs for girls. The National Federation of State High School Athletic Associations has acknowledged its responsibility to assist with this problem. The DGWS is urging that its members cooperate in this project by setting up committees of women in the various states to advise the parent organizations. To set the stage for this action, on July 1, 1964, a Resolution was adopted by the National Council, as follows:

RESOLUTION
ADOPTED BY NATIONAL COUNCIL
Jackson Lake, Wyoming
July 1, 1964

WHEREAS, it is the responsibility of the Board of Education and its duly appointed principals and superintendents to administer the educational program of the school, and

WHEREAS, interscholastic athletics is a part of the educational program of the school, and

WHEREAS, it is the duty, obligation, and responsibility of each school to determine its own program, and

WHEREAS, the administrators of the schools of the several states and provinces have caused to be created the High School Athletic or Activity Associations for the purpose of controlling, organizing, and supervising such interscholastic programs as may be deemed by them necessary and desirable to serve the interscholastic needs of boys and girls, and

---

[2] Orlo Miller, "Sports for Girls," *Wisconsin Journal of Education,* XCVII, No. 11–12 (January, 1965), 12.

WHEREAS, there is an increasing interest in the development of interscholastic school programs for girls; therefore

BE IT RESOLVED that the National Federation of State High School Athletic Associations, assembled in Jackson Lake, Wyoming, on this day, July 1, 1964, hereby recommends and urges that all control and supervision of girls' interscholastic athletics be administered through existing state and provincial athletic or activity associations.[3]

An outstanding example of sensible controls and excellent standards for girls in a secondary school (ninth, tenth, eleventh, and twelfth grades) has been developed by the Advisory Committee on Girls' Sports and Physical Education, The Ohio High School Athletic Association. Stress is placed on a variety of activities rather than on one or two sports, on limitation of the number of practice periods, and on the number of contests played. Moreover, the overly active student is protected from overplay by limiting her to the school squad in a specific activity during the school season. The recommendations of DGWS in relation to certified and qualified faculty women teachers, coaches, and officials are followed. Both the teacher and the player are safeguarded from certain types of exploitation by limitation of paid admissions and by support of the program by school administrative personnel.[4] For younger teachers or for teachers starting an interscholastic program, the Advisory Committee has prepared a booklet discussing the above standards, the organization of a G.A.A., cheerleading, and associated activities.[5] A program such as the one in Ohio throws light upon the path for leadership in interscholastic sports for girls.

Administrative policies and decisions, in the long run, must be based on the stated DGWS principles: namely, fine leadership, a variety of activities, participation by players at all levels of skill, and concern with the total welfare of the player rather than an emphasis upon highly structured competition.

BASES OF PHYSICAL EDUCATION

Currently in physical education, there is a curricular emphasis that requires administrative attention. Growing out of the swing of the pendulum toward purely academic concepts and the growing interest of this profession in establishing itself as a discipline, a renewed depth in the teaching of physical education is emerging. This depth imposes upon the teacher and the administrator the

[3] Used by permission.

[4] Ohio High School Athletic Association, *Constitution and Rules,* Part III, Girls Interscholastic Athletics, 1966–1967.

[5] Advisory Committee on Girls' Sports and Physical Education of the Ohio School Athletic Association, *Guidelines of Girls' Sports Programs in Ohio,* 1966.

need to orient the student in the reasons for physical education in the curriculum, the scientific laws from which movement and exercise patterns are derived, and the resulting analysis of motor movement with individualized student instruction. Professional students who have recently completed their preparation are aware of this emphasis and are increasingly able to meet these demands. The administrator enters the picture in the need for in-service education. In the public schools, coordinators of physical education are finding that, as this emphasis moves from the colleges via recent graduates to the secondary schools and even to the elementary schools, there is need to organize work-study groups or refresher sessions. The men who are experienced coaches have long known how to look at movement and how to analyze it. Women are just beginning to learn this art, with modern dance teachers in the vanguard. Even in the college departments concerned with professional preparation, there is need to arouse the latent abilities of the staff. Staff seminars and staff involvement in study of the problem seems to be the answer both at the public school and the college level. A problem in morale is involved as well as problems in the organization of time for such study, resource materials, and resource speakers or leaders. The administrator must establish a climate in which the task becomes acceptable to the staff and, at the same time, must forward the project.

PHYSICAL EDUCATION—AN ENTIRE LIFE SPAN

The administration of physical education has concerned itself for many years with the school- and college-age spans only. The few research studies of motor movement for the nursery school age were carried out under the auspices of either child psychology or child welfare departments. Recommendations regarding equipment, program, teacher preparation, and the administration of the activities were left to these specialists. They have certainly contributed richly to our knowledge of the preschool child. Along with the development of Operation Head-Start and similar projects, more teachers of physical education are being consulted on the activities feasible for this age. There is more interest in developmental equipment, correct program scheduling, and facilities needed for preschool activities.

The opposite end of the life span is also suddenly in sharp focus. Although the average physical education teacher will not immediately work in nursing home or retirement village recreation programs, this area may provide her with eventual employment either of a voluntary or a financially rewarding nature. As a nation, we are suddenly conscious of the need to remain active if the total life span is to be a vital, satisfying experience. Research reported from the laboratories concerned with heart and circulatory problems and the geriatric findings of the American Medical Association point definitely to the necessity of activity for the young adult on to the close of the life span. Where programs for young adults and oldsters may take place, how they may be financed, equipped, and supervised is usually the work of a community recreation agency. In the interrelationships that exist between public school systems, colleges, and community recreation offices, the administrative details of facilities, supervision, and use of equipment are usually resolved. It is in the area of the attitudes toward these programs that administrators of physical education find themselves currently involved.

Administratively, both these areas have implications for teacher education—in preparation and in in-service programs. Information must be gathered regarding the best facilities, excellent choices of equipment, personnel needed, and the framework for scheduling and time allotments to be included in course offerings or workshop sessions. Administratively, current staff personnel need orientation in these areas, and students preparing to teach need to understand especially the necessity for consideration of programs for the elderly.

FITNESS

Although the current emphasis upon fitness started in 1957, there still are schools around the country that are unaware of this movement. Suffice it to say that, initiated by President Eisenhower and supported and sustained by President Kennedy and President Johnson, the movement has gone beyond its initial concept to encompass total fitness for this nation. Under the auspices of the President's Council on Physical Fitness, testing programs have been set up and national norms established. Starting from a youth fitness concept, the movement has expanded to encompass adults and to include the physical recreation activities in the community. Regional workshops demonstrating the use of the fitness testing procedures and activities that develop fitness, publications both to orient the public and to serve as source materials,[6] and films to stimulate interest in the fitness movement are available. None of these materials would be operative unless both the professional and the

[6] See partial list of available publications on fitness in the Bibliography.

lay publics support the program. The administrator of physical education has responsibilities toward the fitness program as one phase of the total program. Public interest has been aroused in the fitness movement. Judicious use of the testing program gives stimulus to the full program. The broad concept of fitness sponsored by the President's Council is an asset to the work of the administrator. Even as the fitness concept aids the administrator, the administrator aids the fitness program by supporting the Council's work, by providing in-service education for teaching personnel, and by interesting the general public in the national fitness movement.

OTHER STUDENT ACTIVITIES

There are many student activities that do not belong under the umbrella of physical education. The many ramifications of the music program, debate teams, and dramatic productions as well as special interest clubs are examples. But there are also correlative activities, such as drill teams, pep squads, and cheerleaders, that are frequently placed under the sponsorship of the woman teacher of physical education. There are pros and cons regarding the constant use of the physical education teacher as a sponsor. On the pro side, she has knowledge of body reaction and movement that enables her to develop better use of the body in the execution of cheers or routines. She has close contact with the students and often may influence them in the development of school spirit and fine sportsmanship. On the con side, she is involved in activity all day, and superimposing a constant team game schedule on top of her already busy schedule may be physically too demanding unless she is allowed a rest period during the day. If every weekend demands her attendance at games, a certain amount of boredom and even disgust with the situation may result. And last, the general faculty may become indifferent to their responsibilities for school spirit and, particularly, for maintenance of fine behavior and sportsmanship standards on the part of both the school body and the general public. Several solutions of these administrative problems have been offered. One of these is a salary increment for the teacher charged with this responsibility. This solution plainly states that such organizations are "extras" and their sponsorship is a chore. Another solution is the practice of including such a sponsorship in the teaching load and adjusting the teacher's schedule accordingly. This practice is generally believed to be preferred. Regardless of which of the above administrative procedures is in use, rotation of this sponsorship every three or four years should be encouraged. New ideas, new enthusiasm, and new vigor in the organization will help to keep school spirit alive.

There are other administrative duties involved in the best possible program of pep squads and cheerleaders. Standards of selection must be established, practice time must be arranged, and standards (both academic and personal) for participation must be set. The number of individuals allowed to travel to games must be determined, and great care expended to be sure that they are carefully chaperoned and travel under the same conditions as the team. An additional problem is guidance of these young women in crowd psychology. Finally, the administrator in an institution preparing teachers has an additional responsibility—that of seeing that her students receive preparation in this phase of the total program.

TEACHER COMPETENCY

One of the major administrative problems facing physical education today is two-pronged. The first prong is the necessity for teacher education institutions to prepare more competent teachers of physical education. Spurred on by advances in the sciences, by standards for academic excellence, and by the increasingly better programs in elementary and secondary schools, the teacher education program is under pressure to prepare superior teachers. Such teachers must not only be conversant with the advances in general knowledge but must also be prepared to teach more highly skilled students at every level. The administrative problem of how to prepare teachers who can analyze movement and thus improve coordination, heed physiological and anatomical needs, and stimulate appreciation of the body and its aesthetic contributions runs headlong into the second great administrative problem of the day. Teacher education institutions faced with higher enrollments are desperately hunting well-prepared, experienced staff members. It becomes then an administrative responsibility to urge young staff members with potential for advanced graduate study to undertake this preparation. It becomes also an administrative responsibility to state the problems in the field honestly but, at the same time, to point out the advantages of advancement within one's chosen profession.

INCREASED LEISURE

In cycles, an emphasis upon the wise use of leisure time has appeared upon the horizon. At first glance, this would seem to be repetitious. At times, this cycle of emphasis has been frowned upon as a frivolous aspect of our society. At other times, as during the great depression of the early 1930's, it has been hailed as one means of upholding the morale of the people. Today, we are facing shorter and shorter work weeks plus a population explosion in schools and colleges. If the students of today are to be ready to use wisely the increased leisure time of tomorrow, they must have knowledge and skill in activities. Moreover, the population explosion in schools and colleges has resulted in crowded working and living arrangements. The tensions that result may either forward or contribute to the destruction of this civilization. Administratively, we have, therefore, increased demand for open gymnasiums, recreational activities of many types and kinds, and cooperative planning with other agencies concerned with student welfare. To initiate and maintain such a program by asking the teaching staff to assume these additional responsibilities dilutes the program. There is a limit to physical capacity on the part of individuals. Therefore, budgets must be constructed and personnel enlisted to cover these additional needs. Moreover, the teacher education institutions have responsibilities in the orientation of their students to this contingency. This is a real administrative problem involving careful public relations, careful analysis of the specific local situation, and judicious budgeting and personnel practices.

SUMMARY

This chapter has concerned itself with the intermittent problems and certain trends in physical education. These problems and these trends are interrelated with the materials in the various chapters in this book. Without facilities and equipment, personnel, and carefully constructed administrative contacts, one could not develop a fitness program, expand campus recreation, or engage in extramurals. The preparation of teachers with competency, as well as advancements in the field, rests in part upon research. To keep physical education advancing in an affirmative manner, then, the materials presented in this chapter and this book form a web base for ventures that the future may bring.

CONCLUSION

This book has been concerned with the many ramifications of administration of physical education. Since administration has often been defined as "getting things done" and organization as "how to get things done," a heavy emphasis has, necessarily, been placed upon the problems. The neophyte may be appalled or even terrified by the magnitude of the problems. They run the gamut of maturation aspects from the kindergarten child to the advanced graduate student. They range from the classroom, through varied administrative channels, to the contacts with the various publics. They are deeply concerned with tangibles such as facilities and equipment but even more concerned with the intangibles of personnel reactions. Problems of detailed business techniques sit side by side with problems of governmental structure and legal responsibilities. Administrative support of research results in evaluation, and evaluation in turn results in research. This is an almost overwhelming prospect. Administration, however, is an area in which one lives a day at a time as well as with projected planning. Perspective is needed to keep its details in focus. One attempts to solve the problem at hand with the best possible advancement of the whole department as the basic factor in the immediate decision. Life is never dull in administration. Every day brings new challenges. If you, as a neophyte, are professionally ambitious, if you want an alert full life, demanding in time but rewarding in satisfactions, the challenge to prepare for administrative duties is there. Physical education, spurred on by the current interest in physical fitness and the prospects of increased leisure time, is an expanding field. It needs well-prepared persons in its teaching corps and dedicated administrators to forward its causes. We challenge you to join our ranks.

APPENDIXES

APPENDIXES

1. Guiding Principles for Adapted Physical Education [1]

Prepared by the AAHPER Committee on Adapted Physical Education and endorsed by the AAHPER Board of Directors and the Joint Committee on Health Problems in Education of the American Medical Association and the National Education Association.

It is the responsibility of the school to contribute to the fullest possible development of the potentialities of each individual entrusted to its care. This is a basic tenet of our democratic faith.

1. There is need for common understanding regarding the nature of adapted physical education.

Adapted physical education is a diversified program of developmental activities, games, sports and rhythms, suited to the interests, capacities and limitations of students with disabilities who may not safely or successfully engage in unrestricted participation in the vigorous activities of the general physical education program.

2. There is need for adapted physical education in schools and colleges.

According to the best estimates, there are about four million children of school age in the United States with physical handicaps. Only 11 percent of this group requiring special educational services are receiving them through special schools and classes. The vast majority of exceptional children are attending regular schools.

The major disabling conditions, each affecting thousands of children, are cerebral palsy, poliomyelitis, epilepsy, tuberculosis, traumatic injuries, neurological problems, and heart disease. Further evidence indicates that on the college level there is a significant percentage of students requiring special consideration for either temporary or permanent disabilities.

3. Adapted physical education has much to offer the individual who faces the combined problem of seeking an education and living most effectively with a handicap.

Through adapted physical education the individual can: (a) Be observed and referred when the need for medical or other services are suspected; (b) Be guided in avoidance of situations which would aggravate the condition or subject him to unnecessary risks or injury; (c) Improve neuromuscular skills, general strength and endurance following convalescence from acute illness or injury; (d) Be provided with opportunities for improved psychological adjustment and social development.

4. The direct and related services essential for the proper conduct of adapted physical education should be available to our schools.

These services should include: (a) Adequate and periodic health examination; (b) Classification for physical education based on the health examination and other pertinent tests and observations; (c) Guidance of individuals needing special consideration with respect to physical activity, general health practices, recreational pursuits, vocational planning, psychological adjustment, and social development; (d) Arrangements of appropriate adapted physical education programs; (e) Evaluation and recording of progress through observations, appropriate measurements and consultations; (f) Integrated relationships with other school personnel, medical and its auxiliary services, and the family to assure continuous guidance and supervisory services; (g) Cumulative records for each individual, which should be transferred from school to school.

[1] From *Journal of American Association for Health, Physical Education, and Recreation*, April, 1952.

5. It is essential that adequate medical guidance be available for teachers of adapted physical education.

The possibility of serious pathology requires that programs of adapted physical education should not be attempted without the diagnosis, written recommendation, and supervision of a physician. The planned program of activities must be predicated upon medical findings and accomplished by competent teachers working with medical supervision and guidance. There should be an effective referral service between physicians, physical educators, and parents aimed at proper safeguards and maximum student benefits. School administrators alert to the special needs of handicapped children, should make every effort to provide adequate staff and facilities necessary for a program of adapted physical education.

6. Teachers of adapted education have a great responsibility as well as an unusual opportunity.

Physical educators engaged in teaching adapted physical education should: (a) Have adequate professional education to implement the recommendations provided by medical personnel; (b) Be motivated by the highest ideals with respect to the importance of total student development and satisfactory human relationships; (c) Develop the ability to establish rapport with students who may exhibit social maladjustment as a result of a disability; (d) Be aware of a student's attitude toward his disability; (e) Be objective in relationships with students; (f) Be prepared to give the time and effort necessary to help a student overcome a difficulty; (g) Consider as strictly confidential information related to personal problems of the student; (h) Stress similarities rather than deviations, and abilities instead of disabilities.

7. Adapted physical education is necessary at all school levels.

The student with a disability faces the dual problem of overcoming a handicap and acquiring an education which will enable him to take his place in society as a respected citizen. Failure to assist a student with his problems may retard the growth and development process.

Offering adapted physical education in the elementary grades, and continuing through the secondary school and college will assist the individual to improve function and make adequate psychological and social adjustments. It will be a factor in his attaining maximum growth and development within the limits of the disability. It will minimize attitudes of defeat and fears of insecurity. It will help him face the future with confidence.

2. Statement of Policies for Competition in Girls and Women's Sports [*,1]

Approved May 1963 by Division for Girls and Women's Sports Executive Council and American Association for Health, Physical Education, and Recreation Board of Directors

The Division for Girls and Women's Sports of the American Association for Health, Physical Education, and Recreation believes the competitive element in sports activities can be used constructively for achievement of desirable educational and recreational objectives. When favorable conditions are present, competitive experiences may be wholesome and beneficial and result in acceptable conduct and attitudes. Competition in and of itself does not automatically result in desirable or undesirable outcomes.

The adoption of practices best suited for the attainment of desirable outcomes is the responsibility of all associated with competitive events. Sponsoring agencies, players, teachers, coaches, officials, and spectators must share responsibility for valid practices in competitive sports.

DGWS believes participation in sports competition is the privilege of all girls and women. Sound instructional and well-organized intramural programs will answer the needs and desires of the majority of young women. For the college woman and high school girl who seek and need additional challenges in competition and skills, a sound, carefully planned, and well-directed program of extramural sports is recommended. The provisions for extramural sports opportunities should be broad, including such events as sports days, leagues, meets, and tournaments. Development of all participants toward higher competencies and advanced skills should be a major objective in all sports programs.

DGWS advocates the following policies through which desirable outcomes in competition may be achieved.

Definition of Competition

Competition is defined as the participation in a sport activity by two or more persons, in which a winner can result. The educational values of competition are determined by the quality of leadership and of the participation. For the best results, there should be comprehensive physical education, intramural, and extramural programs. The organized competitive programs should offer opportunities in terms of individual ability and should be adapted to the needs and interests of the participants.

---

* This is a revision of the "Statement of Policies and Procedures for Competition in Girls and Women's Sports," which was published in the September 1957 *Journal of Health, Physical Education, and Recreation* and later in 1958 and 1961 editions of *Standard in Sports for Girls and Women*, published by AAHPER. This revised statement is an outgrowth of recent DGWS discussions of major issues, one of which dealt with the needs and interests of the highly skilled girl.

1 Reprinted by permission from *Journal of Health, Physical Education, and Recreation*, September, 1963. Copyright © 1963 by The American Association for Health, Physical Education, and Recreation, National Education Association, Washington, D.C.

283

Forms of Competition

Intramural competition is sports competition in which all participants are identified with the same school, community center, club, organization, institution, or industry, or are residents of a designated small neighborhood or community. This form of competition stresses the participation of "the many." A good intramural program which offers a variety of activities, at various skill levels, including corecreational activities, frequently is sufficient to meet the needs and desires of the majority of girls and women.

It is the responsibility of the school or agency sponsoring the intramural program to provide the time, facilities, and competent leadership, with preference given to professional, qualified women. Intramural programs should be an outgrowth of and a complement to the school physical education program or the organized community recreation program.

Extramural competition is a plan of sports competition in which participants from two or more schools, community centers, clubs, organizations, institutions, industries, or neighborhoods compete. The forms of extramural competition include:

1. Sport days—school or sport group participates as a unit.
2. Telegraphic meets—results are compared by wire or mail.
3. Invitational events—symposiums, games, or matches, for which a school or sport group invites one or more teams to participate.
4. Interscholastic, intercollegiate, or interagency programs—groups which are trained and coached play a series of scheduled games and/or tournaments with teams from other schools, cities, or organizations.

The extramural program is planned and carried out to complement the intramural and instructional programs. For the best welfare of the participants, it is essential that the program be conducted by qualified leaders, be supported by budgeted funds, and be representative of approved objectives and standards for girls and women's sports, including acceptable conditions of travel, protective insurance, appropriate facilities, proper equipment, and desirable practices in the conduct of the events. When the program affords group participation as a team in a series of games on appropriate tournament or schedule basis, additional coaching by qualified staff members must be provided.

It is assumed that the sponsoring organization recognizes its obligation to delegate responsibility for this program to the supervisor or specialist in charge of the girls and women's sports programs. When admission charges are made, the proceeds should be used for furthering the sports programs for girls (instructional, intramural, and extramural).

Adaptation of Competitive Sports for Age-Level Groupings in School Programs

In junior high school, it is desirable that intramural programs of competitive activities be closely integrated with the basic physical education program. Appropriate competition at this level should be comprised of intramural and informal extramural events consistent with social needs and recreational interests. A well-organized and well-conducted sports program should take into account the various skill levels and thus meet the needs of the more highly skilled.

In senior high school, a program of intramural and extramural participation should be arranged to augment a sound and inclusive instructional program in physical education. It should be recognized that an interscholastic program will require professional leadership, time, and funds in addition to those provided for the intramural programs. Facilities should be such that the intramural and instructional programs need not be eliminated or seriously curtailed if an interscholastic program is offered.

Specifically, the following standards should prevail:

1. The medical status of the player is ascertained by a physician and the health of the players is carefully supervised.
2. Activities for girls and women are planned to meet their needs, not for the personal glorification of coaches and/or sponsoring organizations.
3. The salary, retention, and promotion of an instructor are not dependent upon the outcome of the games.
4. Qualified women teach, coach, and officiate wherever and whenever possible, and in all cases the professional background and experience of the leader meet established standards.
5. Rules approved by DGWS are used.
6. Schedules do not exceed the ability and endurance relative to the maturity and physiological conditioning of the participants. Standards for specific sports are defined by DGWS and appear in sports guides, published by the American Association for Health, Physical Education, and Recreation, Washington, D.C.
7. Sports activities for girls and women are scheduled independently from boys and men's sports. Exceptions will occur when the activities and/or time and facilities are appropriate for both.
8. Girls and women may participate in appropriate corecreational activities or teams. Girls and women may not participate as members of boys and men's teams.
9. The program, including health insurance for players, is financed by budgeted school or organization funds rather than entirely by admission charges.
10. Provision is made by the school or organization for safe transportation by bonded carriers, with chaperones who are responsible to the sponsoring group.

In colleges and universities, it is desirable that opportunities be provided for the highly skilled beyond the intramural program. Regulations for the conduct of collegiate competition have been developed by the National Joint Committee on Extramural Sports for College Women [2] and are available from the committee for any specific sport activity. While the statements of NJCESCW apply to approval for state-wide or wider geographical tournaments, the principles may also be applicable to or guide the conduct of local and district tournaments.

In addition to the standards previously listed, other standards pertinent to the colleges are:

1. The amount and kind of intercollegiate competition should be determined by the women's physical education department.
2. The financial arrangements relative to all intercollegiate sports events should be administered with the approval of the women's physical education department.
3. The time involved in relation to intercollegiate competition should not interfere with the academic program of the institution sponsoring the event and should not make excessive demands upon the participants' academic schedules.
4. All housing arrangements relative to visiting participants should be approved by the women's physical education department.

Adaptations of Competitive Sports for Age-Level Groupings in Public and Private Recreation Agency Programs

DGWS recognizes that the sports programs of public and private recreation agencies make a valuable contribution to girls and women. The aims and objectives of community recreation agencies in their conduct of sports programs are similar to those

[2] Composed of representatives of the Division for Girls and Women's Sports, Athletic and Recreation Federation of College Women, and National Association for Physical Education of College Women. Write to American Association for Health, Physical Education, and Recreation, Washington, D.C.

of the schools. By using common rules and applying basic standards in organizing competition, many girls and women can be given the opportunity to develop skills and to enjoy a desirable type of competition.

Students should be informed of the opportunities for participation in the sports activities of these agencies. If a student contemplates entering events which appear to jeopardize her welfare, she should be given guidance which will help her to make wise decisions.

If individuals are grouped according to age and skill ability, the statements of policy outlined above can be applied by these agencies in organizing desirable forms of competition. The formation of leagues is often the organizational structure through which many recreation programs are conducted. The definitions of intramural and extramural competition, as previously stated, may be interpreted to apply to programs provided by public and private agencies.

Modifications will be required in planning policies for competition depending upon the age level involved:

1. For girls under senior high school age, competition may be provided in intra-mural games, that is, games with teams of the same age and ability from the same neighborhood, playground, recreation center, or league. Extramural events consistent with social needs and recreational interests of junior high school age groups may be arranged with similar teams from other playgrounds, centers, or leagues.
2. For girls of senior high school age, it is recommended that all standards listed for senior high school be used for intramural and extramural competition. A player should affiliate with only one team in one sport.
3. For girls over senior high school age, it is recommended that the intercollegiate standards be followed for competition at this age level.

Sponsorship by recreational agencies of the participation of women in tournaments and meets organized at successively higher levels (local, sectional, national) should be governed by the best practices for safeguarding the welfare of the participants. The organization, administration, and leadership of such competitive events should be conducted so that the basic policies of DGWS are upheld.

3. Freshman Scholarship Agreement

March 25, 19____

To Dr. _____ _____
Chairman
Department of Physical Education for Women
University of _____

I accept the Physical Education Scholarship for Freshman Women ($100), University of _____, for the year 19____–19____. I understand that this scholarship has been contributed by the Alumnae of the Department of Physical Education for Women in the interest of preparing teachers in this field. This award carries a moral obligation for preparation in this specific area in the year of its grant.

Recipient's signature _____

Parent's signature _____

4. Rating Form for Professional Students in Physical Education

Student_____ Instructor _____

Class_____ Course_____ Date_____

Mark each item where there is some basis for judgment.

	Poor			Fair			Good			Excellent		
	L	M	H	L	M	H	L	M	H	L	M	H

A. APPEARANCE
1. Dress appropriate for the occasion
2. Neat and well-groomed appearance
3. Good posture and carriage
4. Feminine appearance and manner
5. Appearance and behavior suggest good physical health and vitality
6. Good personal health practices

B. ORAL AND WRITTEN COMMUNICATION
1. Voice quality adequate and pleasant
2. Oral expression well organized and understandable
3. Absence of annoying mannerisms
4. Written communication

C. BEHAVIOR AND ATTITUDES
1. Willingness and ability to work with others.
2. Consideration of others
3. Proficiency in social amenities
4. Respectful of authority and established policies
5. Temperament and/or disposition
6. Absence of annoying personal mannerisms
7. Emotional control and poise
8. Adaptable to varying situations
9. Character

D. PROFESSIONAL QUALITIES
1. Enthusiasm for physical education
2. Well informed about physical education
3. Technical skills and knowledges
4. Acceptance of responsibilities
5. Organizational ability
6. Initiative
7. Resourcefulness and adaptability
8. Ability to accept constructive criticism and to follow through on suggestion
9. Completion of assignments and tasks on time
10. Recognition of own abilities and limitations
11. Pursuance of opportunities beneficial to her as a future teacher
12. Ethical behavior
13. Leadership ability desirable for teaching

E. PROFESSIONAL PROFICIENCY
1. Grade received in course_____
2. Skill, where pertinent_____
3. Knowledge _____

F. GENERAL RECOMMENDATION AS A PROFESSIONAL STUDENT
1. I recommend _____

2. I do not recommend_____

3. I provisionally recommend_____

G. COMMENTS:

5. The Undergraduate Course in Organization and Administration[1]

The four hypothetical situations are used as problem-solving devices in the class.

Situation A: grades 10, 11, 12
Large Secondary School

Enrollment: 860 girls in physical education
1 gymnasium (for girls alone)
1 play room
½ use of swimming pool
1 play area (5 acres)
4 teachers
Population of city: 180,000
Budget: $500 per year

Situation B: grades 7, 8, 9
Junior High School

Enrollment: 350 girls in physical education
1 combined large gymnasium and auditorium (for boys)
1 smaller gymnasium (for girls)
1 playground (2 posts in it); swim at YWCA pool
1 teacher
Population of city: 100,000
Budget: $300 per year

Situation C: grades 1, 2
Two Elementary Schools

Enrollment: 575 boys and girls
Class size: 32
Each school has:
   1 multiple purpose room (shared with music and cafeteria)
   1 play area for own use—gravel and black top
Population of city: 450,000
Budget: $100 for each school

Situation D: grades 1–6
Consultant and Teacher for
Three Elementary Schools

Enrollment, each school: 1–6
Class size: 30
Facilities:
  I. Playroom in basement
    Playground (200′ × 500′)
 II. Combined gymnasium and auditorium (also for music)
    Playground (300′ × 600′)
III. Hallway on first floor
    Classrooms, movable desks
    Playground (200′ × 400′)
No swimming pools
No use of community facilities
Population of city: 40,000
Budget: $50 per school

The class members are divided into four groups and assigned one of the above situations. A unit on program planning is studied; this includes the study of principles, procedures for planning, program content, special programs, restricted programs, extracurricular programs, relationships of health to physical education, health services and health education, and the teacher's schedule. Each group charts a total program, a plan for use of facilities, and the teacher's schedule for its situation.

The class group is assigned a second situation. A unit on facilities and equipment is studied; this includes space needs such as storage, dressing rooms, lockers, showers, baskets, padlocks, costumes, swimming pool, and play areas; this covers policies for purchase of equipment and supplies and for care of equipment. Then, each group draws up an ideal outdoor and indoor facility for its particular situation.

[1] Prepared by Ruth D. Levinson, Assistant Professor of Physical Education for Women, University of Nebraska, Lincoln, Nebraska.

The class groups move on to their third specific situations. A unit on public relations is studied; this includes scope and basic principles, such as media, ethics, and possible interrelationships and outcomes. Each group designs a sample brochure to advertise some phase of that situation's program, writes short articles feasible for newspaper publicity, and arranges a mock panel discussion or hearing before a board of education or a PTA on some related topic, such as need for facilities in Situation D.

Again, the class groups interchange situations. A unit on administrative responsibilities is covered; this includes rules and regulations, safety, legal liability, the protection program, inventories, budget, care of plant, office planning, and preliminaries and ending activities for the school year. Each group prepares a year's budget with a five-year plan for purchases and allocations, dependent upon money available and program plans for the specific situation.

Individual assignments as well as group assignments are made in each unit. For example, in Unit I, Program Planning, each student finds five principles, one of which must be original, for program planning in her assigned unit. In Unit II, Facilities and Equipment, students visit different facilities in the community to observe their best features and to note needed improvements. Each class member is asked to prepare the essential equipment needed for a class of thirty-five in one or two activities, such as folk dance and archery, and to include three comparative prices on all items and to list two or three important details on care and repair of equipment. For Unit III, Public Relations, the student states her policies in regard to public relations and how she implements her procedures for good public relations with the administration, the students, the parents, the school paper, the community newspaper, and the custodial staff. For Unit IV, Administrative Responsibilities, a safety code is written to cover an assigned situation for either use of a piece of apparatus or general safety.

Throughout the course, students are reminded that all problems cannot be anticipated, but that with careful thought and planning based on sound principles, one can attempt to solve any problem. Returned questionnaires from graduates who have been asked to evaluate their professional preparation have indicated that the above course plan has so far permitted them to approach organization and administration with confidence.

6. Rules Governing the Use of the Pool

A. Admittance to the Pool:
1. Foot conditions of all who use the pool are carefully checked at the opening of each semester, but unfavorable conditions may develop after this checkup. Persons with blistering, peeling, wart, or wartlike conditions of the feet are excluded from the pool, showers, and locker rooms in bare feet. Whenever any unfavorable condition of the foot appears, report this to your instructor before class. To prevent athlete's foot, be sure to dry your feet thoroughly—especially between the toes.
2. If there is any question about your entering the pool because of some unfavorable condition, such as a cold or similar infection, a skin rash, inflamed eyes or like condition, consult your instructor before dressing for class.
3. Tape, corn plasters, bandages, and the like must be removed before entering the pool.
4. Dispose of chewing gum before entering the pool. Wrap it in a piece of paper and put it in the wastebasket.
5. Spitting or otherwise polluting the pool water is forbidden; use the overflow trough if necessary.
6. The instructor must be the first person to enter the pool and the last person to leave it. Students please note.

B. Swimming Equipment:
1. Bathing caps must be worn at all times to protect the pool from hair.
2. Each swimmer furnishes her own bathing cap. Your name must be on the cap. (Adhesive tape may be used for the inside of cap.)
3. Bring a box large enough to accommodate all your valuables (jewelry, wallet, watches, etc.).
4. It is recommended that a head scarf be worn to protect your head if hair is not completely dry when leaving building.

C. General Procedure:
1. Pick up suit from the matron at main desk. Only those suits furnished by the University may be worn. Sizes run small. Ask attendant for one size larger than you usually wear. Suits also come in Medium for short girls and Long for medium and tall girls.
2. Take suit to booth in dressing room.
3. Remove clothes. Do not wear jewelry to the pool; you are responsible for your own property.
4. Place your valuables in a box and lock your basket.
5. Before taking shower, use the toilet whether or not you feel you have to. This is a definite must.
6. Next, go to the shower room and take a good soapy shower. Soap is furnished in each shower booth.
7. *Do not put on your bathing suit until after you shower.*
8. In returning from the pool, take one towel from the main desk and carry it to the shower with you. It can be kept dry by throwing it over the curtain.
9. Wet suits may be worn only between shower and pool rooms. Do not enter any other part of dressing rooms with a wet suit on.
10. As soon as you remove your wet suit, put it in a special container at entrance to showers.
11. Before dressing after a swim, it is advisable to take another shower to remove all trace of pool water from the body. Chlorine may be irritating.

12. Do not leave towel in dressing room or shower room. There are large containers provided for them.
13. Lock up property before you leave.

D. Pool and Dressing Room Regulations:
   1. No one wearing street shoes will be allowed in the pool room. All spectators will be restricted to the balcony, and bathers to the platform.
   2. Do not put waste materials in the suit container or towel carriers; use the cans under the mirrors.
   3. Smoking is forbidden in the dressing rooms and pool room.
   4. No glass articles may be taken into the dressing rooms or showers. Report breakage of any glass articles, or the spilling of any fluid, to the matron at once, so that it will not be tracked around.
   5. Be sure to read all notices posted on the bulletin board opposite the counter. You are responsible for information posted there.
   6. Each girl is responsible for obtaining and learning her locker combination.

E. Special Rules for Menstrual Period:
   1. During the menstrual period, you need not swim. Report to class as at other times and observe the classwork. Dress in your regulation physical education costume and remove shoes and stockings.
   2. Do not take any books or schoolwork to the pool. You are to observe classwork and pay close attention to all class instruction.
   3. If you desire to swim during your menstrual period, *internal* sanitary protection must be used.

F. Absence from Class:
   1. When you are absent from class for a reason that is unavoidable, explain the situation to your instructor, and if possible present a written excuse.
   2. When you are absent from class without good reason, expect to receive a zero for that day's classwork.
   3. Recreational swims are scheduled on Tuesdays from 8:00–9:00 P.M. If you have had excessive absences or observations, it is advisable that you attend these sessions for extra practice.
   4. Your instructor will inform you of her requirements for making up work missed.

G. Roll Call and Class Dismissal:
   1. For one-hour classes, roll is called promptly at five minutes past the half-hour; class is dismissed at five or ten minutes after the hour.
   2. For hour-and-a-half classes, roll is called promptly at five minutes past the half-hour. Class is dismissed on the half-hour.
   3. Do not be tardy.

H. You will be graded on:
   1. Classwork.
   2. Skill test.
   3. Knowledge test.

I. Safety Rules To Follow:
   1. Swim only when an instructor is on duty.
   2. If you are a beginner, swim only in shallow water. Do not go in deep water by a hand-over-hand method or by hanging onto other swimmers.
   3. Do not run on the stairs, dressing room floor, or the pool deck.
   4. No ducking or splashing is allowed.
   5. Do not yell unless in actual danger.
   6. Do not jump or dive on swimmers.
   7. Do not swim under the diving board.

8. Only one person at a time is allowed on the diving board.
9. Dive only in deep water.

J. Bring to next class meeting:
   1. Regulation costume.
   2. Cap.
   3. Box for valuables.
   4. Locker combinations.

7. Rules for Lifeguards

A. Work Assignments:
   1. All lifeguards shall have filed an application with the Swimming Chairman, including name, address, phone number, current schedule, and have identified themselves by presenting a current Red Cross L.S. or W.S.I. card.
   2. After receiving work assignments, the lifeguard shall be expected to remain on duty during the school term in which she agrees to serve. She shall uphold the same standards of attendance as the instructor. In case it is absolutely necessary for a lifeguard to be absent, the following procedures apply:
      a. She shall secure a substitute lifeguard from the approved list posted.
      b. She shall attempt to notify her instructor ahead of time.
      c. In the event that she is unable to find a substitute lifeguard, she shall report this to the Swimming Chairman twenty-four hours in advance of her absence.
      d. In case of sudden illness, the Swimming Chairman or class instructor shall be notified immediately.
   3. The lifeguard shall report on time to the pool room in costume. Repeated tardiness for work warrants a dismissal as does even one absence not announced in time to secure a substitute.
   4. The lifeguard shall report at the same time as the instructor and shall be dismissed at the end of the period or at the instructor's discretion.
   5. At the close of each work period, the lifeguard is responsible for filling out her employment card, which is kept at the matron's desk. The matron will send the card to the Department of Physical Education for Women at the end of the month. The check may be procured at the Administration Building by the lifeguard on the 15th of the following month.

B. Rules for the Lifeguard:
   1. Dress for work in the special booth reserved for lifeguards. Do not go back of the counter; that place is reserved for the exclusive use of the attendant and the faculty members.
   2. Wear a one-piece bathing suit or a tank suit. (Carry a whistle at all times.) Whenever possible, an A.R.C. emblem should be worn.
   3. Station yourself between the deep and shallow ends and on the side opposite the instructor or as otherwise directed by the instructor.
   4. Be alert and be ready for quick and efficient action.
   5. Know and enforce the regulations for use of the pool, and uphold the regulations when using the pool.
   6. Know that the lifesaving equipment is in place for use. Never allow anyone to play with this equipment. Keep a rescue pole by your side.
   7. Be on duty at all times. Avoid the temptation to converse socially with the class or swimmers.
   8. Always face the swimmers.
   9. At no time should you leave the pool room when you are on duty unless you advise the instructor. This would be in case of emergency only. You should have no personal phone calls during the time you guard.
   10. Never swim alone in the pool unless an instructor or another lifeguard is present. Never swim on duty except in case of emergency. After all swimmers have left the pool, you may swim with permission and in the presence of the instructor.
   11. Keep control of the situation. Prevent accidents by removing possible causes

of accidents. Report to the instructor or Swimming Chairman any suggestions regarding repair or replacement of equipment.

12. Enforce the rule that swimmers who are not able to take care of themselves in deep water must remain in shallow water. Swimmers may not advance to deep water by holding on to sides of pool or other swimmers.

13. Be able to account for swimmers at all times. Keep constant check and count of all present.

14. After the swim period, make a careful check of the water before leaving the pool area. Be sure that all swimmers leave the pool room before you leave and that all are in the dressing room before you leave the stairway.

15. In case of accidents, the following applies:
    a. In case an individual needs help, extend the pole to her and pull her to the edge of the pool. *Enter the water only as a last resort.*
    b. Know the proper procedure in case of accidents. Review the procedure advocated by the A.R.C. in order to be prepared for quick and effective action.
    c. In case of any emergency, clear the pool of swimmers and notify the instructor immediately.
    d. A list of emergency phone numbers is located near the phone on the matron's deck.

C. Rules for Guarding During Recreational Swimming:

1. Station yourself on the side nearest the door for the first ten minutes. For the remainder of the time, station yourself on the opposite side.

2. Do not give swimming instruction unless requested by the instructor.

3. Do not carry on conversations with swimmers. Talk to them only as is necessary to see that rules are obeyed and safety measures observed.

4. Request that those who will not obey pool rules, after a warning, leave the pool. The names of such violators should be left with the Swimming Chairman. A list of violators will be furnished to the matron.

5. In case of accident, proceed as follows:
    a. If the injury is slight, such as skin abrasions or bruises, send the individual to the locker room matron for first-aid treatment and then to the Health Center. Fill in an accident form provided by the matron.
    b. If the injury is more serious, request the swimming office attendant to call a physician from the approved list posted in the dressing room. Notify the Chairman of Physical Education for Women. Fill out the accident form.

6. Remember: *you are the first person in the pool room and the last to leave.*

8. Liability Factors

Common Law or Sovereign Immunity	Immunity Removed to Extent of Insurance Policy Coverage	Respondent Superior	Common Law or Sovereign Immunity Unaffected by Insurance
Alabama	Arkansas	Alaska	Idaho
Colorado	Indiana *	Arizona	Iowa
Delaware	Minnesota *	California *	Maryland
Florida	New Hampshire	1963—Compre-	Montana *
Georgia *	New Jersey *	hensive Govern-	Nevada
Kentucky *	North Carolina *	ment Tort Lia-	New Mexico
Louisiana *	Oregon *	bility Act	Oklahoma
Maine	Tennessee *	Hawaii	Pennsylvania *
Massachusetts	Vermont	Illinois *	Texas
Michigan *		New York	West Virginia
Mississippi		Ed. Law	Wyoming
Missouri		552560,3023	
Nebraska		Washington	
Ohio *			
Rhode Island			
South Carolina			
South Dakota			
Virginia			

* Cases cited.

California
    a. Accidents occurring during physical education classes generally have immunity from suit—for example, *Redlands High Sch. Dist. v. Superior Court of San Bernardino County*, 20 Cal. 2d 346, 125 P.2d 490 (1942).
    b. Athletic injury—may or may not be able to sue—depends on the negligence if the proximate cause of injury—for example, *Welsh v. Dunsmuir Joint Union High Sch. Dist.*, 326 P.2d 633 (Cal. App. 1958).

Georgia
    Athletic injury; school immune from suit. *Hale* v. *Davies* (1952) 86 Ga. App. 126 70 SE2d 923.

Illinois
    Ill. Rev. Stat. c.122, 56-35.1 (1959).
    a. *Molitor* v. *Kaneland County Community Unit*, Dist. 18, Ill. 2d 11, 163 N.E.2d 89, 97 (1959). School bus case. Illinois Supreme Court, without depending on an insurance statute, concluded, ". . . the rule of school district tort immunity is unjust, unsupported by any valid reason and has no place in modern society."
    b. Prior case. *Thomas* v. *Broadlands*, 348 Ill. App. 567, 109 N.E.2d 636 (1952). A school district carrying public-liability insurance waived its immunity from tort action to the extent of such insurance.

Indiana
    a. Generally under statute expressly providing that insurer waived defense, there was no immunity to extent of insurance coverage;

insurance was not intended merely to protect officers and agents. *Flowers* v. *Board of Community of Vanderburgh County* (Ind.), 168 N.E.2d 224.

b. Athletic injury. Sovereign immunity. *Hummer* v. *Sch., City of Hartford County,* 124 Ind. App. 30, 112 N.E.2d 891 (1953).

Kentucky   Kentucky Court of Appeals held that under certain conditions members of boards of education may be personally liable for the negligent acts of their employees if the board failed to exercise ordinary care in selecting competent people. *Whitt* v. *Reed,* 239 S.W.2d 489 (1951).

Louisiana   A committee of legislators determines if certain facts justify waiver of the sovereign immunity of Louisiana. If determined in the affirmative, normally a concurrent resolution of the legislature is prepared, allowing suit to be filed.

Michigan   a. Accidents—physical education classes. Generally, immunity from suit. *McDowell* v. *Brozo,* 285 Mich. 38, 280 N.W. 100 (1938).
b. Athletic injury. School immunity. *Williams* v. *Detroit,* 364 Mich. 221, 111 N.W.2d 1 (1961).

Minnesota   Accidents—physical education classes. Generally, immunity from suit. *Makovich* v. *Independent Sch. Dist.,* 177 Minn. 446, 225 N.W. 292 (1929).

Montana   Accidents—physical education classes. Generally, immunity from suit. *Rhoades* v. *Sch. Dist. of Roosevelt County,* 115 Mont. 352, 142 P.2d 890 (1943).

North Carolina   Athletic injury. School immunity. *Smith* v. *Hefner,* 235 N.C. 1, 68 S.E.2d 783 (1952).

Ohio   Accidents—physical education classes. Generally, immunity from suit. *Shaw* v. *Bd. of Educ.,* 17 Ohio L. Abs. 588 (App. 1934).

Pennsylvania   Athletic injury. School immunity. *Martini* v. *Sch. Dist. of Olyphant* 83 Pa. D. & C. 206 (1902).

Tennessee   Athletic injury. School immunity. *Reed* v. *Rhea County,* 189 Tenn. 247, 225 S.W.2d 49 (1949).

Washington   Accidents—physical education classes. Generally, immunity from suit. *Dead* v. *Sch. Dist. of Lewis County,* 7 Wash. 2d 502, 110 P.2d 179 (1941).

STATES WITH QUALIFYING FACTORS

Arkansas   Sovereign immunity. 1941: If insurance is carried, direct cause of action against the insurer is allowed.

Connecticut   1949: Save harmless statute protects only teachers and administrative personnel. 1964: Boards of education may insure to protect teachers and employees. 1964: Transportation of schoolchildren as governmental duty—no defense in case of injury.

Florida   Sovereign immunity. 1963: Schools may purchase general liability insurance. Liability insurance mandatory for school buses. Immunity does not extend to personal tort of governmental employees.

Kentucky   Sovereign immunity is removed to extent of insurance policy coverage. Immunity does not extend to personal tort.

Louisiana   Sovereign immunity may be waived.

Minnesota   Two divisions. Sovereign immunity is unaffected by insurance; immunity is removed to the extent of the policy coverage.

Missouri   Governmental agencies may not waive immunity in carrying insurance, but employees may be liable if negligent.

North Dakota   No specific laws either granting or denying immunity. Political subdivisions of state may insure to cover possible liability.

Washington   Two decisions. Sovereign immunity is removed to extent of liability
                  coverage; Washington Code—suits may be maintained for damages
                  suffered at the hands of their school boards.

Wisconsin   Two decisions. Sovereign immunity is removed to extent of insur-
                  ance coverage; sovereign immunity is unaffected by insurance. Safe
                  place statute is subject to limited application.

9. Detailed Legal Definitions[1]

1. *Negligence.* Generally, negligence refers to the failure to exercise that degree of care which a reasonable, prudent, and ordinarily careful person would exercise, as rendered appropriate by the particular circumstances. There are degrees of care, and failure to exercise proper degree of care is negligence, but there are no degrees of negligence.

> EXAMPLE: Classification of negligence as "gross," "ordinary," and "slight" indicates only that under particular circumstances great care and caution, or ordinary care, or slight care are required, but failure to exercise care demanded is negligence.

2. *Contributory Negligence.* Any want of ordinary care on the part of the person injured (or on the part of another whose negligence is imputable to him) which combined and concurred with defendant's negligence, and contributed to the injury, and as an element without which the injury would not have occurred.

3. *Assumption of Risk.* In a primary sense, assumption of risk means that the plaintiff, in advance, has expressly given his consent to relieve the defendant of an obligation of conduct toward him, and to take his chances of injury from a *known* risk arising from what the defendant is to do or to leave undone. The result is that the defendant is relieved of all legal duty to the plaintiff; and being under no duty, he cannot be charged with negligence.

4. *Act of God.* An accident without human intervention; an exclusive operation of the forces of nature of such character that it could not have been prevented by any reasonable degree of care or by any amount of foresight.

5. *Attractive Nuisance.* The doctrine that a person maintaining on his premises a condition, instrumentality, or other agency which is dangerous to young children because of their inability to appreciate peril and which may reasonably be expected to attract them to the premises owes duty to exercise reasonable care to protect them against such attraction.

6. *Tort.* A legal wrong committed upon a person or property. There are three elements of every tort action:

1. Existence of legal duty from defendant to plaintiff
2. Breach of duty
3. Damage as proximate result

There always must be a violation of some duty owing to the plaintiff, and generally such duty must arise by operation of law and not by agreement (contract) of the parties.

7. *Vicarious Liability.* The principle of vicarious liability is imputed negligence. Imputed negligence means that, by reason of some relation existing between A and B (respondent–superior), the negligence of A is to be charged against B, although B has played no part in it.

8. *Proprietary Function.*

> EXAMPLE: A municipality engaged in functions that are ordinarily exercised by private persons and which have no relation to public health or police power is

---

[1] Prepared by William Barrett Schenk, student in law.

engaged in proprietary functions as respects liability of the municipality for negligence of its servants.

9. *Waiver.* The intentional or voluntary relinquishment of a known right.

EXAMPLE: A person is said to waive a benefit when he renounces or disclaims it, and he is said to waive a tort or injury when he abandons the remedy which the law gives him for it.

10. *Laws.* That which must be obeyed and followed by citizens, subject to sanctions or legal consequences, is a law. With reference to its origin, law is derived either from judicial precedents, from legislation, or from custom.

EXAMPLE: An enabling law is any statute enabling persons or corporations to do what before they could not do.

11. *Regulations.* A rule or order prescribed for management or government—a regulating principle.

EXAMPLE: Rule of order prescribed by superior or competent authority relating to action of those under its control.

12. *Court Decision.* A judgment or decree pronounced by a court in settlement of a controversy submitted to it, and by way of authoritative answer to the questions raised before it. (A finding, as by a court, upon either a question of law or fact arising in a case.)

13. *Court Opinion.* The statement by a judge or court of the decision reached in regard to a cause tried or argued before them, expounding the law as applied to the case, and detailing the reasons upon which the judgment is based.

14. In Loco Parentis. In place of a parent; instead of a parent; charged factitiously with a parent's rights, duties, and responsibilities.

15. *Contract.* An agreement between two or more persons, upon sufficient consideration (consideration is something which the law regards as legally binding between the parties—a benefit or a detriment); to do or not to do a particular thing. The writing which contains the agreement of parties, with the terms and conditions, and which serves as proof of the obligation.

10. Staff Responsibilities

Department of Physical Education for Women

Committees:

Major Curriculum: _____, Chairman; _____, _____, _____, _____.

Service Program: _____, Chairman; _____, _____, _____, _____.

Testing Committee: _____, Chairman; _____, _____, _____.

Graduate Program: _____, Chairman; _____, _____, _____.

Ad Hoc Committees:

Study of Body Mechanics Course: _____, Chairman; _____. _____, _____.

Swimming Study: _____, Chairman; a consultant on testing, and all staff members teaching swimming.

Advisor, ARFCW Conference: _____.

NOTE: As Chairman, _____ becomes an ex-officio member of all committees and desires to attend as many meetings as possible.

Staff Meetings: Fridays as scheduled at 1:00 or 1:30 P.M. Minutes, _____.

General Functions:

Care and upkeep of the building (equipment rooms and storage cabinets in your section are also your responsibility). *Please check weekly:*

Facilities taken care of by Matron I .... _____
Facilities taken care of by Matron II .... _____
Facilities taken care of by Matron III .... _____
Facilities taken care of by Custodian ..... _____
Care and marking of grounds .... _____
Departmental library .... _____
Departmental publicity .... _____

Club Advisers:

W.A.A. .... _____, assisted by _____, _____ (intramurals).
Orchesis .... _____.
Aquaquettes .... _____.
Lincoln Board of Women Officials: 8 staff members.

Sponsors:

Freshman Council (service classes) .... _____.
Camp Counselors .... _____.

Advising for Majors:

Junior division work .... _____, _____
Physical education majors and minors .. _____ (Chairman); assisted by
                                          _____ Seniors
                                          _____ Juniors
                                          _____ Sophomores
                                          _____ Freshmen
Graduate students .... _____, Chairman; _____,
                                          _____.
Physical education club .... _____, _____.
University High School Coordinator ... _____.
Lincoln Public Schools Coordinator .... _____.

Chairmen of Activities: Each person who teaches an activity is a member of that
    committee. _____ (Chairman) ex officio on all committees.

Ag college work .... _____
Archery .... _____
Badminton .... _____
Basketball .... _____
Body mechanics .... _____
Bowling .... _____
Canoeing (including canoes, trailer) .... _____
Dance (modern, folk, social) .... _____
Fencing .... _____
First class meetings .... _____
Golf .... _____
Gymnastics .... _____
Hockey .... _____
Individual gymnastics .... _____
Lacrosse .... _____
Recordings .... _____
Recreational sports .... _____
Soccer and speedball .... _____
Softball .... _____
Square dancing .... _____
Stunts and tumbling, trampoline ...... _____
Swimming coordinator .... _____
Tennis .... _____
Track .... _____
Volleyball .... _____

Committees will meet, so far as possible,
on Fridays at 1:30 P.M.,
alternating with staff meetings.

11A. Application for School Physical Education and Physical Fitness Program Banner and Award[1]

This is to certify that we have evaluated our program in light of the standards developed by the Standards Committee of the Governor's Fitness Council and comply with the requirements.

....
Physical Education Instructor

....
Principal or Superintendent

....
Name of School

....
Address

The committee welcomes comments accompanying this application explaining your school's program.

[1] Used by permission of State of Nebraska; Department of Health; Division, Health Education; **State** Capitol, Lincoln.

11B. A Guide for Evaluating Physical Education Programs [1]

(Adopted from the evaluating criteria of the American Association for Health, Physical Education, and Recreation)

School's Name .... Address .... Signature of Representative ....

It should be understood that these are minimum standards. It is hoped that many schools will surpass the minimum and will continue to improve each semester.

To qualify for the citation, elementary schools should comply with **FIVE** of the first six standards; secondary schools should comply with **NINE** for the banner. The committee welcomes comments accompanying this application explaining your school's program on the back of this page.

YES   NO

....

1. Teacher-pupil ratio in a physical education class should not exceed 40 pupils.

   a. Average size physical education class:

   Elementary (K-6)............   High School (7-12)............

2. There is balance in the physical education program with emphasis given to individual body building activities as well
   as to team sports and it is under a professionally qualified physical educator who follows an approved guide.   ....

   a. Person who is general supervisor of physical education classes or teachers:

   Elementary............   Secondary............

   b. Basic guide followed:............

   c. Check areas of activity in your program:

Elementary	Secondary	Secondary
☐ 1. Low organized games & relays	☐ 1. Touch or flag football	☐ 11. Calisthenics
☐ 2. Track and field	☐ 2. Track and field	☐ 12. Soccer or speed ball
☐ 3. Self-testing	☐ 3. Testing	☐ 13. Field hockey
☐ 4. Rhythm	☐ 4. Rhythm	☐ 14. Bowling
☐ 5. Basketball	☐ 5. Basketball	☐ 15. Deck tennis
☐ 6. Flag or touch football	☐ 6. Softball	☐ 16. Handball
☐ 7. Softball	☐ 7. Tumbling & Apparatus gymnastics	☐ 17. Fencing
☐ 8. Tumbling	☐ 8. Wrestling	☐ 18. Tennis
☐ 9. Wrestling	☐ 9. Swimming	☐ 19. Shuffleboard

3. Co-educational activities are included in the instructional program and are co-operatively planned and conducted by the men and women instructors.　.........　.....

   a. List some co-educational activities carried out:

4. Modified or adapted activities are provided for students with special needs as based on information from medical data.　.........　.....

   a. Briefly describe some plan you use for taking care of students with special needs:

5. A fitness test is given at least annually (twice per year is desired) and covers such components of fitness as muscular strength, endurance, speed, and agility.　.........　.....

   a. Name of test used.................... b. Dates administered..............

6. Efforts are made to publicize the physical education activities through demonstrations and public appearances and through local publications or news media.　.........　.....

   a. List several specific instances:

7. Appropriate credit is given for class instruction in physical education and is required for graduation from junior and senior high school.　.........　.....

   a. Amount credit given................ b. Amount credit accepted for graduation....................

8. Activities such as band, marching, cheerleaders, driver education, and interscholastic athletics are not substituted for physical education.　.........　.....

9. Physical education class participation is required for a minimum of 8 semesters in grades 7-12 and two days each week.　.........　.....

   a. How many semesters of physical education are required 7-12?.....................

   b. How many days per week required for each child?....................

10. An intramural program is open to boys and girls and provides competitive participation opportunities.　.........　.....

   a. List two or three activities in which intramural competition is provided:

11. Appropriate uniforms and showering are required of all participants in secondary schools.　.........　.....

   These awards are made available by the Woodmen of the World Life Insurance Society, Omaha, Nebraska

305

[1] Used by permission of State of Nebraska; Department of Health; Division, Health Education; State Capitol, Lincoln.

12. Body Mechanics

Department of Physical Education for Women

Did you enjoy this unit of activity?   Yes _____   No _____

Regardless of the above answer, what phase or phases
of this work did you like best?

least?

Regardless of the above answer, what phase or phases
of this work were most valuable to you?

least valuable to you?

Comments or suggestions:

*Please do *not* sign this sheet*

---

13. Evaluation

Department of Physical Education for Women

Class: Sophomore _____
Other _____

DIRECTIONS: We would like to ask for your cooperation in planning a program which will meet your needs and interests. With your help in answering this questionnaire, we can evaluate our present program. Names of students will not be requested. The results of the questionnaire will not be used for individual classes but will be tabulated for the total department.

I. a. In *each* category, check the activities which you have had in college classes. Then in *each* category, place an asterisk (*) beside the one you like best.

Group Activities

1. Basketball   1. _____
2. Folk dance   2. _____
3. Hockey   3. _____
4. Modern dance   4. _____
5. Softball   5. _____
6. Speedball   6. _____
7. Square and social
   dance   7. _____
8. Volleyball   8. _____

Individual and Dual Sports

1. Archery   1. _____
2. Badminton   2. _____
3. Bowling   3. _____
4. Duckpins   4. _____
5. Fencing   5. _____
6. Golf   6. _____
7. Tennis   7. _____

Body Building Activities

1. Body mechanics   1. _____
2. Individual
   gymnastics   2. _____
3. Physical fitness 3. _____
4. Tumbling–
   trampolining   4. _____

Water Sports

1. Canoeing   1. _____
2. Lifesaving   2. _____
3. Swimming   3. _____
4. Synchronized swim-
   ming   4. _____
5. Water safety
   instructor   5. _____

b. Of *all* the above activities, state the activity you liked best. Why?

307

c. Of *all* the above activities, state the activity you liked least. Why?

II. Do you think you received the following benefits from class?
    Check the word "much," "some," or "none" after the objectives listed below:

	Much	Some	None
1. Skill and knowledge to participate in the activity reasonably well	1. _____	_____	_____
2. Chances to have fun	2. _____	_____	_____
3. Meet people and make new friends	3. _____	_____	_____
4. Opportunity for physical activity	4. _____	_____	_____
5. Other benefits derived from class:			

_____
_____
_____
_____
_____

III. Do you have any additional suggestions which would help to make the physical education program more beneficial to you?

14. Appraisal of Physical Education Programs[1]

This checklist synthesizes the recommendations made by the Washington Conference concerning principles underlying desirable policies and practices in instructional programs of physical education for college men and women. It is designed as a convenient tool for program appraisal to be used by administrative and faculty personnel in departments of physical education in appropriate institutions of higher education. In using this instrument, each item should be discussed fully and consensus reached concerning the extent to which the principle is operative within the departmental structure of policies and practices. No objective standards have been established for determining an over-all categorical rating for any department. The values accruing from the use of the checklist come from the subjective evaluation of departmental policies and practices as they relate to the instructional program.

To what extent are the following general principles operative within the departmental structure of policies and practices as they relate to the instructional program of physical education?

PHILOSOPHY AND OBJECTIVES	Completely (5)	To a great degree (4)	To a moderate degree (3)	Very little (2)	Not at all (1)
1. The educational philosophy of the department has been formulated in writing and is subscribed to whole-heartedly by the instructional staff.					
2. The departmental philosophy is in harmony with the over-all educational philosophy of the college or university as stated in the appropriate publications of the institution.					
3. The departmental philosophy is compatible with the principles set forth in the Report of the President's Commission on Higher Education as they relate to the education of college men and women. ..					
4. The major objectives of the instructional program have been formulated in writing, and these specific objectives are compatible with the over-all educational philosophy of the department and the institution.					
5. The major objectives of the instructional program cover the potential contributions of physical education in the areas of: a. Effective movement b. Skill in specific activities c. Physiological function d. Human relations e. Knowledges, insights, understandings					

[1] Used by permission, "Criteria for Appraisal of Instructional Programs of Physical Education in Colleges and Universities," *Physical Education for College Men and Women* (3d printing; Washington, D.C.: American Association for Health, Physical Education, and Recreation, 1965). Conference report.

To what extent are the following general principles operative within the departmental structure of policies and practices as they relate to the instructional program of physical education?

ADMINISTRATION

	Completely (5)	To a great degree (4)	To a moderate degree (3)	Very little (2)	Not at all (1)
6. In the development and conduct of the programs of physical education, the administrator is committed to action through a democratic process which includes both faculty and students.					
7. The department is guided by a sound philosophy of physical education. A concerted attempt is made to interpret a broad concept of physical education to faculty, students, administration and community.					
8. The administrator gives consideration to the problems of men and women in regard to policy, budget, use of facilities, equipment, scheduling of classes, intramural programs and makes provision for instruction in co-educational activities.					
9. The standards in the institution relating to staff qualifications, teaching load, size of classes, retirement, academic rank and salaries apply equally to staff members in the physical education department.					
10. The department promotes continuous in-service education to stimulate professional growth and improved service to students.					
11. The basic instructional program is co-ordinated with other areas (intramural athletics, intercollegiate athletics, teacher education, etc.).					
12. The source of financial support for the physical education program is the same as that for all other instructional areas of the institution.					
13. Instruction in physical education, properly adapted, is required of all students throughout their undergraduate college careers.					
14. All entering students are given a thorough physical and medical examination by home or staff physician prior to participation in the physical education program (followed by periodic examinations).					
15. Exemption from participation in the physical education program for medical reasons is predicated upon the carefully co-ordinated judgment of the medical and physical education staff.					
16. Students are permitted to substitute freshman and varsity sports in season, using the same intercollegiate sport only once during the year, for the purpose of meeting their physical education requirement, but return to class at the end of their sport season.					

To what extent are the following general principles operative within the departmental structure of policies and practices as they relate to the instructional program of physical education?

	Completely (5)	To a great degree (4)	To a moderate degree (3)	Very little (2)	Not at all (1)
17. It is the policy of the department *not* to accept veteran experiences, military drill, R.O.T.C., band and other extracurricular participation for the required instructional program of physical education.					
18. Credit and quality or grade point value is granted on the same basis as any other area in the educational program.					
19. Facilities and equipment are adequate with respect to quality and quantity.					
20. Guidance and counseling of students is an integral part of the physical education program.					
21. Adequate supervision is provided for teaching done by graduate students and teaching fellows.					
22. Comprehensive and accessible records are maintained to indicate student accomplishments within the program.					
23. The department of physical education conducts program of organized research.					

PROGRAM

24. The program provides instruction in activities for every student.					
25. The program provides for orientation of each student with regard to purposes, policies, and opportunities in physical education. (This may be accomplished by orientation week programs, medical and health examinations, courses, group and individual conferences, handbooks and printed material, and demonstrations.)					
26. The program offerings are well rounded, including body mechanics, swimming, team games, rhythms, individual and dual activities, with basic requirements for each student set up according to his needs.					
27. The program provides specific counseling and guidance (planned and incidental, group and individual) on a very definite pattern with appropriate referrals to other campus agencies (student health, counseling bureau, etc.).					
28. The activities selected make full use of accessible community facilities.					
29. The activities selected make full use of local geography and climate.					

To what extent are the following general principles operative within the departmental structure of policies and practices as they relate to the instructional program of physical education?

	Completely (5)	To a great degree (4)	To a moderate degree (3)	Very little (2)	Not at all (1)
30. The program provides opportunities through co-educational classes for teaching men and women to develop skills and to enjoy together those activities which bring life-long leisure time satisfactions.					
31. The activities selected offer opportunities for creative expression and for the development of personal resources.					
32. The program provides instruction for efficient body movement in physical education and daily living. . .					
33. The activities selected promote healthful functioning of organs and systems of the body within the limits of present physical conditions.					
34. Some of the activities selected encourage all students to develop relaxation skills and to understand their importance; and provide specific opportunities for relaxation and rest where such is indicated. . . .					
35. The physical education instruction program provides a means of introducing students to the activities of the intramural program, and encourages them to participate in it.					
36. The physical education instruction program introduces students [to], and encourages their participation in, the various recreational activities of the campus and community.					
37. The physical education instruction program is integrated with other college programs and services concerned with health education.					
38. Teaching methods provide progressive learning experiences through which each student derives the satisfaction in achievement which is essential for continued participation after college.					

EVALUATION

39. The philosophy and objectives of a department are reviewed and re-evaluated periodically.					
40. All the objectives, viz., skill, knowledge, attitudes, habits, etc., are included in: a. The evaluation of the program. b. The final rating (or grade) given a student. The objectives are weighted according to the emphasis given in each course.					
41. Selection and use of evaluation techniques are cooperatively planned within the department.					

To what extent are the following general principles operative within the departmental structure of policies and practices as they relate to the instructional program of physical education?

	Completely (5)	To a great degree (4)	To a moderate degree (3)	Very little (2)	Not at all (1)
42. Evaluative measures are selected in the light of probable psychological and physiological reactions and result in stimulation of faculty and student interest and enthusiasm.					
43. Evaluation of student status and progress is determined at the beginning, during and at the termination of the course.					
44. Evaluative procedures are used to determine strengths and weaknesses of individual students and class groups and lead to guidance and help for the individual student.					
45. Evaluative procedures are employed to determine strengths and weaknesses of the program: a. For the college student b. For post-college life					
46. Evaluative measures are employed only if the results are to be used in some way.					
47. Objective measurement is used whenever possible.					
48. If objective measurement is not possible, subjective judgment is used for purposes of appraisal.					
49. Teachers are familiar with the best available evaluation techniques and use research findings in so far as possible.					
50. All students and faculty in a course participate in the evaluation of student accomplishments and learning, teaching effectiveness and course content.					

15. Confidential Statement

THE UNIVERSITY OF_____
Department of Physical Education for Women

Name_____

School_____

Please check one category for each item.

Qualities	Superior	Above Average	Average	Below Average	Poor	No Opportunity To Evaluate
GENERAL						
Understanding of students						
Cooperation with colleagues, parents						
Knowledge of subject matter						
Professional attitude						
Understanding of total school program						
PERSONAL						
Appearance (social, professional)						
Emotional maturity						
Integrity						
Self-confidence						
Sense of humor						
Resourcefulness						
Enthusiasm and interest						
PROFESSIONAL						
Preparation of teaching assignments						
Ability to discern and provide for individual differences and needs						
Ability to handle discipline problems						
Ability to evaluate pupil progress						
Teacher-pupil relationship						
Willingness to assume additional school responsibilities						
Professional promise						

Are you willing to renew this teacher's contract?

As you recall, were the recommendations for this teacher:
        (a) exaggerated   (b) fair   (c) underestimated

Additional Comments:

Signed: Position:

Date: Address:

16. DGWS Guidelines for Interscholastic Athletic Programs for Junior High School Girls[1]

Principles

During the junior high school years [2] girls should have the time and opportunity to explore a great variety of sports. Because of growth and development patterns, this is an age when many goals can be accomplished through team sports and a time when skills of individual sports should also be sampled and developed. Therefore, the Junior High School sports program for girls should involve opportunities to participate in many kinds of sports and in a variety of sports situations.

It is also recognized that some girls with high skill potential will wish to extend their training and competitive experiences under competent leaders outside the jurisdiction of the school.

A wide variety of activities should be offered and available to all students in the school instructional and intramural programs. Opportunities for interschool competition may be provided in the form of a limited number of sports days at the end of the intramural season. The following guidelines are recommended:

1. Competitive sports opportunities for junior high school girls should be planned as a program separate and different from the program of competitive athletics for senior high school girls whether or not the state high school athletic organization includes the junior high school level.

2. Sports competition should be planned for the values offered to the participant rather than as a spectator sport or as a training program for senior high school teams.

3. Extramural programs should not be organized until there are broad instructional and intramural programs and a sufficient allotment of time, facilities and personnel for new programs.

Interscholastic Athletic Programs for Junior High School Girls

1. One or two sports days following the end of the intramural season will in most cases give enough breadth to the opportunity for student competition in sports at this age. If a more extensive schedule is planned, individual participation should not exceed more than one contest per week and three contests per sport season.

2. The wide variation in growth and development within this age grouping necessitates equating of competitors with reference to skill level, age, and/or size.

3. Travel should be kept to a minimum by competing only with other schools in the vicinity. Travel should be in school buses or with bonded carriers.

4. The responsibility for leadership of the local girls interscholastic program should be delegated to the women physical education teachers. The school administration should delegate to them the major responsibility for planning, organizing, coaching, and supervising the program with the understanding that the ultimate authority remains in the hands of the administration.

5. The program, based on the needs and interests of the girls, should include those individual and team activities for which qualified leadership, financial support, and adequate facilities are available.

6. The entire financing of the girls' sports program should be included in the total school budget. Any monies collected should go into the general fund.

[1] Used by permission of DGWS, AAHPER.

[2] Although the pattern differs, junior high is used here to include grades 7 through 8 or 9.

7. DGWS approved standards should be used in all sports. It is strongly recommended that DGWS rules be used in those sports in which DGWS publishes rules.

8. The administration should provide a healthful, safe, and sanitary environment for all participants.

Standards

Participants

1. Participants must be bona fide students of the school which they represent. Students under temporary suspension or probation for disciplinary reasons should not be allowed to participate.

2. Participants must have amateur standing in the interscholastic sports in which they participate.

3. Written permission of the parent or guardian is required for all participants.

4. A physician's certification of a girl's fitness for participation shall be filed with the administration prior to the first practice in a sport. The examination must have been made within the time period specified by local regulations. Written permission by a physician should be required for participation after a serious illness, injury, or surgery.

5. Participants should carry some type of accident insurance coverage that protects them during athletic competition.

Leadership

1. The interscholastic program should be directed, coached, and officiated by qualified women whenever and wherever possible. No program should be expanded past the ability of the girls' department of physical education to direct it.

2. All coaches should be certified teachers employed by the local board of education. If teachers other than trained women physical educators are used to coach, they should work closely with the girls' department.

3. A woman faculty member appointed by the principal shall accompany and supervise girls' teams at all contests.

4. Officials should hold a current intramural or above DGWS rating or an equivalent rating in the specific sport and should be registered with the appropriate administrative or regulatory bodies.

5. A doctor should be on call for all contests, and someone who is qualified in first aid procedure should be in attendance.

6. In case of question as to fitness for play, the official has the right to overrule the coach for the protection of the welfare of the girl.

Administration

1. All games and contests in which school teams participate must be under the direct sponsorship and supervision of the schools involved. No postseason games for teams or individuals should be permitted.

2. Girls may participate on only one interscholastic team during a season. They may not take part in a contest on any out-of-school team until the school sport season is completed. A girl is considered a member of a team when she participates in her first contest.

3. Interscholastic competition should be limited to those sports for which DGWS publishes rules and standards, and they should be used in administration of the program.

4. Awards when given should be inexpensive tokens of a symbolic type, such as ribbons, letters, and small pins. The giving of other types of awards as well as fundraising for expensive or elaborate awards is considered a violation of this guideline.

Questions on interpretations of the high school recommendations should be directed to Lucille Burkett, Shaker Heights High School, Shaker Heights, Ohio.

17. DGWS Statement of Beliefs[1]

WE BELIEVE that opportunities for instruction and participation in sports should be included in the educational experiences of every girl. Sports are an integral part of the culture in which we live. Sports skills and sports participation are valuable social and recreational tools which may be used to enrich the lives of women in our society.

WE BELIEVE that sports opportunities at all levels of skill should be available to girls and women who wish to take advantage of these experiences. Competition and cooperation may be demonstrated in all sports programs although the type and intensity of the competition will vary with the degree or level of skill of the participants. An understanding of the relationship between competition and cooperation and of how to utilize both within the accepted framework of our society is one of the desirable outcomes of sports participation.

WE BELIEVE in the importance of physical activity in the maintenance of the general health of the participant.

WE BELIEVE that participation in sports contributes to the development of self confidence and to the establishment of desirable interpersonal relations.

For these reasons, WE BELIEVE that girls and women of all ages should be provided with comprehensive school and community programs of sports and recreation. In addition, they should be strongly and actively encouraged to take part in such programs.

PROGRAM

We believe that sports programs for girls and women should be broad, varied, and planned for participants at differing levels of skill. There should be full awareness of the wide span of individual differences so that all types, ages, and skill levels are considered in the planning of sports programs. In conducting the various phases of sports programs, principles must guide action. These principles should be based on the latest and soundest knowledge regarding

1. growth and development factors
2. motor learning
3. social and individual maturation and adjustment
4. The values of sports participation as recognized in our culture.

Elementary Schools (grades 1–6)

We believe in planned, comprehensive, and balanced programs of physical education for every girl in the elementary program. These should provide experiences in basic movements—for example, skipping and simple dance steps, bending, reaching, and climbing—and in a wide variety of activities which require basic sports skills such as catching, throwing, batting, and kicking.

We believe that intramural sports experiences in appropriately modified sports activities should supplement an instructional program for girls in grades 4, 5, and 6, and that in most cases these experiences will be sufficiently stimulating and competitive for the highly skilled girl. We believe extramural sports activities, if included in the upper elementary grades, should be limited to occasional play days (sports groups or teams composed of representatives from several schools or units), sports days, and invitational events.

[1] Used by permission of DGWS, AAHPER.

Secondary Schools (grades 7–12)

We believe that in secondary schools a program of intramural and extramural participation should be arranged to augment a sound and comprehensive instructional program in physical education for all girls. Extramural programs should not be organized until there are broad instructional and intramural programs and a sufficient allotment of time, facilities, and personnel for new programs.

Colleges and Universities

We believe that college and university instructional programs should go beyond those activities usually included in the high school program. There should be opportunities to explore and develop skills in a variety of activities, with emphasis on individual sports. It is desirable that opportunities for extramural experience beyond the intramural program be accessible to the highly skilled young women who wish these opportunities.

Forms of Competition

INTRAMURAL COMPETITION is sports competition in which all participants are identified with the same school, community center, club, organization, institution, or industry, or are residents of a designated small neighborhood or community.

EXTRAMURAL COMPETITION is a plan of sports competition in which participants from two or more schools, community centers, clubs, organizations, institutions, industries, or neighborhoods compete. The forms of extramural competition include

1. Sports Days—school or sports group participates as a unit.
2. Telegraphic Meets—results are compared by wire or mail.
3. Invitational Events—symposiums, games, or matches to which a school or sports group invites one or more teams or individuals to participate.
4. Interscholastic, Intercollegiate, or Interagency Programs—groups which are trained and coached play a series of scheduled games and/or tournaments with like teams from other schools, cities, or organizations.

INTERNATIONAL COMPETITION involves players from different nations and provides sports experiences for individuals or groups with exceptional ability and emotional maturity. This type of competition under some conditions could include secondary school girls, but usually it is planned for more mature participants.

CO-RECREATIONAL ACTIVITIES are designed to give boys and girls opportunities to participate on the same team against a team of like composition, provided the activities do not involve body contact. The basis for formation of teams should be to promote good team play. We believe that girls should be prohibited from participating (1) on a boys' intercollegiate or interscholastic team; (2) against a boys' intercollegiate or interscholastic team; and (3) against a boy in a scheduled intercollegiate or interscholastic contest.

ADMINISTRATION

We believe that certain SAFEGUARDS should be provided to protect the health and well-being of participants. Adequate health and insurance protection should be secured by the institution. First aid services and emergency medical care should be available during all scheduled interscholastic sports events. Qualified professional leaders should ensure a proper period for conditioning of players, a safe environment including equipment and facilities, a schedule with a limited number of games, and similar measures.

We believe that sports OFFICIATING should be the responsibility of those who know and use DGWS approved rules. Officials should hold current ratings in those sports in which ratings are given.

We believe that the entire FINANCING of girls and women's sports programs should be included in the total school budget. It is suggested that income be handled as a regular school income item.

We believe that the SCHEDULING of sports activities for girls and women should be in accordance with their needs and that their schedule should not be required to conform to a league schedule established for boys' and men's sports.

We believe that excellence of achievement should be given RECOGNITION and that the intrinsic values which accrue from the pursuit of excellence are of primary importance. We believe that, when awards are given, they should be inexpensive tokens of a symbolic type, such as ribbons, letters, and small pins.

We believe that expert teaching and quality programs generate their own best PUBLIC RELATIONS. It is suggested that an effective plan be developed for interpreting the values of the sports program to parents, teachers in other fields, and interested members of the school or college community, including the press. A procedure which has proved successful is to invite key groups to a selection of demonstrations and sports events at different levels, so that they may see effective programs in action.

LEADERSHIP

We believe that good leadership is essential to the desirable conduct of the sports program. The qualified leader meets the standards set by the profession, including an understanding of (1) the place and purpose of sports in education, (2) the growth and development of children and youth, (3) the effects of exercise on the human organism, (4) first aid and accident prevention, (5) understanding of specific skills, and (6) sound teaching methods. Personal experience in organized extramural competition is desirable for the young woman planning to become a leader or teacher of women's sports. The leader should demonstrate personal integrity and a primary concern for the welfare of the participant.

POLICY-MAKING

And, finally, we believe that all leaders, teachers, and coaches of girls and women's sports should be encouraged to take an active part in the policy decisions which affect planning, organizing, and conducting sports programs for girls and women. Leaders should make sure that qualified women are appointed to the governing sports bodies at all levels—local, state, national, and international—to ensure that programs are in the best interest of those who participate.

DGWS GUIDES—contain the official rules, articles on coaching, officiating, and valuable information on aquatics, archery, badminton, basketball, bowling, fencing, field hockey, golf, gymnastics, lacrosse, outing activities, riding, soccer, softball, speedball, tennis, track and field, volleyball, and winter sports.

18. Guidelines for Interscholastic Athletic Programs for High School Girls [1]

In May 1963 the DGWS approved a statement of policies for competition in girls and women's sports. One part of this statement suggests the possibility of including interscholastic programs, as one of the forms of competition appropriate for girls, to complement the intramural and instructional programs offered in each school.

As prerequisites for an interscholastic program the DGWS recommends,

"For the best welfare of the participants, it is essential that the program be conducted by qualified leaders, be supported by budgeted funds, be representative of approved objectives and standards for girls and women's sports, including acceptable conditions of travel, protective insurance, appropriate facilities, proper equipment, and desirable practices in the conduct of the events."

The increased interest throughout the nation in developing interscholastic programs for high school girls prompted the DGWS to hold a Study Conference on Competition for Girls and Women in February 1965 to establish recommended guidelines for such programs.

These guidelines are to be considered as minimum. It is strongly urged that no individual and/or school attempt the establishment of interscholastic programs if these minimal requirements cannot be adequately met. Further requirements, beyond those suggested by DGWS, may be established as seems appropriate under varying local conditions.

The nature and growth of girls interscholastic programs will vary. In many schools lack of the recommended basic requirements and/or lack of interest on the part of the girls may delay the development of an interscholastic program. In other situations an interscholastic program may be started in one sport only, with other sports added as seems desirable.

In all cases, a thorough understanding and knowledge of these recommendations is essential for women physical educators desirous of developing such programs as well as for the school administrators ultimately responsible for such programs.

Principles

Competitive sports are an important part of the total physical education program for high school girls. A program of intramural and extramural participation should be arranged to augment a sound and inclusive instructional program in physical education. The interscholastic program should not be promoted at the expense of the instructional or the intramural programs.

As the interscholastic program is expanded, the State High School Athletic Association will be the regulatory body for its member schools. For schools that are not members, a regulatory body may need to be formed. The State Department of Education should be involved.

1. Existing legislative and administrative bodies for interscholastic athletic programs will retain ultimate control of the total program for girls within the state. However, a women's advisory board composed mainly of women high school physical educators will be formed to propose policies to these administrative and legislative groups and to review policies approved by them.

2. Total responsibility for the administration and supervision of the local inter-

[1] Used by permission of DGWS, AAHPER.

320

scholastic athletic program is vested in the local school administration and the appropriate persons designated by the administration.

3. The responsibility for leadership of the local girls interscholastic program should be delegated to the women physical education teachers. The school administration should delegate to them the major responsibility for planning, organizing, coaching, and supervising the program with the understanding that the ultimate authority remains in the hands of the administration.

4. The program, based on the needs and interests of the girls, should include those individual and team activities for which qualified leadership, financial support, and adequate facilities are available.

5. The entire financing of the girls' sports program should be included in the total school budget. Any monies collected should go into the general fund.

6. DGWS approved standards should be used in all sports. It is strongly recommended that DGWS rules be used in those sports in which DGWS publishes rules.

7. The administration should provide a healthful, safe, and sanitary environment for all participants.

Standards

Participants

1. Participants must be bona fide students of the high school which they represent. They shall not have attended high school for more than eight semesters after entering the ninth grade. They must be successfully carrying full academic loads. Students under temporary suspension or probation for disciplinary reasons should not be allowed to participate.

2. Participants must have amateur standing in the interscholastic sports in which they participate.

3. Written permission of the parent or guardian is required for all participants.

4. A physician's certification of girl's fitness for participation shall be filed with the administration prior to the first practice in a sport. The examination must have been made within the time period specified by local regulations. Written permission by a physician should be required for participation after a serious illness, injury, or surgery.

5. Participants should carry some type of accident insurance coverage that protects them during athletic competition.

Leadership

1. The interscholastic program should be directed, coached, and officiated by qualified women whenever and wherever possible. No program should be expanded past the ability of the girls department of physical education to direct it.

2. All coaches should be certified teachers employed by the local board of education. If teachers other than trained women physical educators are used to coach, they should work closely with the girls department.

3. A woman faculty member appointed by the principal shall accompany and supervise girls teams at all contests.

4. Officials should hold a current intramural or above DGWS rating or an equivalent rating in the specific sport and should be registered with the appropriate administrative or regulatory bodies.

5. A doctor should be on call for all contests, and someone who is qualified in first aid procedure should be in attendance.

6. In case of question as to fitness for play, the official has the right to overrule the coach for the protection of the welfare of the girl.

Administration

1. All games and contests in which school teams participate must be under the direct sponsorship and supervision of the schools involved. No postseason games for teams or individuals should be permitted.

2. Girls may participate on only one interscholastic team during a season. They may not take part in a contest on any out-of-season team until the school sport season is completed. A girl is considered a member of a team when she participates in her first contest.

3. Competition should be limited to a geographical area which will permit players to return at reasonable hours. Safe transportation should be assured.

4. The maximum length of a sport season should be twelve weeks, with the first three weeks devoted to training and conditioning. The participant should take part in no more than five participation periods per week including games or contests. There should be no more than two games per week, which should not be played on consecutive days. Standards for specific sports are listed in the current DGWS guides.

5. Interscholastic competition should be limited to those sports for which DGWS publishes rules and standards, and they should be used in administration of the program.

6. Awards when given should be inexpensive tokens of a symbolic type, such as ribbons, letters, and small pins. The giving of other types of awards as well as fund-raising for expensive or elaborate awards is considered a violation of this guideline.

Questions on interpretations of the high school recommendations should be directed to Lucille Burkett, Shaker Heights High School, Shaker Heights, Ohio.

19. Guidelines for Intercollegiate Athletic Programs for Women [1]

In response to an increasing interest throughout the nation, the following guidelines have been developed to assist institutions now operating or planning to operate an intercollegiate athletic program for women. They are presented for consideration as minimum standards with the understanding that additional standards are also suggested or imposed by local, state, or regional collegiate groups. They should not be interpreted as directives. Rather their purpose is to give assistance at the point where an extended program is desired to meet students' needs.

An intercollegiate athletic program for women should be an extension of an existing intramural program and in addition to established instructional and intramural offerings. Extended programs should not be attempted without adequate leadership, facilities, and budget in addition to what is needed for the basic programs.

Two other statements are relevant in planning the extended intercollegiate program. One is the newest DGWS "Statement of Policies for Competition in Girls and Women's Sports," approved in 1963, particularly the following quotation:

"For the best welfare of the participants, it is essential that the program be conducted by qualified leaders, be supported by budgeted funds, be representative of approved objectives and standards for girls and women's sports, including acceptable conditions of travel, protective insurance, appropriate facilities, proper equipment, and desirable practices in the conduct of events."

The second is the DGWS "Belief Statement," revised in 1965, which sets forth a total philosophy for the participation of girls and women in sports programs. (Both are available from AAHPER.)

The underlying aim of any sports program is to provide a wide range of opportunities for all students who wish to participate at levels appropriate to their individual skills. In starting or expanding the athletic program, satisfying this aim should be worked out within the limits of budget and available qualified leadership. Any expansion should also be based on a careful consideration of student interests.

Administration

The intercollegiate athletic program should be specifically designed for women, and its administration and organization should be the responsibility of the department of physical education for women. It is also the responsibility of the physical education faculty women to recommend and formulate policy for the expanded program to be submitted to the appropriate policy-approving authority of the institution.

Budget

The budget for women's intercollegiate athletics should be part of the budget of the institution so that the program is assured. A separate budget item should be specifically designated for this program. (This does not preclude the use of state monies, student fees, gate receipts, and other sources of income, but the program should not depend solely on fluctuating sources of income.) The budget should be administered by the women's physical education department as part of overall administration.

[1] Used by permission of DGWS, AAHPER.

Scheduling

Contests should be scheduled among schools having players of comparable ability in order to equate competition. In order to make this possible, scheduling in each sport need not be with the same institutions each season.

Scheduling with collegiate institutions is recommended. However, when budget is inadequate for travel, limited scheduling with outside organizations (i.e., church, industrial leagues, etc.) in the local area may be desirable. Scheduling should allow opportunities for participants of intercollegiate teams to meet on an informal social basis.

Health and Safety

Adequate health and insurance protection should be provided by the institution for all members of athletic teams. First aid services and emergency medical care should be available during all scheduled intercollegiate athletic events.

Tournaments

Problems surrounding the development of regional and national tournaments are so varied that the matter of intercollegiate tournaments needs further study. At this time it is recommended that tournaments be confined to participation within limited geographic areas.

Leadership (teachers, coaches, and officials)

1. Good leadership is essential to a desirable sports program. The qualified leader meets the standard set by the profession through an understanding of (a) the place and purpose of sports in education, (b) the growth and development of children and youth, (c) the effects of exercise on the human organism, (d) first aid and accident prevention, (e) understanding of specific skills, and (f) sound teaching methods. It is desirable that, when possible, leaders of women's sports have personal experience in organized extramural competition. The leader should demonstrate personal integrity and a primary concern for the welfare of the participant.

2. The program should be under the direct supervision of the women's physical education department. Qualified women should teach, coach, and officiate wherever and whenever possible, and in all cases the professional background and experience of the leader must meet established standards of the physical education profession.

3. It is strongly recommended that an official's rating be considered a prerequisite for coaching in order to enhance the coach's understanding of the official's role.

4. Intercollegiate events should be officiated by DGWS nationally rated officials. In those sports where DGWS does not rate officials, an equivalent rating is acceptable.

5. If a nonstaff member is teaching or coaching, a woman member of the physical education faculty should supervise and chaperone the participants. Cooperative institutional efforts should be devoted toward preservice and inservice programs and clinics for leaders and teachers.

6. DGWS-approved rules should be used in the conduct of all intercollegiate sports events.

Participation

1. Intercollegiate participation should not interfere with primary educational objectives.

    a. A student may not participate as a member of an intercollegiate athletic team and at the same time be a member of a team in the same sport outside her institution.

    b. Local policy-making groups may wish to qualify this policy for occasional individual students.

2. The athletic schedule should not jeopardize the student's class and study time.

  a. The length of the season and the number of games should be established and agreed upon by the participating schools.

  b. The length of the season will vary according to the locale and sport but should not exceed twelve weeks, including at least three weeks of preliminary conditioning and instruction.

  c. Standards for specific sports concerning number of practices and/or contests per week are found in the DGWS guides.

3. Women should be prohibited from participating

  a. on a men's intercollegiate team.

  b. against a men's intercollegiate team.

  c. against a man in a scheduled intercollegiate contest.

4. To be eligible to participate in intercollegiate athletics, the individual must be a full-time student of the institution and maintain the academic average required for participation in all other major activities. Undergraduate students only are eligible to participate in the intercollegiate athletic program. For the purposes of eligibility, an undergraduate student is defined as one who has not received the B.A. degree or its equivalent.

5. Transfer students are immediately eligible for participation following enrollment in the institution.

6. A medical examination is a prerequisite to participation in intercollegiate athletics. This examination should be given within the six-month period prior to the start of the sports season each year. Where health examinations are done by the family physician, a covering letter explaining the program of activities and an examination which would include the information needed is suggested. Written permission by the physician should be required for participation after serious illness, injury, or surgery.

7. A participant in intercollegiate athletics maintains amateur status if she has not received money other than expenses as a player, instructor, or official in any sport.

8. There should be no scholarships or financial assistance specifically designated for women athletes. This does not preclude women who participate in the intercollegiate athletic program from holding scholarships or grants-in-aid obtained through normal scholarship programs of the institution.

Questions on interpretations of the college recommendations should be directed to Marguerite Clifton, Purdue University, Lafayette, Indiana.

Bibliography

ABERNATHY, RUTH. "Implications for Physical Education in Current Developments in American Education," *American Academy of Physical Education, Professional Contributions No. 7.* Washington, D.C.: American Association for Health, Physical Education, and Recreation, 1961.

AMERICAN ASSOCIATION FOR HEALTH, PHYSICAL EDUCATION, AND RECREATION. *Current Administrative Problems,* Yearbook. Washington, D.C.: AAHPER, 1960: RUTH ABERNATHY, "Substitution in the Curriculum for Physical Education"; FRANCES TODD, "Girls Sports"; GEORGE I. WERNER, "Excuses from Physical Education Classes"; GORDON G. WOEPLER, "Scheduling Physical Education Classes."

AMERICAN ASSOCIATION FOR HEALTH, PHYSICAL EDUCATION, AND RECREATION AND THE NATIONAL SCHOOL PUBLIC RELATIONS ASSOCIATION. *Putting PR into HPER.* Washington, D.C.: AAHPER and NSPRA, March, 1953.

AMERICAN ASSOCIATION FOR HEALTH, PHYSICAL EDUCATION, AND RECREATION, DEPARTMENT OF THE NATIONAL EDUCATION ASSOCIATION. *Exercise and Fitness.* Washington, D.C.: AAHPER, 1958.

————. *Fit for College.* Washington, D.C., AAHPER, 1959.

————. *Graduate Education in Health Education, Physical Education, Recreation Education, Safety Education, and Dance.* Washington, D.C.: AAHPER, 1967.

————. *Graduate Study in Health Education, Physical Education, and Recreation.* Washington, D.C.: AAHPER, 1950. Report of a National Conference.

————. *Physical Education for College Men and Women.* Washington, D.C.: AAHPER, 1965. Report of a National Conference.

————. *Professional Preparation in Health Education, Physical Education, and Recreation Education.* Washington, D.C.: AAHPER, 1962. Report of a National Conference.

AMERICAN ASSOCIATION OF SCHOOL ADMINISTRATORS. *Public Relations for America's Schools.* 25th Yearbook, 1950.

AMERICAN EDUCATIONAL RESEARCH ASSOCIATION, and ESPENSCHADE, ANNA S. *What Research Says to the Teacher. Physical Education in the Elementary Schools.* Washington, D.C.: National Education Association.

AMERICAN MEDICAL ASSOCIATION. *7 Paths to Fitness.* Chicago: AMA.

ANDERSON, VIVIENNE, and DAVIES, DANIEL R. *Patterns of Educational Leadership.* Englewood Cliffs, N.J.: Prentice-Hall, Inc., 1956.

ANDREWS, GLADYS, SAURBORN, JEANNETTE, and SCHNEIDER, ELSA. *Physical Education for Today's Boys and Girls.* Boston: Allyn & Bacon, Inc., 1960.

ASHTON, DUDLEY. "Action Research in Rhythmic Testing," *Journal of Health, Physical Education, and Recreation,* XXXI, No. 8, November, 1960.

BACON, HAROLD D., and MAYER, TOM. "You Don't Have To 'Baby' Your Gym Floor," *Journal of American Association for Health, Physical Education, and Recreation,* XXVI, No. 3, March, 1955.

BERNARD, EDWIN J. "Simple Resource Filing Techniques," *Journal of Business Education,* March, 1956.

BOURQUARDEZ, VIRGINIA, and HEIDMAN, CHARLES. *Sports Equipment, Selection, Care, and Repair.* New York: A. S. Barnes & Co., Inc., 1950.

BUCHER, CHARLES A. *Foundations of Physical Education.* 3d ed. St. Louis: The C. V. Mosby Co., 1960.

BUIKEMA, KENT A., and SMITH, JAMES E., JR. "Effective Staff Utilization," *Journal of Health, Physical Education, and Recreation*, XXXIV, March, 1963.

California Physical Performance Test. Sacramento: California State Department of Education, 1958.

CASTETTER, WILLIAM B. *Administering the School Personnel Program.* New York: The Macmillan Co., 1962.

COLLINS, MARY. *Cheerleader's Handbook.* Fond Du Lac, Wis.: National Sports Company.

COPLAN, ARLO H. "The Ugly Gym Teacher," *The Physical Educator*, XXI, No. 3, October, 1964.

COWELL, CHARLES C., and SCHWEHN, HILDA M. *Modern Principles and Methods in Secondary School Physical Education.* 2d ed. Boston: Allyn & Bacon, Inc., 1964.

CULP, ROBERT L. "The 'Story' Behind the Publicity Releases," *The Physical Educator*, XIX, No. 1, March, 1962.

DAUER, VICTOR P. *Fitness for Elementary School Children.* Minneapolis: Burgess Publishing Co., 1965.

DAVIS, ELWOOD C., and WALLIS, EARL L. *Toward Better Teaching in Physical Education.* Englewood Cliffs, N.J.: Prentice-Hall, Inc., 1961.

"DGWS Statement on Competition in Girls and Women's Sports," *Journal of the American Association for Health, Physical Education, and Recreation*, XXXVI, No. 7, September, 1965.

ELSBREE, WILLARD A., and REUTTER, E. EDMUND, JR. *Staff Personnel in the Public Schools.* Englewood Cliffs, N.J.: Prentice-Hall, Inc., 1958.

EVAUL, THOMAS W. "The Automated Tutor," *Journal of Health, Physical Education, and Recreation*, XXXV, (March, 1964), 27.

"Focus on Facilities," Symposium, *Journal of the American Association for Health, Physical Education, and Recreation*, XXXIII, No. 4, April, 1962.

FORSYTHE, CHARLES E. *The Athletic Director's Handbook.* Englewood Cliffs, N.J.: Prentice-Hall, Inc., 1956.

FREDERICK, A. BRUCE. "Don't Throw Those Bats Away," *The Physical Educator*, XIX, No. 2, May, 1962.

————. "Homemade Equipment and Supplies for Physical Education," *The Physical Educator*, XXI, No. 2, May, 1964.

FREDERICK, ROBERT W. *The Third Curriculum.* New York: Appleton-Century-Crofts, Inc., 1959.

GEORGE, JACK F., and LEHMAN, HARRY A. *School Athletic Administration.* New York: Harper & Row, Inc., 1966.

GRIFFITHS, DANIEL E. *Human Relations in School Administration.* New York: Appleton-Century-Crofts, Inc., 1956.

HAGA, ENOCH J. "Single Entry Bookkeeping of 1875—Still Useful," *Journal of Business Education*, XXXVI, May, 1961.

HALSEY, ELIZABETH, and PORTER, LORENA. *Physical Education for Children, A Developmental Program.* Rev. ed. New York: Holt, Rinehart & Winston, Inc., 1963.

HARLACHER, ERVIN L. "Physical Education Facilities for a Junior College," *Journal of American Association for Health, Physical Education, and Recreation*, XXXIV, No. 2, February, 1963.

HAVEL, RICHARD C., and SEYMOUR, EMERY W. *Administration of Health, Physical Education, and Recreation for Schools.* New York: The Ronald Press Co., 1961.

HEILMAN, CHARLES, and BOURQUARDEZ, VIRGINIA. "Some Standards Are Needed," *Journal of Health, Physical Education, and Recreation*, XX, No. 2, February, 1951.

HEWITT, JACK E. "A Coeducational Gymnasium," *Journal of American Association for Health, Physical Education, and Recreation*, XXVII, No. 1, January, 1956.

HOWARD, GLENN W., and MASONBRINK, EDWARD. *Administration of Physical Education.* New York: Harper & Row, Inc., 1963.

HUELSTER, LAURA J. "Substance of the Image—College Teachers of Physical Education," *The Physical Educator*, XXI (May, 1964), 54.

HUGHES, WILLIAM LEONARD, FRENCH, ESTHER, and LEHSTEN, NELSON G. *Adminis-*

tration of Physical Education—For Schools and Colleges. New York: The Ronald Press, Co., 1962.

JENSEN, CLAYNE. "Evaluate Your Testing Program," *The Physical Educator,* XXI, No. 4, December, 1964.

JONES, JAMES J., and STOUT, IRVING W. *Public School Relations—Issues and Cases.* New York: G. P. Putnam's Sons, Inc., 1960.

KENYON, GERALD S. "The Fallacy of Accuracy," *The Physical Educator,* XX, No. 4, December, 1963.

KEPPEL, FRANCIS. *Personnel Practices for Public Education.* Pittsburgh: University of Pittsburgh Press, 1961.

KNEZEVICH, STEPHEN J. *Administration of Public Education.* New York: Harper & Row, Inc., 1962.

LEIBEE, HOWARD C. *Tort Liability for Injuries to Pupils.* Ann Arbor: Campus Publishers, 1965.

LINSLEY, JOHN W. "Creative Approach to Management," *Office,* LIX, No. 1, January, 1964.

LOKEN, NEWT. *Cheerleading.* 2d ed. New York: The Ronald Press Co., 1961.

LUMPKIN, MARGARET C. "Feminize Your Facilities," *Journal of American Association for Health, Physical Education, and Recreation,* XXVI, No. 6, September, 1955.

McGRAW, LYNN W. "Principles and Practices for Assigning Grades in Physical Education," *Journal of Health, Physical Education, and Recreation,* XXV, No. 2, February, 1964.

MATHEWS, DONALD K. *Measurement in Physical Education.* 2d ed. Philadelphia: W. B. Saunders Co., 1963.

METCALF, O. E. "School Laundries Are Good Business," *The Physical Educator,* XVII (May, 1960), 55.

MILLER, ARTHUR G., and MASSEY, M. DOROTHY. *Methods in Physical Education for the Secondary School.* Englewood Cliffs, N.J.: Prentice-Hall, Inc., 1963.

NIXON, JOHN E., and JEWETT, ANN E. *Physical Education Curriculum.* New York: The Ronald Press Co., 1964.

NOLTE, MERVIN CHESTER, and LINN, JOHN PHILLIP. *School Law for Teachers.* Danville, Ill.: The Interstate Printers and Publishers, Inc., 1963.

OBERTEUFFER, DELBERT. "Implications for Physical Education in the Current Re-Examination of American Education," *American Academy of Physical Education, Professional Contributions No. 7.* Washington, D.C.: American Association for Health, Physical Education, and Recreation, 1961.

"Penny Wise and Pound Foolish," *Today's Secretary,* February, 1965.

Planning Facilities for Health, Physical Education, and Recreation. Chicago: The Athletic Institute, 1962 and 1965.

PRESIDENT'S COUNCIL ON PHYSICAL FITNESS. *Adult Physical Fitness, A Program for Men and Women.* Washington, D.C.: Government Printing Office, 1963.

————. *Fitness for Leadership* (Suggestions for Colleges and Universities). Washington, D.C.: Government Printing Office.

————. *Fitness of American Youth* (A Report to the President of the United States on the Fort Ritchie Meeting). Washington, D.C.: Government Printing Office, 1958.

————. *Physical Fitness Elements in Recreation* (Suggestions for Community Programs). Washington, D.C.: Government Printing Office, 1962.

————. *Vim* (A Complete Exercise Plan for Girls Twelve to Eighteen). Washington, D.C.: Government Printing Office.

————. *Youth Physical Fitness, Suggested Elements of a School-Centered Program.* Washington, D.C.: Government Printing Office, July, 1961.

Profiles of Significant Schools. High Schools, 1962. A Status Report on Educational Change and Architectural Consequence. New York: Educational Facilities Laboratories, 1962.

PURVIS, ELGIE G. "Sixth Sense—Secretarial Sense," *Journal of Business Education,* XXXVI, January, 1961.

RAY, ROBERT F. "Trends in Intercollegiate Athletics," *Journal of the American Association for Health, Physical Education, and Recreation*, XXXVI, No. 1, January, 1965.

RICHARDSON, DEAN. "A Start in Selective Retention," *Journal of the American Association for Health, Physical Education, and Recreation*, XXXVI, No. 1, January, 1965.

SALT, E. BENTON, FOX, GRACE I., and STEVENS, B. K. *Teaching Physical Education in the Elementary School*. 2d ed. New York: The Ronald Press Co., 1960.

SCOTT, HARRY A., and WESTKAEMPER, RICHARD B. *From Program to Facilities in Physical Education*. New York: Harper & Row, Inc., 1958.

SCOTT, M. GLADYS, and FRENCH, ESTHER. *Measurement and Evaluation in Physical Education*. Dubuque: W. C. Brown Co., 1959.

SHAPIRO, FRIEDA S. "Your Liability for Student Accidents," *NEA Journal*, LIV, March, 1965.

SHEPARD, NATALIE MARIE. *Foundations and Principles of Physical Education*. New York: The Ronald Press Co., 1960.

SHROYER, GEORGE. "Legal Implications of Requiring Pupils To Enroll in Physical Education," *Journal of Health, Physical Education, and Recreation*, XXXV, May, 1964.

"Sports Opportunities for Girls and Women," *Journal of American Association for Health, Physical Education, and Recreation*, XXXV, No. 9, November–December, 1964.

STOUT, EVELYN E. *Introduction to Textiles*. 2d ed. New York: John Wiley & Sons, Inc., 1965.

STROMGREN, GEORGE. "Injury Prevention Check-Up Program," *Journal of Health, Physical Education, and Recreation*, XXXV, May, 1964.

Values in Sports. Washington, D.C.: AAHPER, 1962. A report of a Joint National Conference of the Division for Girls and Women's Sports and the Division of Men's Athletics, June 17–22, 1962, Interlochen, Michigan.

VOLTMER, EDWARD F., and ESSLINGER, ARTHUR A. *The Organization and Administration of Physical Education*. 4th ed. New York: Appleton-Century-Crofts, Inc., 1967.

WESSELS, R. G. "The Responsibility of Purchasing," *Office*, LIX, No. 1, January, 1961.

WILEY, ROGER C. "Student Accident Insurance in the Public Schools," *The Physical Educator*, XX, May, 1963.

WILLGOOSE, CARL E. *Evaluation in Health Education and Physical Education*. New York: McGraw-Hill Book Co., 1961.

WILLIAMS, JESSE FEIRING. *Principles of Physical Education*. 8th ed. Philadelphia: W. B. Saunders Co., 1964.

WILLIAMS, JESSE FEIRING, BROWNELL, CLIFFORD LEE, and VERNIER, ELMON LOUIS. *The Administration of Health Education and Physical Education*. 6th ed. Philadelphia: W. B. Saunders Co., 1964.

ZEIGLER, EARLE F. *Administration of Physical Education and Athletics, The Case Method Approach*. Englewood Cliffs, N.J.: Prentice-Hall, Inc., 1959.

Index

DATE DUE

MR 28 78			
GAYLORD			PRINTED IN U.S.A.